EARL J. GLADE:

AN INSIDE STORY OF CHURCH AND STATE, POLITICS, AND MEDIA

TIM LARSON AND CRAIG WIRTH

EARL J. GLADE:

AN INSIDE STORY OF CHURCH AND STATE, POLITICS, AND MEDIA

TABLE OF CONTENTS

Earl J. Glade was instrumental in helping push (or pull) Utah into the modern world. His influence extended to broadcasting, government, religion and education. He understood those institutions, and he recognized that they offered a synergy of ecumenism necessary to build cultural and functional bridges across boundaries of communication, politics, economics and social interaction.

Glade understood that bridge building was vital for the success of his country, state, city and, especially, his LDS religion. His was a broad and interwoven worldview. He and his cohort of contemporary visionaries interacted amicably and respectfully to achieve community improvements for the benefit of all. As a result, both the local community and the entire state became century-long beneficiaries of Earl Glade's vision.

Over many years of observation, I became convinced that those who contributed most to Utah's history were individuals who, like Glade, found ways to dissolve barriers between the influence of the LDS Church and the interests of groups not affiliated with the Church. Influential bridge-builders from outside the Church included such individuals as businessman I. J. Wagner, newspaper publishers John F. Fitzgerald and Jack Gallivan, banker George Eccles, and Chamber of Commerce leader Gus Bachman. (*Time* magazine called Fitzgerald the "peace maker.") Earl J. Glade was a devoted LDS Church insider who worked with all these community leaders – and others – to identify and move toward common community improvement goals. He never lost faith in his religion, and he never lost faith in his fellow citizens.

Glade is known equally well for his pioneering broadcast efforts and his long-time service as an elected official. He was attracted to broadcasting in the 1920s when radio was in its infancy. He recognized early on that radio would become the most powerful communication tool in history during the 1920s, '30s, '40s and early '50s. He sensed, also, that broadcasting was destined to be a powerful economic force – even more powerful than newspapers of the 19th and early 20th centuries. In addition, he believed radio could become a powerful information tool for his church, as well as an economic contributor to the church's financial success. Indeed, he spent a great deal of time and effort convincing Church leaders about the value of radio. (In the process, he encountered considerable opposition from less visionary leaders, as chronicled in the following pages.)

Earl Glade's early background was as a teacher, a businessman, and a promoter, all of which served him well when he approached LDS Church leaders to enter (or re-enter) radio station operation. He convinced them that the station they owned (soon to be KSL) should be a commercial operation, not simply a source of Church information. He argued that only by affiliating with a national network could the station build up a large audience of listeners – Mormon and non-Mormon -- for Church programming such as semi-annual conference meetings and weekly Mormon Tabernacle Choir broadcasts. Glade used his remarkable sales ability to convince Church leaders that in order to be economically viable, the station would necessarily broadcast popular programs and types of advertising not in keeping with Church teachings – coffee and tobacco, for instance. He used those same skills to sell advertising time to local business establishments. He invested a large part of the station's advertising revenue in uniquely local programming such as the KSL Orchestra, the KSL Players, and original KSL radio drama or comedy. Later, Glade convinced Church leaders to invest large sums in technology so KSL could become one of the nation's first "clear channel" stations, broadcasting with 50,000 watts, the maximum power allowed for any domestic broadcaster.

While he was building KSL, Glade was the primary announcer. Everything was "live" in those days. Glade's voice was heard throughout the day and evening – before, after, and between programs. He performed commercials, made announcements, and voiced transition segments from program to program. His voice was not so powerful as it was sincere. It carried believability and credibility matched by few others. His use of language was impeccable, concise, exact . . . but without pretentiousness. Before long, everyone living in or around Utah recognized the radio voice of Earl J. Glade. (That voice recognition would serve him well in countless public speaking engagements and, later, in his political career.)

I grew up listening to the voice of Earl J. Glade. Only later, though, would I learn about his contributions as a pioneer broadcaster and as a community leader. Years later, one of my mentors, Arch L. Madsen – also a broadcast pioneer – talked about Earl Glade with reverence and respect. Madsen often talked about Glade's leadership in bringing the CBS network to Utah, about his untiring efforts to give the Mormon Tabernacle Choir national exposure, about his struggles with certain LDS Church leaders over programs and advertising, about his conflicts with his superiors over how the station should be operated, and about his belief in the power of broadcasting as a tool for Church growth. Indeed, according to Arch Madsen, without Earl J. Glade KSL would never have survived. Without Glade, KSL would never have become a powerful influence in the broadcast world. Without Glade, LDS Church broadcasting would never have developed into a nationwide radio and television broadcast group with stations from New York to Los Angeles.

And yet, powerful individuals within the LDS Church would eventually come between Earl Glade and his love of broadcasting. He was forced to find a second career in politics and community leadership. He became a three-term mayor of Salt Lake City, a two-term Regent of the University of Utah, and an elected member of the Utah State House of Representatives. Some called Glade "the conscience of Salt Lake City." As mayor, he spoke with the same clarity and sincerity he had employed on radio. He led the city through the closing months of World War Two, the Korean War, and the difficult transition from wartime to peace. He led the city through one of its greatest growth spurts. He oversaw costly flood repairs and vital infrastructure developments. He provided unfailing support for Utah youth during challenging times. He used his remarkable public speaking skills to uplift, encourage, and reassure the citizenry. And he freely shared his inherent generous, warm and compassionate nature in both good times and trying times.

Somehow during all of these activities, Earl Glade found time to serve as president of the Salt Lake Chamber of Commerce, chairman of the Selective Service (draft) Board, chairman of the Salt Lake Youth Council, member of the LDS General Deseret Sunday School Board, director of the Salt Lake Council of the American Red Cross, member of the Salt Lake Council of Boy Scouts of America, and chairman of the Compliance Committee of the National Association of Broadcasters, among others.

Many Utah historians overlook Earl J. Glade and his significant contributions. He did not seek personal recognition, and he seemed to care little about promoting his considerable legacy. Even so, he received an honorary doctorate from the University of Utah, and he was inducted into the Utah Broadcast Hall of Fame. Brigham Young University offers a broadcasting scholarship in his name, and the Jesse Knight Building at BYU houses Earl J. Glade Hall. Along the way, he received dozens – perhaps hundreds – of honors, awards, and other symbols of appreciation.

However, until this current volume by Tim Larson and Craig Wirth, no one has pursued the sometimes-elusive research necessary to chronicle the lifetime contributions of Earl Glade. In the following pages, Larson and Wirth provide an overview of Glade's vital contributions to ecumenism, to economic development, to community growth, to his church, and most importantly, to the history of broadcasting in Utah and the nation. They discuss his recurring conflicts with certain LDS Church leaders, and they recognize the role of other Church leaders in assisting Glade through end-of-life financial struggles

The record of Earl J. Glade was not an easy story to uncover, but Larson and Wirth doggedly pursued the task over more than a decade. The result is a significant contribution to understanding twentieth-century Utah. The book offers appropriate recognition of the impact broadcasting had on the state and its institutions, and it chronicles the vital role played by a modern pioneer named Earl J. Glade.

G. Donald Gale, Ph.D.
Vice President, Bonneville International
Corporation/KSL (Retired)

ACKNOWLEDGMENTS

We dedicate this book to Patricia Curtis, the youngest of seven of Earl and Sarah Glade's children who died in April 2016 at the age of 93. She shared her remembrances of growing up in the Glade family, gave us access to letters, photos and personal memorabilia, and encouraged us to write about the sunshine and shadows of her father's life.

We thank Richard L. Curtis, Patricia's son, for renewing our interest in Earl J. Glade. He contacted us several years ago wanting to learn more about his grandfather's broadcasting endeavors. In this book we expand our treatment of Glade and KSL to include his political and LDS church endeavors as well.

In five trips to the National Archives and Records Administration (NARA) in Suitland and College Park, Maryland, to research a comprehensive Utah radio history book, the authors obtained copies of the first KZN/KSL licenses and associated Earl J. Glade Federal Radio Commission and Federal Communications Commission appearances and correspondence, helpful in writing this book. They are too many to name, but we are grateful to the NARA workers for their professional support in accessing pertinent documents stored in isolated boxes in the vast NARA federal complex. (We also thank the people at a retail store nearby the Suitland NARA who graciously exchanged our dollar bills for dime-rolls so we could photocopy 3,000 pages of material at 10-cents a copy, some essential to this endeavor.) We mined the extensive J. Willard Marriott Library *Utah Broadcast History Collection* and the *Everett L. Cooley Oral History Collection* for carefully preserved Glade and KSL documents and remembrances.

Two people at the Marriott Library encouraged and supported us throughout our comprehensive Utah radio history research from which this Glade biography evolved. The late Roger Hansen, while J. Willard Marriott Library's Director, encouraged us and provided financial support for travel and collection acquisition. And Gregory Thompson of Marriott Library Special Collections has, for decades, encouraged and supported us, and joined us at the NARA sites. The contacts he introduced, his Utah history expertise and his keen editorial sense, have been immeasurably helpful. Paul Mogren of Marriott Library Special Collections, always supportive of our research, was our go-to individual to obtain daily access to Glade and Utah broadcast history related documents.

Kirk H. Bandley, archivist at the University of Utah's Archives/Records Management Center, was amazing in his knowledge of the center's records and holdings concerning Glade. He was always available and immensely helpful, especially in giving us access to Glade's University of Utah teaching records and his Board of Regent contributions.

The professionals at the Utah State Historical Society, especially Gregory Walz and Anthony Castro, also served us well. We obtained photos, minutes of the Salt Lake City Commission meetings presided over by Glade, and other KSL and Glade associated documents, photos and other materials from them.

The late Arch Madsen, while Bonneville International Corporation (BIC) president, gave access to the Radio Service Corporation Board of Director minutes beginning when it was formed in the 1920s to oversee what became KSL. He also gave us financial support to write about Glade for whom he had enduring admiration. The late Blaine Whipple, a past BIC Senior VP of Finance, who worked with Glade, provided personal remembrances and pertinent business information concerning Glade after he returned to KSL in the early 1960s.

Linda Davies, a special university student and professional colleague provided essential radio station ownership research as well as counseled us on LDS people, issues and pertinent beliefs. And thanks to Ivor Sharp daughter, Lucien Lloyd, and her sisters for donating to Marriott Library their father's personal diary and relevant KSL business papers and correspondence, essential to informing a part of the KSL story never before told.

We thank retired Bonneville International Corporation executive and U ambassador, Don Gale, as well as Robert K. Avery and the late Malcolm Sillars, colleagues in the University of Utah Department of Communication, for critiquing early manuscript drafts of this book and for their editorial support and encouragement. And we are indebted to the talented Les Roka for his significant editorial support in preparing this book for publication.

The above people along with others were invaluable to our efforts, but we take full responsibility for the book's content.

Tim Larson and Craig Wirth

SECTION I

GLADE'S COMING OF AGE

CHAPTER 1
THE EXEMPLARY YOUNG MAN OF UTAH

Earle J. Glade is an exemplar of Utah's remarkable history. He spans most of the first century of modern Utah's development. He was born in Ogden on December 2, 1885, in the Territory of Utah, a decade before Utah became the 45th state. His coming of age coincided with Utah's coming of age. He prominently shaped Utah's unique church-state-business relationship, combining his interpersonal and public relations skills to navigate trends and patterns in business, community service, government and politics as he and Utah matured. He served higher education, joined the prohibition movement, crusaded for youth morality, engendered patriotic support for three wars, and supervised the expansion of services and infrastructure as a public official at the local and state levels. Most prominently, he joined Utah's first technical revolution by developing the region's most powerful radio station and shepherding its growth from the earliest formative years of the industry to its golden age.

Glade's family, typical of many late nineteenth century Utah families in the transition years culminating in statehood, was influenced by mining, the state's second largest industry at the time. When Earl was a youngster, his father James, a baker, moved the family to Park City, where they lived for about ten years serving silver miners. During that time, the still callow young Earl had his first "real" job – as a mudder, or mud-hen, and oiler in the Daly West Concentrating Mill, an ore mill. His job was to keep the sluice valve open so the sloppy mud and ore could slip through without becoming clogged.

He reported later that sometimes the mud would "accidentally, of course, slip through and splatter on Salt Lake highbrow student visitors." Splattering mud on highbrow students, if it actually happened and wasn't merely self-effacing banter, likely was a rare personal incident of thoughtlessness on Earl's part. Even as a boy, Earl exhibited his definitive sense of kindness. In 1898, Glade, then 13, wrote to his Aunt Mary Jane Glade Litson: "Happiness is the perfume that one cannot shed over another, without a few drops falling on one self."

Hopeful and opportunistic, Glade in his actions and attitude embodied the aspirations and character of his era, representing members of a generation of young Utah men who didn't necessarily follow a life-long, hardscrabble family job path into farming or mining. Not overly concerned with tradition at the time, he became interested in Utah's nascent lines of work –advertising and sales promotion, teaching, political consulting, media development, and community activism. In his lifetime, in countless speeches, radio shows and devoted public service, Glade tirelessly evinced his commitment to democracy, to national security, to America's veterans, to education, to Utah's youth, to fair treatment of people, and did so with passion and eloquence.

As Mark Twain and Charles Dudley Warner wrote in *The Gilded Age*, "To the young American [man] … the paths to fortune are innumerable and all open; there is invitation in the air and success in all his wide horizon."[1] Today we understand how Glade assiduously reenacted the age-old rite of the young in search of fresh opportunity. Opportunity in Glade's time was plentiful, producing a generation of men for whom work became an adventure. Glade came to maturity in the latter part of the Gilded Age, and as an adult, maximized the gift of serendipity to exploit the work opportunities of a new century.

Work abounded in farming and mining, but young Glade and many in his cohort, as noted above, did not choose that direction.[2] Unconventional, he certainly was not anti-social. The 17-year-old hardly had time to unpack his bags at Brigham Young University, when Glade found a tireless path for involvement. Leveraging his modest height, he took advantage of muscles formed from mudding to join BYU's basketball team. For him, it wasn't enough to just play the game; the young Glade became the secretary of the Intercollegiate State Basket Ball League, where, in 1903, he helped draw up a twelve game season. The league represented the major LDS academies and universities in Utah, including Brigham Young College of Logan, the Latter Day Saints University of Salt Lake City, Weber Stake Academy of Ogden, and BYU. Still in his teens, Glade was appointed to the League's executive committee, serving side by side with the physical education directors and coaches of the participating schools.

An *Ogden Standard Examiner* article from November 30, 1903, stated: [Glade's team] is the only team in the league that is in any kind of shape to play ball." Actually, official play was postponed until January of 1904 to give the other institutions' teams time to catch up. However, Glade, already honing his skills as a future advertiser and civic cheerleader, amplified the anticipation for League play: "The season promises to be one of the hardest fought since the introduction of basket ball.[3]

Glade smartly championed basketball at this time, as it became the most popular sport, after the BYU Board had banned football at the school. Glade and his team used the new Training School Building's second story gymnasium as their home court. One could imagine the "slight" advantage he and his

A Young Earl J. Glade
(Glade Family Collection)

teammates had over the interstate rivals. The court was nine-feet smaller than the other gyms, and partisan fans stood at the very edges of the playing floor during a game. Glade's committee had voted that the championship team would get a pennant as a permanent reminder of a championship season. Few records appear to exist indicating the Park City teen's performance, but the League lasted only three years, and BYU carried home the championship two of those three years.[4]

In Utah's important transition years that would stretch from statehood through the post WWI era, Glade also saw a different path when it came to family dynamics. Although wanting to please yet restless, the student Glade was looking for an alternative to the traditional callings of the time, as evidenced in an inscrutable letter he wrote to his father, Park City baker. Sent from Provo on May 2, 1904, the letter was written on Glade's stationery with the top featuring a caricature of a fence-sitting black Cheshire cat:

"I am like a Cheshire Cat.
Our 'Den' will grin, upon
receiving an answer to
this untimely epistle."
Bachelor's Den
Smith & Glade, Provo

We assume Smith was his roommate. The letter followed:

Dear Father,

I have been waiting for a letter from you, but it appears I have waited in vain. I guess you heard the account of the track meet with the L.D.S.A and the BYU. We beat them by the score of 71-73. Probably you have heard how I won the mile race. I simply took a big lead and held it, and beat the other fellow by 175 yards. It was a big day and I looked for you down [here], but we failed to find you.

Now here is something more important. I have received a call to go on a mission to Switzerland and Germany. Now what am I to do about it? Today, I had a conference with President [Counselor to BYU President Brimhall] Keeler and President Brimhall, and they told me to accept it. Both of them were very kind and ~~sent~~ gave me lots of encouragement. Of course, I shall abide by your judgment if it were contrary to the King of Spain. Kindly write me soon as you possibly can and let me have particulars.

There is another thing if I can get $600 here next year would you object to my going to Chicago, (Kingships Studios) if I pay my own expenses? If President Brimhall won't let them take me on a mission, he will probably offer the above. They want me to teach correspondence and Theology next year classes among other work. In order to do it right, I ought to have further training. And there are two other university boys that are also going. Of course this only surmises if they don't want me on the mission I should like to go to Kinships.

My health is perfectly good. I have had pain in the back but I got an Alleach's Porous Plaster and placed on it, and it is helping me wonderfully. If you ever get a pain in the back try one they only cost 15.

... How are you feeling and how is your work serving you? I had to make a speech in devotional exercises this morning about that <u>wonderful race</u>. Made me kind of shivery.

When I got the call to go on this mission I could hardly stand up. It simply took the breath out of me.

Regarding the mission and about going to Chicago I wish you to please let me know as soon as you possibly can ... [but I] don't want you to kill yourself to help me on a mission. This is all for this time so good bye with love to all.

Sincerely I am your affectionate Earl.[5]

His father replied promptly and favorably. As with his promotional efforts for basketball, when he was called to an LDS mission in Germany, the enterprising Glade found ways to raise money for the mission. He organized a summer-time dance in Park City, a town still recovering from an 1898 fire that destroyed Main Street and many dozens of buildings and residences. Knowing that the rough mining town had far more men than women, and in order to increase the number of ladies in attendance that could be wooed by prospective suitors, he announced all women would be admitted without charge to the dance. He then levied a 50-cent admission fee (a steep charge at the time) to the men who knew this was a rare chance to witness so many women in town. The *Park Record* carried his announcement of the event. "A Social Dance"

Prior to the dance, to cement his connection to the mining town, Glade also announced in the paper a month before the dance that he and his high school friend, Fred Richmond, would be spending their summer vacations in Park City. Richmond, Glade and Sadie Rasband, Glade's future wife, graduated in 1903 from Brigham Young Academy in Provo. Richmond and Glade graduated in Commerce at BYA, and Rasband in Music. They were in the last graduating class at BYA before it became Brigham Young High School.

For his mission, Glade, who said that he never experienced seasickness, traveled to London by ship and then continued by train to France and Zurich. He left the other Park City "boys" in Switzerland to serve his LDS mission in the Mannheim Branch in Southwest Germany, likely supported to some extent from his dance promotion earnings. Much later, when he was mayor, Glade adeptly recalled his German language skills, reportedly surprising some German visitors to the Salt Lake City council chambers by welcoming them in their native language.

Glade's LDS mission to Germany was valuable for the formative lessons he would apply throughout his life. It would be the only time in his adult life that his religious views and opinions would not be on the side of the majority of those in his surroundings. For three years, Earl J. Glade was not in the majority. He wasn't even welcomed in Germany as a Mormon missionary.

But a hallmark of Glade's worldview was improvisation. In a December 8, 1904, letter to his grandmother, the LDS missionary said he adopted an assumed name to hide his real reason to be in Germany:

*We are in these cities entirely unknown to the government
officials, as the elders have been banished. In fact my name
has been changed to Wilhelm Seiter. ... In Strassburg we are
registered as students of the Deutch and French languages. We*

The assumed name was hardly a capricious practice. Missionaries had to be discreet in their work. In July 1910, Mormon missionaries were expelled from Germany amid allegations they were recruiting women to become polygamous wives in Utah. That move prompted the British Parliament to wonder whether England should follow suit.

Curiously, the politician assigned to oversee the British investigation? A young man named Winston Churchill. The future prime minister took to the task with his usual aplomb and thoroughness, but the final report was lost — until it was unearthed recently by Utah researcher Ardis Parshall. "Churchill did take seriously the request that he investigate Mormon missionary practices," Parshall

Glade's LDS mission class, 1904. (Third row, second from left) Family Photo

explained in a paper during a 2016 Mormon History Association conference at the Snowbird resort in Utah. "Churchill's inquiry took several forms. First was an investigation of actual Mormon proselyting activities in England. How extensive were those activities? Who were the men who conducted them? What did they teach?"

Members of Glade's family recall his adopted German last name as Zurite, but in the letter to his grandmother, he relates it as Seiter, a difference that may have resulted from his stylistic penmanship. He lived on a modest $15 a month, but at one point when the funds from Park City were exhausted, Earl J. Wilhelm Seiter persisted by taking a part-time job in a furniture factory delivering goods by push-cart.[8]

A November 1906 letter from the shy Sarah Elizabeth ("Sadie") Rasband to Glade, two years into his mission and a year before they were married, referred to his adopting new names.

Rasband also wished him a somewhat tongue-tied but loving birthday greeting as he turned 21. Sadie was seven months older than Glade.

> *Your note containing your new name and address came Thursday for which I was thankful, as I didn't like to write you until after its arrival. I am very sorry for the inconvenience under which you are obliged to labor and my prayer constantly is for your protection and success. However it really is laughable the strange names you adopt, you surely should have been a girl don't you think so yourself? I am sending you just a tiny box to let you know that I have not forgotten that you will soon be twenty-one years of age. If you were home I <u>might</u> give you about twenty-one kisses. Now then there are not many young men receive that promise at that age. I know that sounds queer but I don't exactly mean it as it is written. I mean there are not many young men who receive such a promise from the certain young lady from whom they would be most happy to receive it. Now there is <u>that</u> right? We are well and very busy but will write you a letter as soon as possible. With love and best wishes for a happy birthday Yours Sadie[9]*

Glade, whose stoicism was impressive for a man of his young age, learned on his mission that in the business of persuasion one should always be prepared for disappointments and to adapt accordingly to the dynamics of a progressively complex world. His faith was foremost in his survival kit. He later explained that nearly every emotion, the ability to adapt to adverse situations, and each creative opportunity throughout his life had foundations in his faith. "Our religion has long stressed the significance of creative attitudes and of manual skills and dexterities. … Thus, that which we create is recreated in our own personalities."[10]

The young man adapted well, pushing a cart around Germany, posing as Wilhelm Seiter to spread the Good News for the amelioration of mankind. In future decades, anyone who would ever agree or disagree with Glade, oppose or join him in political battles, or conduct church, public or private business with him, would see first-hand his remarkable capacity to adapt, as needed.

Glade returned to Utah, completing a personal mission in which he had won the heart-and-hand of the Park City letter writer. The *Park Record* carried the news of this newly prominent young couple.

MARRIAGE LICENSE

Application No. 4882

THE STATE OF UTAH, COUNTY OF SALT LAKE.

To Any Person Legally Authorized to Solemnize Marriage, Greeting:

You are hereby Authorized to Join in Holy Matrimony

Mr. Earl J. Glade, of Park City in the County of Summit, and State of Utah, of the age of 21 years, and Miss Sarah E. Rasband, of Park City in the County of Summit, and State of Utah, of the age of 22 years.

Witness my hand and official seal this 10 day Sept. 1907

J. G. Eldredge, County Clerk, Salt Lake County, Utah.

By Watkins, Deputy Clerk.

STATE OF UTAH, COUNTY OF SALT LAKE } ss.

I hereby certify that on the eleventh day of Sept. in the year of our Lord one thousand nine hundred and seven, at Salt Lake City in said County, I, the undersigned, An Elder of the Church of Jesus Christ of Latter-day Saints, did join in the Holy Bonds of Matrimony according to law Earl J. Glade, of the County of Summit, State of Utah, and Sarah E. Rasband, of the County of Summit, State of Utah. The nature of the ceremony was according to the rites of the Church of Jesus Christ of Latter-day Saints, and was a present mutual agreement of marriage between the parties for all time.

We were married as stated in this Certificate, and are now husband and wife.

Signed, Earl J. Glade, Groom.

Signed, Sarah E. Rasband, Bride.

In the presence of George Romney, Witness.

John W. Woolley, Witness.

John R. Winder, An Elder of the Church of Jesus Christ of Latter-day Saints.

Frederick Rasband, Sadie's father, ordained Glade an LDS Elder on July 24,1909, nearly two years after Earl and Sadie were married.

Bishopric of Park City Ward
Sarah's father Federick Rasband, Bishop (left), Earl's
farther James R. Glade, Counselor, and James A.
Barton, Counselor (right)
(Glade Family Collection)

Soon, the Glade family branch added fresh branches. Starting with twins Melba and Melva that same year, the couple had seven children – the youngest, Patricia, born in 1923, died in April 2016 at the age of 93. Glade's father was 20 when Earl was born, and nearly 40 in 1904 when he received his son's letter requesting missionary counsel. Earl was the first of eight children --seven boys-- born to James Richard and

Anna Louise Glade.

Of Earl and Sadie's own seven children, James Richard Glade would live to see only the twin granddaughters. He died on July 16, 1910, at age 46, soon after moving his family to Provo where he bought a small farm. More trying was that Earl had four brothers ranging from two to twelve when their dad died, leaving a 44-year-old widow with very young children to raise. On a "Mothers of Today" program broadcast on KSL Radio on Sunday, January 9, 1944, Glade's mother said that as each Glade boy married, "the next eldest took over as head of the house to help the younger ones along." No record could be found to confirm his involvement, but the 25 year-old Glade, although already married and out of the family home, likely helped his widowed mother during this distressing time in their lives. Anna Louise Glade married educator Leonard John Nuttall in September 1931 and lived to 93, her death in April 1964 coming only two years before Earl's.

Glade's skills as an orator are well documented but he also had an elegant way with words on paper, both in content and style. He polished his skills while teaching commerce and penmanship classes after attending the Rochester Business Institute in New York in 1903. This was followed by a 1904 stint at the Columbus, Ohio, Zanerian School of Design, a school that taught ornamental penmanship and evolved into today's Zaner-Bloser Company, the nation's largest supplier of handwriting manuals. He spent the next two decades in education, first as a student and then as teacher. He taught at BYU and was head of its department of business education from 1911 to 1914 during his student days there. He took a short break in 1911 to attend the University of Chicago to study commerce, and in 1914 was president of the National Education Association's business section in St. Paul, Minnesota, although this seemingly didn't take him away from Provo for extended periods.

Many considered BYU more immediately as a religious seminary than as a comprehensive institution of higher education at the time. Glade graduated from BYU in 1914 at 29, and three years later, when the United States entered World War I, Glade would lend his considerable community activist skills to funding. Meanwhile, Sadie had graduated from BYU in 1908.[12]

Glade's imprint at BYU is still felt today. He was a pioneer manager from about 1912 to 1915 of what was then called the Student's Supply Association, which is now the BYU bookstore. The BYU Bookstore gives 1912 as the start date, but family accounts attribute Glade's employment at the Student's Supply Association a bit earlier. The bookstore's website gives Glade credit for charting the course for the store's financial stability in those early days. Glade's extensive portfolio of business fame started in the pencils, pens and paper business but soon his academic career would take a new path when he moved his family to Salt Lake City in 1915.

The reason Glade moved north, among other factors, may have had its genesis beginning in 1909 when a controversy at BYU over evolution was brewing. At services that year commemorating the centennial of Charles Darwin's birth, BYU Professor Ralph V. Chamberlin, formerly chair of the University of Utah biology department and dean of its medical school, publicly pronounced Darwin one of the greatest scientific minds of his era. Several months later the First Presidency of the LDS Church, consisting of Joseph F. Smith and his counselors, sanctioned an official anti-evolutionary statement on the "origin of the physical man." The statement defended a spiritual creation, the creation of man in the image of God, and Adam as the "primal parent of the race." The controversy among some BYU faculty and the LDS leadership festered for several years, triggering the departure of many BYU teachers, some of whom cited the banishing of "academic liberty" at the school. Beginning in 1911, Professor Chamberlin and colleagues resigned or were encouraged to conform or leave as a result of their evolutionary beliefs. Although their positions on evolution are not publicly known, Dr. Harvey Fletcher, credited with being the father of stereophonic sound, left for a position at Western Electric, and Glade left for Salt Lake City and the Gillham Advertising Agency. Glade moved onto the University of Utah campus, as BYU was floundering in the aftermath of the controversy.[13]

In 1916, Glade was appointed an instructor in the University of Utah's School of Finance and Commerce where he worked as an adjunct until 1929. He soon introduced the University of Utah's first courses in advertising, salesmanship, insurance, and office management. In 1917, he developed the

Business Department's first advertising course, in which he touted the economic, psychological and physical factors in advertising and gave students hands-on practice for advertising display and campaigns. The course, as he described it, involved a "comprehensive advertising laboratory in which the student had access to actual working exhibits from the studies of recognized specialist throughout the world."[14]

Glade was a self-styled pioneer of advertising in the field in Utah and the nation. He saw advertising as a higher calling – an enterprise that fit well into his dearly loved LDS principle that held at its core personal growth and improvement and positive movement forward. He later wrote:

> *Advertising, at its best, is one of the most potent elevators of living standards in the world today. Further, it is the world's champion builder of payrolls. What this means to humanity, is possibly most appreciated by those who know the significance of work as a true friend of man. As an energizer to achievement and to improvement; as a stimulant to constructive activity, advertising is incomparable.[15]*

Glade also introduced the school's first course in salesmanship in 1917, which was intended "not only for 'the man-on-the-road' but also for every one who enters business." Emphasis was on such matters as building, presenting and controlling the sales argument and managing the sales interview.[16]

In 1918, Glade added a course in the principles of economics to his academic stable. He promoted this course as a general study of business activity from the standpoint of the public welfare, a subtle tribute to his belief in helping others progress and improve by serving the greater good of all. Glade's economics course was a prerequisite for the more advanced business and marketing courses taught by, among others, Dr. George Thomas, the dean of the Commerce School who in 1922 became president of the University of Utah, a position he held for two decades.[17]

By 1919, Glade was diversifying the curriculum in ways that were novel for the time. In one course, students specifically discussed business problems in the West and particularly Utah with its unique population and religion. He added advanced courses in advertising. By late 1920, he reportedly had a record-breaking enrollment in his advertising class, registering students who represented many downtown Salt Lake City and Ogden businesses.[18]

By 1924, there were courses dealing with insurance institutions and various kinds of property and life insurance, as well as a course highlighting the principles of office administration, location, layout, training and, most importantly, communication.

Perhaps, it is an odd fact that those who accomplish the most often spend years fumbling and stumbling to find what it is they can achieve. The first half of life involves much experimentation with numerous examples of trial and error. While teaching at the University of Utah, the peripatetic Glade also played musical chairs at a rapid pace with a myriad of consulting and advertising enterprises. In 1916, he opened the Glade Efficiency Service, and, with L.D. Billings, provided advertising and stenographic services. In 1918, the company became Glade Services, and he added Examiner of Disputed Documents and Secretary Utah State Fair Associates to his entrepreneurial efforts. In 1919, he joined with John D. Giles to form the Glade and Giles Advertising Agency, with offices on what today is the City Creek Center on Main Street. Giles left in 1922 and the Earl J.

Glade Advertising Sales Promotion and Business Counsel evolved. In 1923, Glade became managing editor of the *Sugar House Times* newspaper and President of the Glade Realty Company with

Glade's Home Library
(Salt Lake Tribune, December 1, 1940)

offices in Sugarhouse. And in 1924, he returned to the agency business with the Glade Advertising Co. In that same year, he launched his radio career at KFPT, later to become KSL, and embarked on the principal achievement that would absorb his talents for the next two decades.

Glade's academic and business ventures were punctuated by constant demands for him to speak at school, civic, professional, and religious events. He seemed to spend as much time in the public arena as he did in his business and academic pursuits. He prepared his speeches using carefully selected information and quotes from books in his home library.

He would read volumes, write article after article, and give speech after speech based on his readings and study. He had a deep, compelling intellect; his speeches were intellectually sound and concerned the political, cultural, and social issues of the time, consistently

The Glade Family Home, 2610 Highland Dr.,
Circa 1925 (top) and 2016 (bottom), (Larson Collection)

buttressed at least implicitly by an LDS doctrinal or religious principle or value. Earl J. Glade was a collector of scholarly and inspirational material that frequently was used in his nearly weekly speeches to civic, charitable, business and religious groups. His library in his long time residence at 2610 Highland Drive in Salt Lake City held a portion of his book collection.

As an aside, although Glade gave hundreds of speeches and appeared on the radio airwaves tens-of-hundreds of times over several decades, he was rarely an impromptu speaker. He carefully prepared and wrote out each of his speeches, talks and sales pitches to assure that his messages were focused, well organized and persuasively targeted. He likely memorized great parts of his presentations but by all accounts did not speak off-the-cuff, and ad libbed only occasionally.

Glade wrote in his lengthy treatment entitled, "Truly Great Men Recognize Spiritual Power," that LDS Church President Heber J. Grant had presented him with a book, *Lincoln, A Man of God*, by Dr. John Wesley Hill. He held Lincoln's need for religion as "the greatest attribute that can be ascribed to the martyred president. I am thankful to President Grant for pointing it out." [19] Glade saw religion as a necessary part of business and civic leadership, and often used his religion's media holdings, buildings, and events to present his beliefs and opinions.

Ever since Brigham Young served both as territorial governor and as President of the Church of Jesus Christ of Latter-day Saints in the middle to late 1800s, to the casual observer it has been nearly impossible to discern a meaningful distinction in Utah among religion, government, and politics. Glade certainly was no different, but he proved to be more adept than many who followed as community leaders up until the current time. No matter the venue, he advocated Mormon principles and thinking in Utah and often applied them to controversial issues of public importance. One such controversial issue was prohibition, the topic of the next chapter.

CHAPTER 2
THE PERSUASIVE ADVOCATE
WHETS HIS POLITICAL AMBITIONS

In 1916, Glade, the non-drinking, LDS returned missionary cultivated a statewide political profile, venturing into the subject of prohibition, an opportunity for LDS dominated Utah to shine positively in the national spotlight. Even after 20 years, the state still suffered the sting of not only having to bury polygamy by religious decree but also by a popular but failed official national Constitutional Amendment, in order to gain acceptance into the United States.

Two camps divided Utah. The Greater Utah Development League represented those wishing to keep Utah "wet" such as miners who still wanted to whet-the-whistle at the end of a work shift. However, Development League members found their formidable foe in the Prohibition and Betterment League of Utah, which was led by Glade. A couple of cities – most notably, St. George – had already turned off the taps, giving Glade a head start in his efforts.

Now 31, Glade spent the summer of 1916 drumming up support with naturally sympathetic LDS church members and honing his skills as a persuasive speaker and promoter of the anti-spirits rallies. One such event came when he was called to pitch-hit at the last minute for Heber J. Grant, then a member of the church's First Presidency, at a meeting of the Bear River Stake Tabernacle in Garland, Utah, where nearly 1,000 people had assembled. The stake president, M. H. Welling, announced the disappointing news that Elder Grant was absent, but that Glade, the manager of the Prohibition and Betterment League of Utah, would speak in the church leader's place.

> *Mr. Glade occupied almost an hour, and brought out very successfully why the people of Utah should suppress the liquor traffic and support only candidates who would stand for state-wide prohibition ... The Honorable W. S. Hansen handed out resolutions. The newspaper reported the crowd was ready to sign. The prohibition Bateson rally had been a success. ...Not one dissenting vote was cast against it. Several good musical*

*numbers were rendered under the direction of Professor
George O. Nye.[1]*

The meeting heightened Glade's profile. The wide-open town of Park City summed up the prohibition fight, giving the odds to Glade, its former resident. The *Park Record* forecasted the "last call" for alcohol because Glade was in charge. It wrote:

> *Earl J. Glade, a Park City boy, has been appointed manager
> of the prohibition campaign launched by the Prohibition and
> Betterment League of Utah, and the chances are Mr. Glade
> will, to a very great extent, kill the work of Robt. W. Brown,
> who is spending his time and great sums of money for the
> Greater Utah Development League, whose object is against
> statewide prohibition. It is almost a certainty the next State
> legislature will put Utah in the "dry" column.[2]*

Less than two weeks later, Glade spoke to even larger crowds, condemning the sale and use of alcohol in Utah, while promoting the 18th Amendment favoring prohibition. Glade reeled off facts on liquor traffic and the positive results that would accrue by prohibiting its sale and use. For instance, in a July 30, 1916, speech delivered in the Tabernacle, he referenced the moves in European nations to abolish liquor immediately after World War I. He opened his remarks, stating that if "in the game of death [war] sobriety is indispensable, it is obvious that in the game of life it is even more indispensable." Glade presented statistics that purported to show that alcohol "undermines the activity of the user and incapacitates him to bear responsibility." He cited Kansas, a state that had practiced prohibition for many years, as having only 1 in 800 feebleminded people, while New York State, "where the saloons are dishing up their beverage unmolested," had 1 in 200 such people. Kansas also was touted as the wealthiest state in the union, with one automobile for every eight people. Glade said that social liberty and the greater good trump personal liberty when it comes to liquor sales and use. He made a strong appeal to Utah's young men and women to speak out for passage of a statewide prohibition law, exhorting them to vote only for politicians who favored that cause.[3]

Utahans glimpsed what Glade's students already had witnessed in the classroom – a passionate, tireless advocate with a persuasive command of the language who never shied away from the chance to proselytize a worldview framed by classic LDS values. His public appearances in 1916 introduced Glade to the state's political arena, demonstrating how adept he was in reaching out beyond LDS Church venues with his message to find allies in the Democratic Party. His appeal now extended beyond Utah's borders.

Glade was elected to be an officer in the National Young Men's Democratic League in a meeting at the National Democratic Club in New York. He was one of two westerners among the east coast power brokers directing the youth of the Democratic Party and actively worked for Progressive Movement leader President Woodrow Wilson's run for a second term. The other westerner was from the much larger state of California. Glade's passion at Utah's prohibition rallies had drawn a great deal of attention.[4]

Back home, Glade joined the campaign of Simon Bamberger in his campaign to become the state's next governor. A political oddity in Utah, Bamberger was a German-born Jew who, at one time, was the sole Democratic member of the State Senate from Salt Lake County. Ironically, Bamberger ran against Nephi Morris, a prohibitionist who also was LDS. Glade liked the odds. Bamberger, a railroad and mining executive, had already slugged it out with Alfred McCune, a Mormon with deep pockets, in the primary.

While he followed his religious teachings, Glade learned that successful politics in Utah at the time meant not blindly following candidates merely because they were Mormon. Glade's

Simon Bamberger
4th Governor of Utah
(bing.com/images)

21

strong affiliation with the non-Mormon Bamburger did not turn heads. Glade appreciated the significance of the population data suggesting a non-Mormon Democrat from Salt Lake represented an opportunity for success, especially when that Democrat also was a staunch Prohibitionist. Bamberger believed as Glade did, that even though he didn't carry the Mormon name that he could do well in a state that already had a significant number of non-Mormons, especially in mining which was among the state's largest industries. Historian Gene Sessions described the Mormons and non-Mormons of the time around World War I as approaching parity and cooperating in "a largely congenial manner in a progressive society and burgeoning economy." [5]

One might quickly embrace the impression that the answer to who exerts considerable power in politics, the government, the media, the culture, and religion in Utah always has been the same (that is, the LDS church) since statehood was achieved in 1896. This is not true. For instance, Utahans of late might be surprised to learn the LDS Church members did not constitute the largest share of demographics in early Utah. The average Utah resident at statehood and beyond into the twentieth century was neither a member of the Church of Jesus Christ of Latter-day Saints nor married. The collective *he* (and there were more men, despite a common belief plural marriages meant more women in Utah) was neither a farmer nor a dweller of a single-family house in the country. And, perhaps most surprisingly to today's political observers, *he* was not always a life-long Republican.

With Glade's help, Democrat Bamberger trumped Republican Morris's claim to be the best choice to dry up Utah. Glade, Bamberger, Secretary of State candidate Harden Bennion and other members of the Prohibition and Utah Betterment League went to town with the flair of a vaudevillian troupe. Political scholars point to Glade's own 1952 gubernatorial campaign against J. Bracken Lee as one of colorful speeches and events. However, Glade's brand of political panache already had been established in 1916, with the Bamberger campaign.

One campaign visit to the Uintah Basin typified Glade's sense of dramatic timing in the political arena. The party, consisting of Glade, Bamberger, Bennion, and Robert Siddoway of the Utah Prohibition and Betterment League, motored across the desert to their first stop in the old eastern Utah town of

Jensen. To add to the trip's impact, they pulled over in Fort Duchesne to telephone the waiting crowd in Jensen with a public announcement of their progress. Jensen area Democrats rushed to their jalopies and headed to an appointed meeting place at a well-known bridge in time to caravan back to Jensen en masse for a grand arrival. They precisely ended the Jensen rally with enough time to rush the group to Vernal. They arrived on stage just as the picture show ended at the Orpheus Theater, taking advantage of the full theater of people who would continue their applause for rousing speeches and a tenor solo by Siddoway. [6]

Glade told the group that Bamberger not only had the will to enforce prohibition, but also possessed the power to do so. Bamberger echoed Glade, announcing he wouldn't employ men who drank liquor, or even those who visited saloons for milder beverages. He added that he wouldn't even employ men who smoked cigarettes, and that his Lagoon Amusement Park was absolutely liquor free.[7]

With Glade's help, Bamberger, the popular amusement park and railroad owner and capitalist, easily won. Additionally, Glade and his followers were successful in achieving statewide prohibition; in 1917, Utah became the twenty-fourth state to do so. On January 16, 1919, Utah became the thirty-fourth state to ratify the Eighteenth Amendment and on that same day, Missouri and Wyoming added their consent, providing the number of states needed nationwide to prohibit the production and distribution of intoxicating beverages. The Amendment went into effect a year later on January 17, 1920. Interestingly, in the 1920 elections, wet Democrats in many states with large urban populations thumped dry Republicans running for office, while in Utah a dry Democrat won. Utah's political peculiarities so familiar to today's observers already were norms a century earlier.

On the heels of the Eighteenth Amendment came the Nineteenth Amendment, which was proposed on June 4, 1919, stating that the right of citizens of the United States to vote shall not be denied or abridged by the United States or by any State on account of sex. On October 4, 1919, Governor Bamberger signed the resolution ratifying the Susan B. Anthony Amendment, as the Nineteenth was called, to the federal constitution providing for equal suffrage for women. Utah was the seventeenth state to ratify the Amendment. On August 18, 1920, Tennessee, by a one-vote margin became the thirty-sixth state to ratify it. On August 26, the Amendment was certified and adopted.

Glade was not involved with promoting the Nineteenth Amendment in Utah. It wasn't because he necessarily disapproved of the Amendment; there was not a need to promote it. In Utah the story of women's voting rights was unique because the right to vote for women was granted fifty years prior to the ratification of the Nineteenth Amendment. On February 12, 1870, the Territory of Utah's Legislative Assembly passed a law granting women twenty-one and over the right to vote. To be clear: It wasn't that the LDS Church and the Utah Territorial leaders were forward thinking on the women suffrage issue as much as they likely wanted to show that polygamy did not enslave women. Seven years later, the U.S. Congress passed the Edmunds-Tucker Act in reaction to the practice of polygamy in Utah. That Act repealed Utah's law on women's right to vote. However, when Utah became a state in 1896, the Utah Constitution granted equal voting rights to both men and women. When the Nineteenth Amendment became law in 1920, it gave Utah women the right to vote in federal elections, a right, sans a decade or so, they had had statewide for most of the previous fifty years.[8]

In 1921, building on what officials saw as the moral turpitude of liquor, Utah also passed legislation to prohibit smoking in public places. But after the chair of the Republican Party was arrested for smoking a cigar after dinner, Salt Lake residents took a page out of the Glade-Bamberger political primer of movie-theater politics by rallying in protest of the law at a packed Orpheum Theater in Salt Lake City.[9]

Glade, busy with duties as the national officer of the Young Democrats, did not retreat from Utah's political spotlight even before Bamberger's election. Glade relished his status as a popular University professor and speaker. Among many speeches he gave during this period, one in particular showed the thinking of the times while resonating with his firmly established worldview that reflected his commitments to the LDS Church's teachings. After only a year at The University of Utah, on November 9, 1917, Glade made what was described as a stirring address at a student assembly. He spoke soon after the United

States had entered World War I, emphasizing the importance of promoting national unity, not only in feeling and spirit, but in language as well.

Glade lamented that certain industries were becoming entirely dominated by foreigners, who retained their native tongues and customs. Deploring those conditions as indicative of a lack of national solidarity, he said the war would undoubtedly remedy this state of affairs by eradicating all un-American speech and mannerisms from our national life. According to Glade, lecturer and journalist Bret Harte and actor Douglas Fairbanks, and "that good old western tongue which gives the 'r' a square deal" typified the language for America. Interestingly, these were immigration related issues resurrected by some as a significant problem facing the United States nearly a hundred years later, well into the twenty-first century. In his speech, Glade concluded by urging an appreciative attitude toward the government by all Americans and discouragement of all pessimistic utterances, which sow dissension and discontent among the nation.[10]

His views of national unity and the elimination of dissent at a time of crisis were formulated during WWI, but he would ratchet them up twenty-four years later as he saw America on the cusp of another World War. By then, he would have a powerful forum, radio, which could be heard from one end of the country to the other and well out to the islands in the Pacific Ocean. Glade would give an electronic spark to his philosophy, his religion, and his salesmanship via the new technology sweeping the nation.

SECTION II

THE RADIO BROADCASTER

CHAPTER 3
GLADE AS RADIO PIONEER
AND THE BIRTH OF KSL

Glade quickly learned to parlay his ability to network politically with business associates and associations. On December 4, 1919, he was elected president of the Salt Lake Kiwanis Club at its first annual election of officers in the Newhouse Hotel. He also was an officer in the Commerce Club of Salt Lake, the precursor to the Salt Lake Chamber of Commerce. He leveraged these connections to his Salt Lake and state inner circles. For instance, as a Bamburger favorite, he joined the Governor and others on the committee that planned the January 1920 grand jubilee to celebrate the fiftieth anniversary of the completion of the Utah Central Railroad from Ogden to Salt Lake City, not to be confused with the transcontinental rail at Promontory which was completed a year before in 1869. Of course, Glade fortified his affiliates within his church, speaking at missionary send-offs and at Sunday School activities, among other venues, and beginning twenty-years of service as a member of the General Board Deseret Sunday School Union.

The engaging Glade was a catalyst for uniting people in a cause. His inexhaustible penchant for promising business opportunities, combined with his communication and promotional skills, connections to people in high places, focus on personal growth, and a proclivity for scattering the seeds of his worldview to the masses all coalesced seamlessly. Not stultified by precedent or tradition, he would create the foundation of one of the most respected radio broadcasting stations in America.

Glade is remembered as the pioneer developer of KSL AM radio and was its beloved station manager or corporate officer for several decades. Glade did not put KSL's predecessor station, KZN, on the air in 1922, and was not involved with the station until the mid1920s, although in virtually every newspaper or public iteration of his accomplishments, the credit for founding KZN/KSL has been invariably and erroneously listed.

Once joining KSL in 1924, however, Glade did build the station's infrastructure and shape its advertiser supported business configuration and subsequent audience reach. Most importantly, he gave KSL its *voice* by creating sustainable programming, not the least of which was and remains the Mormon Tabernacle Choir national radio network broadcast, discussed later, begun in 1929.

We don't exactly know the precise moment Glade threw almost all his enthusiasm towards the fledgling broadcasting industry. Certainly, his fascination with the spoken word, his performance flair, and advertising and promotional skills must all have contributed to more than a curiosity about the new radio business.

In 1922, Utah had its first two major radio broadcasting stations (KDYL and KZN), and Glade, although not yet involved in broadcasting, already had several years' experience in media with the *Sugar House Times* newspaper, his teaching, and his various advertising companies and entrepreneurial endeavors. We don't know the first verified example of Glade's salesmanship success, but we do know the next two decades would be unparalleled in Utah broadcast history. Glade's son and namesake, Earl Jr., who also had a distinguished broadcasting career in Boise and at KBYU credited advertising experiences at Gillham Advertising Agency as whetting his father's appetite for the medium. Certainly, at the time radio wasn't seen as an advertising goldmine, but Glade must have recognized opportunity. If not the first, he absolutely is among the first few radio sales people in Utah, along with the flamboyant Sid Fox of KDYL.

Because Glade is a Utah radio legend, several stories have been magnified as bigger than life about his connection to KSL. Just as there are references by well-meaning historians that credit him to being a founder of KSL, or its predecessor, KZN, there also are stories chronicling his immediate conversion to the magic of radio much the same way a kid impulsively joins the circus at the sight of a circus parade. There is probably more than a modicum of truth in any legends surrounding this fabled radio pioneer.

For example, while Glade wasn't on the roof of the old Union Pacific building the night KZN went on the air on May 6, 1922, he certainly helped "evolve" the modern KSL empire beginning in 1924.

KSL Dedication on the Union Pacific Building Roof Top, LDS President Heber J. Grant May 6, 1922, (bing.com/imgages)

He didn't just abandon his day-job and run off to radio, but he did recognize radio's business potential. We can't completely verify the story, but one account of how Glade joined radio is worth repeating, as it reflects the passion he showed for radio as an advertising medium from his first exposure to it.

A little background is helpful. KSL started as the LDS Church-owned KZN in May of 1922. The church-owned *Deseret News* was responsible for its operation during its first two years. KZN operated with a power of 500 watts at 833 kilocycles in the AM spectrum. The station, however, didn't live up to the Church's original expectations, especially as a proselytizing medium, and in 1924 was given over to two bright radio amateurs, John N. Cope and Lionel B. Cornwell to operate. Cornwell played a less active role in the station, providing some operational funds as needed, while Cope became totally involved technically and financially along with other family members in its early development. The new owners changed the KZN station call-letters to KFPT on June 13, 1924, operating on a new frequency at 1149 kilocycles.

This is the point at which Glade, ever watchful and alert to opportunity, reportedly became involved. A story later related by Cornwell on audiotape has Cope doing a radio demonstration at the University of Utah, attended by Glade then 38 and a business instructor at the school. Glade watched the setup activities and reportedly was full of questions about everything. He was so interested in the business potential of radio that "on-the-spot" he asked to join Cope on a commission basis to sell KFPT (later changed to KSL) to sponsors.[1]

As Cornwell relates the story, soon after becoming associated with KFPT, Glade went to the J.G. McDonald Chocolate Factory, which was founded in 1901, to get a commitment from the candy company to sponsor a weekly performance of the J. G. McDonald Orchestra on the station. With Glade's introduction, Cope subsequently was invited to the McDonald home to discuss this radio novelty with McDonald's dinner guests. "By the Waters of Minnetonka" reportedly was played over the station and was dedicated to Mrs. McDonald. Cornwell recounts the McDonalds then received a call from a friend in Los Angeles, owner of Jones Drug Stores, who said KFPT reception in Los Angeles – some 700 miles away – was great. The J. G. McDonald sponsorship was confirmed that evening. "Glade was magic from the beginning," according to Cornwell.[2]

We are sure of one fact: As of November 17, 1924, Glade became an officer of KFPT when Cope's company was incorporated as the Radio Service Corporation of Utah (RSC) and Glade received an RSC contract to work at KFPT. As indicated in the meeting's minutes, John Cope, in addition to corporation president, was appointed the KFPT technical director, with direct supervision over all station operations. Although a participant at the station for a time prior, at the same meeting Glade, for the first time, officially was recognized as part of the KFPT staff. He was appointed sales manager and advertising counsel and a sales agent for RSC. Unlike the few other employees who were salaried, Glade's compensation was determined on a commission basis. He earned 15-percent of the actual cash payments RSC received and was paid a $25 per month retainer fee. Glade agreed to devote himself diligently to the interest of RSC, and if he didn't, RSC could make their mutual agreement "null and void."[3]

KFPT seemingly fared very well financially with Glade as the "diligent" ad salesperson. There, however, was at least one dissatisfied Salt Lake City radio listener who let the U.S. Commerce Department's Bureau of Navigation, the federal government unit in charge of radio at the time, know how he, and by extension all KFPT listeners, felt about what he perceived as the station's advertising excesses.

> *Like thousands of others here [Salt Lake City], I have a small radio set. I purchased it for the purpose of amusement, as well as for educational reasons ... Some time ago parties were given a license and broadcasted programs from this point, their Station is known as K.F.P.T. and their programs were amusing as well as instructive and every listener in enjoyed them. Things have changed, this station is nothing more than an advertising agency for everything from electrical supplies, 'Two suit Pants,' Rubber horns, musical instruments, automobile repair shops, and in fact everything that one is willing to pay them their price of $30.00 per hours for broadcasting. These advertising stunts are on the air every night from 7 until 12 P.M. [sic] and with such volume that it is only the extremely high priced set that can successfully tune them out, and one has little choice in the matter, listen to a dance programe [sic] under the auspices of some candy manufacturer [presumably J.G. McDonald Chocolate Factory], or other advertisement, or shut of[f] your instrument, and regret your investment.[4]*

Not everybody, however, was as unhappy with KFPT's programming as Mr. Purvis (the letter writer) of 3rd Avenue in Salt Lake City. Fans appreciated the station's willingness to broadcast religious programming geared towards the large LDS audience in Utah and surrounding states. Although Cope's Radio Service Corporation owned and operated the station, station officials felt a connection to the LDS Church, which had basically deeded them the station through the church-owned *Deseret News*. Glade would be one to recognize the power of radio as an electronic pulpit for LDS ministry throughout his career.

KFPT received hundreds of telegraphic, telephonic and written statements from people in states on the East and West Coasts, the Midwest, Hawaii, Alaska, and British Columbia expressing great pleasure with the first-ever radio broadcast of the semi-annual LDS church conference on KFPT in October 1924. Reportedly, in addition, there were at least a dozen businesses in Salt Lake and Ogden that broadcast the conference to hundreds of people who never before had been to or heard such services. The entire proceedings were "radiocast" using a direct hookup from the main pulpit of the Tabernacle on Temple Square for the live presentation. In addition, some people, homebound and unable to attend the conference due to illness, were especially pleased to have the convenience.

One such person was Charles W. Penrose, the second counselor to the LDS president, who listened from his bedroom.

> *President Penrose commented on the power of radio to do for*
> *thousands of others –some ill, possibly, and unable to attend*
> *service in person; some remotely situated from Salt Lake–*
> *what it had done for him. As Station KFPT's representative*
> *left the Penrose home that evening, the great man said, "That*
> *is wonderful. ... I certainly thank you; it [the radio broadcast]*
> *has been one of the most thrilling experiences of my life."[5]*

The success of the conference broadcast likely influenced LDS President Heber J. Grant's decision to inaugurate an hour-long regular Sunday evening broadcast from the KFPT studios consisting of a sermon and sacred music, possibly a precursor to the national Mormon Tabernacle Choir broadcasts. The potential of radio to preach the gospel was just coming to be understood by the principals and was projected to be enormous. Glade saw radio as "selling" the message of a higher calling.

> *These programs of discourse and sacred music are brought to*
> *the very fire-sides of thousands of people who otherwise would*
> *be very difficult to reach. In the privacy of their own homes*

*they are often willing, if not eager, to listen to the gospel
message. Many an indifferent person has openly admitted that
radio has done more to convince him of the immortality of
things and of the existence of Diety than any other
intermediary.*[6]

In the same 1925 document, Glade also offered a suggestion of "selling"
radio based on ratings. While there were no scientific ratings or measurements
of listeners at the time, Glade cited radio experts in an audacious claim: "To
state that station KFPT has an audience of over a million, is no exaggeration."
He could have been correct, as the few existing stations of a thousand-watts
could find nightly reaches halfway across the country, with lack of interference
from other stations on their frequencies. The *Ogden Standard-Examiner*, for
example, listed programs from stations in Los Angeles that could be heard in
Salt Lake City in the 1920s.

Glade was proud of KFPT from his very first days at the station and wrote
that it rated among the fifty finest stations of upwards of 500 watts in the United
States at the time. While he didn't offer proof as to which others rated it among
the top 10 percent, almost everyone acknowledged that Glade absolutely
believed it in 1925. Soon, largely through Glade's enthusiasm and persuasion,
LDS Church leaders decided to get back into radio broadcasting and reclaim the
station they gave away several years before to achieve that goal. Glade
orchestrated the unusual business arrangement that led to the church's re-entry
into broadcasting. He persuaded the LDS Church to give a $5,000 interest-free
loan --one credible source says it, instead, was a $10,000 loan – to RSC to get a
new 1,000-watt transmitter. In the loan agreement, the Mormon Church had an
option to acquire 50 percent stock ownership in RSC after a year. Cope
remained as technical director, and Glade became KSL's general manager.[7]

The agreement also occasioned new call letters. On June 25, 1925, KFPT
officially became KSL, and the station moved its facilities to the LDS Church-
owned offices in the basement of the Vermont Building on the corner of South
Temple and Richards Street in Salt Lake City, across from the south entrance to

Temple Square, and increased power to 1,000 watts. In 1925, KSL listeners tuned their receivers to 1000 kilocycles on the proverbial "dial."

To round out the changes in frequency, on June 15, 1927, KSL's frequency was changed to 990 kilocycles, the power and call letters remaining the same. After the Federal Radio Commission took over regulatory responsibilities for radio by virtue of the Radio Act of 1927, an increase of power to 5,000 watts was granted KSL and a change to 1130 kilocycles occurred on November 11, 1928.

On April 18, 1931, Glade, with Utah Senator William H. King in tow, appeared before the Federal Radio Commission (FRC) and gave assorted reasons why KSL should be granted authority to increase its power from 5,000 watts (5 kilowatts) to 50,000 watts (50 kilowatts), to become the most powerful radio station in the Intermountain West. Glade argued to the FRC commissioners that KSL was located in not only the geographical, but also the educational center of a region of mountains and plains, and the main outlet for people living in a vast area inadequately served by broadcasting stations. It is not exactly clear what Glade said to the commissioners, but it was reported that he "asserted that there was every equitable reason why KSL should be permitted to install the maximum power allowed under the Federal Radio Act of 1927." He said it would be an injustice to listeners to deny the 50,000-watt application. At the same hearing, a FRC chief examiner argued that KSL should be allotted only 25,000 watts instead of 50,000, and, for whatever reasons, stations in Los Angles and Hollywood should be given the valuable maximum power allocations.[8]

Glade overcame FRC objections, and KSL, operating on 1130 kilocycles, was one of nine U.S. radio stations authorized by the Federal Radio Commission on October 16, 1932, to operate using the maximum power of 50,000 watts, culminating more than a year of controversy over the issue. These nine radio stations joined only a few others located in New York, Chicago, Los Angles, and other large cities allowed to operate using 50,000 watts day and night on a clear-channel frequency. KSL would invest $200,000 ($3.3 million in today's equivalence) to install high-powered equipment at its transmitter site eight miles west of Salt Lake City on 500 South Street, and at its studio in the Vermont (later the Beneficial Life Building) Building in downtown Salt Lake City, now part of the City Creek mixed-use complex. When KSL went full power, thousands of people and advertisers residing in remote areas of the Intermountain West heard their first daytime radio broadcast, along with listeners as far away as the Marshal Islands and beyond in the Pacific, in Wisconsin and further east, in Canada to the north, and deep into Mexico to the south could hear KSL at night.

At the KSL dedication on October 2, 1932, using a down-link through KHJ in Los Angeles and promoted as being broadcast coast-to-coast on the Columbia Broadcasting System Network, several dignitaries reverently paid tribute to what they saw as an awe-inspiring technical feat. Included were Utah Senator Reed Smoot, Utah Governor George H. Dern, Salt Lake City Commissioner John M. Knight speaking for Mayor Louis Marcus, Salt Lake Chamber of Commerce President A.S. Brown, and Radio Service Corporation President and LDS Presiding Bishop Sylvester Q. Cannon. William S. Paley, the legendary CBS founder and president, also telegrammed a congratulatory message.

Excerpts from their remarks attest to the supreme importance to the Intermountain West, the LDS Church and to radio's listeners the exponential increase in KSL's transmitting power would represent. After a musical introduction, with a voice reminiscent of FDR's later *Day of Infamy* speech, announcer Dave Elton opened the dedication ceremony attended by 150 musicians and nearly 1,000 guests gathered in what was referred to as the KSL Hotel Utah studios.

[Announcer]
Western America of the mountains and plateaus greets
America from coast-to- coast through the voice of the mighty
station of the Rocky Mountains --the new 50-thousand-watt
KSL of Salt Lake City.

[Musical interlude]
Tonight, radio history is made in the West. Tonight the pioneer
station of the Rocky Mountains climaxes more than a decade
of radio achievement by taking its place among America's
radio stations of greatest power. Tonight another glorious
chapter is added to a colorful story. From a box on the roof of
the early struggling days of the 1920 decade, through a
teeming, throbbing colossus of modern communication,
grounded to the shore waters of the Great Salt Lake, and
shadowed by sky piercing towers, monuments to modern
enlightenment. From a fantastic novelty, used curiously by
some, doubtfully by most, one of the greatest community
building factors between the Mississippi and the Pacific Coast
—that is the record of KSL, oldest and largest commercial
broadcasting station in Intermountain America and an affiliate
of the Columbia Network

Senator Smoot next solemnly spoke:

My fellow citizens, I congratulate Utah and the Rocky
Mountain States upon the installation of this powerful radio
station. Our common heritage and birth, our unity of purpose,
which made possible the conquest of this vast territory, have
been preserved and perpetuated by our systems of
transportation and communication. The increased power of
KSL will to a great extent be the means of enlightening the
people of the world concerning the high ideals for which Utah
stands. What wonders hath God wrought!

George H. Dern, governor of the state of Utah had been "unavoidably detained." He sent this word of greeting quoted by the announcer:

Salt Lake City Commissioner John M. Knight represented Salt Lake City Mayor Louis Marcus in his absence:

*Good evening ladies and gentlemen, it is a pleasure for me to
represent the Salt Lake City Commission in dedicating the new
50-thousand-watt plant of KSL. I realize in part what this
great station will mean to Salt Lake City. Every half-hour, I
understand, the Federal Radio Commission requires the
station to identify itself. At least ten times daily, therefore, the
name of our fair city is hurled into the either to find its way to
the very ends of the continent. This in addition to the fine
programs released from this powerful plant makes thousands
of friends for Salt Lake City. Almost every day score of these
radio friends are visiting us in person. May I say for the
Mayor and the Commission that they are, indeed, welcome. I
hope the Columbia Broadcasting System will accept the thanks
of the City for its gracious cooperation tonight and on
numerous other occasions. I certainly congratulate the
Columbia System on its Salt Lake City outlet, K-S-L. Our
municipality is proud to take part in this 24-hour dedicatory
celebration.*

A.S. Brown, president of the Salt Lake Chamber of Commerce followed Commissioner Knight:

*Literally hundreds of thousands of western Americans to
whom radio has become so large a part in their lives will
enjoy more than ever the vast improvement in transmission
and reception made possible by this new station. The officials
of the Columbia Broadcasting System are most certainly to be
congratulated on this powerful Mountain State outlet for their*

*splendid programs. Tonight we are particularly proud to claim
as our own Earl J. Glade, Managing Director of KSL, who
since he assumed his managerial duties has always striven to
further the interests and welfare of this marvelous region and
its people, and who tonight is seeing the culmination of his
fondest dream, a dream primarily conceived in the interest of
the public who have been and are now being so satisfactorily
served by KSL. Truly a dreamer who has made his dream
come true. The Chamber of Commerce of Salt Lake City
wishes KSL good luck. And God speed for a glorious future.*

Radio Service Corporation (RSC) President and KSL Board Chairman Sylvester Q. Cannon iterated the essential work that took place to bring about this endeavor, how well managed the work proceeded, how important the power increase was to the KSL radio listeners, how every order of the Federal Radio Commission had been followed, and how special the KSL affiliate was to the Columbia Network and vice versa.

*To all the listeners of this program, I desire to say that we're
happy in the completion of this outstanding installation of the
50-thousand-watt transmitter on the shores of Great Salt Lake.
In spite of the prevailing adverse conditions, this construction
work consisting of the very latest and best Western Electric
Equipment, housed in a very commodious fireproof building
adequately served by duplicate telephone and power lines and
reached by the federally laid road known as the KSL Highway,
has been carried through to completion during the last six
months. Station KSL is located in the heart of the
Intermountain Territory in the almost exact center of the
eleven Rocky Mountain and Pacific Coast states. Its mission is
to serve most effectively the interest of the largest possible
number of listeners both day and night throughout this section.
We welcome any suggestions, commendations or criticisms of
programs. For it is our desire constantly to present a variety
of representative programs of most general interest. This
station is one of the pioneer broadcasters of the country. It has
grown steadily and consistently from 500-watts to its present
power of 50-thousand-watts. It has promptly complied to every
order and regulation of the Federal Radio Commission. It has*

constantly sought modestly to best serve public interest, convenience and necessity. To this end also we have after extended consideration for several months past affiliated with the Columbia Broadcasting System in order to bring the fine programs produced over that network to millions of listeners in this territory who for lack of sufficiently powerful stations have heretofore been unable to hear these blended broadcast. In behalf of our Board of Directors, representative of all interests of this community, and the community itself, I thank you for your interest in this station and to speak for you the continued fine service rendered by KSL during the eleven years of its existence.

In addition, Columbia President William S. Paley's telegram was read touting how important the greatly powered KSL station was to his four-year-old network's mission to serve the listening public.

On the occasion of the dedication of KSL's new 50-thousand-watt transmitter, it is a privilege and a pleasure for me to congratulate the management and staff of this giant among America's broadcasters. KSL's accomplishments are a matter of American radio history. And its increased power and facilities can only prove of great benefit to countless listeners who will receive from it the best in radio entertainment and the highest type of cultural advantages. Since KSL became a member of Columbia's International Network, its listeners have had constantly available Columbia's varied program features and in return KSL furnishes to the nation's wide audience an outstanding weekly program --the broadcast of the great Tabernacle Choir and Organ. It is our hope in the future to broadcast additional programs which through the medium of KSL will bring to the nation the voice of the Great West. To KSL and its vast audience, I extend Columbia's greeting and best wishes.

Announcer Dave Elton concluded the dedication ceremony:

Western America of the mountains and plateaus is saying goodnight to America from coast-to-coast. The pioneer station of the Rocky Mountains is proud of its mighty record of achievement since the early days of commercial broadcasting. Is proud of its affiliation with the great Columbia Network. KSL of Salt Lake City dedicates its 50-thousand-watts of power to the service of Western America.

Your announcer, Dave Elton.
This is the Columbia Broadcasting System

It was an exceptional moment of national prominence for Utah and Salt Lake City. An article in Portland's *The Morning Oregonian* two weeks after KSL began broadcasting at 50,000 watts further testifies to the station's expanded and welcomed coverage and of the respect Glade enjoyed far beyond Salt Lake into the Pacific Northwest at the time.

For Pacific coast and mountain region radio listeners the biggest event of the week was the appearance on the dial of a new plaything —50,000-watt KSL at Salt Lake City. Grounded on the shore of the inland sea in soil that is 26 per cent salt solution KSL is supposed to deliver the sock of a station almost twice the power and it delivers after dusk in the Pacific northwest a signal that is strong and comparatively free from fading. The dedication program lasted 27 hours [and during the ceremonies, KSL was christened with salt water] ...While KSL's local programs may not be as interesting to northwest listeners as local productions of stations nearer home, it will release some programs of the Columbia network which never have been heard in some portions of this territory before, or if so never with such brilliance and depth of tone. Presiding frequently at KSL's microphone is its managing director, Earl J. Glade. Diminutive and dynamic, he has the gift of making friends over the air. A promoter and idealist, Mr. Glade... [sold] the first radio time in the inter-mountain region [and] was promoted from the ground up through the early days of radio starvation. He not only sold, but he sang, announced and collected and produced —way back when radio was a one-man show.[10]

Later, on March 29, 1941, in accordance with the terms of the 1938 Havana Treaty, which classified AM channels and set the maximum interference levels permitted from other stations, the KSL frequency was moved to 1160 kilocycles and the station continued with clear-channel status using a new 50,000-watt transmitter placed in operation a year earlier. With exception of the period during World War II, when power was reduced in accordance with FCC dictates (FCC Order #107), the 1160 assignment and the 50,000-watt power output, the largest power, with one exception, allocated to U.S. AM stations even to this day, has since been maintained.

In 1936, Glade boldly attempted to make KSL "America's station." At the time there still were vast regions outside KSL's primary and secondary Intermountain coverage area that could not economically support a local station, did not receive satisfactory daytime signals, and depended on clear channel stations for even sparse nighttime coverage. Glade proposed to make KSL radio available in the daytime to the people in these un-served areas and across several states. On September 1, 1936, he applied to the recently constituted FCC for authorization to operate KSL with a power of 500,000 watts, ten times the highest power allowed AM stations at that time and to the present.

When Glade applied for superpower status in 1936, WLW in Cincinnati was the one exception to a maximum 50,000-watt allocation, as mentioned above. It was the only U.S. broadcasting station licensed to use 500,000 watts of power, having earned approval in 1934. Powell Crosley, who manufactured Crosley radio sets and who introduced the Crosley Shelvador refrigerator --with shelves in the door and a built-in radio-- and the Crosley automobile held the license for WLW. Unlike Glade, Crosley didn't necessarily want the huge power increase in order to reach un-served radio listeners in regions surrounding WLW as much as to allow him to manufacture cheaper, less receptive radio sets. Using higher power, WLW could be heard at greater distances by listeners using less expensive Crosley radios, a benefit for listeners and a way simultaneously to increase profits for Crosley's radio manufacturing and broadcasting enterprises.[11]

In April of 1941, KSL filed a new petition of its 500,000-watt application, which had been held in limbo for five years. No FCC action was taken on either the original application or the petition until both were dismissed on August 12, 1942, in accordance with the February 23, 1942, Memorandum Opinion of the Commission, stating in substance that no future authorizations involving the use of any scarce materials would be issued during World War II. As it turned out, no 500,000-watt license except that allotted to WLW on an experimental basis was ever approved, and its superpower license was not renewed after the war.

Interestingly, in 1960, WLW again proposed to upgrade its super-power radio status to a 1 million watts (1000kW) operation, which included a pitch to the FCC to not duplicate WLW's 700kHz clear channel frequency in Cedar City, Utah. That is, WLW said that a station if licensed to Cedar City and emanating from there on clear-channel 700kHz would serve at night only 31,999 persons, in contrast to the 14,111,520 persons served at night if the boosted WLW 1000kW signal emanated from Cincinnati at 700kHz. WLW's proposal was never approved and the 700kHz clear-channel much later was licensed as KALL radio serving Salt Lake City, U of Utah sports, and environs.[12] KALL now has the same 50,000 watts of power as KSL, although KALL operates with 1000 watts using a directional pattern at night to avoid long distance interference with other stations on the same frequency.

Glade's actions in the previous two decades discussed above provided KSL its infrastructure and a powerful 50kW presence in the Intermountain West and beyond, that has reverberated to this day. In the next chapter, we return to 1925 and chronicle Glade's involvement in the development of KSL's profitable and sustainable business enterprise. His work in this aspect did more work to strengthen KSL's brand than at perhaps any other time in the station's long history.

CHAPTER 4
UTAH'S RADIO ENTREPRENEUR

With its renewed interest in owning KSL for its vast reach and proselytizing potential, if not for its future income potential, LDS church leaders took note of at least one investor who agreed. In 1925, John F. Fitzpatrick, secretary of the Salt Lake Tribune Publishing Company, observed that while the station was in debt, the future looked bright enough for him to take on the investment risk. Fitzpatrick invested $1,050 (about $14,000 in today's equivalence) of Tribune Publishing Company money and in doing so brought the Tribune's financial investment in KSL's operating company, Radio Service Corporation (RSC), to 20 percent. A newspaper again would invest in KSL, but this time it was not the Mormon owned *Deseret News*.

A year later, the LDS church exercised its option to buy a majority of RSC stock (50.2 percent) and, after retiring the $5,000 loan and paying an additional $2,500, released the Copes and others from their controlling interest in RSC. No record is readily available that explains the details of how a fair market value for KSL was determined, but it is thought that John Cope did not find the buyout totally to his satisfaction or benefit, possibly leaving him at least disappointed with the new RSC majority owners.

Cope continued as a KSL employee until the December 4, 1928, RSC Board meeting, when he resigned both as RSC vice president and as KSL technical director. He changed his mind, however, and was allowed to withdraw his resignation as technical director at the January 30, 1929, RSC Board meeting. It is not exactly clear why John Cope subsequently left KSL a year later in January 1930, but it appears linked to disagreements with RSC principals over station operations and stock ownership. Cope left KSL for the Northwest and eventually ended up in Los Angeles with Cecil B. DeMille's Paramount and had a distinguished career, with audio credits for more than a hundred films, many of them among the greatest classics of American cinema. These include *The Last Outpost* (1935); *The Road to Singapore* (1940), with Bob Hope, Bing Crosby, and Dorothy Lamour; *Samson and Delilah* (1949), directed by Cecil B. DeMille;

Sunset Blvd. (1950) and *Sabrina* (1954), directed by Billy Wilder; *White Christmas* (1954), with Bing Crosby, Danny Kaye, and Rosemary Clooney; and *Rear Window* (1954) and *To Catch a Thief* (1955), directed by Alfred Hitchcock.

Earl L. Mathewson replaced Cope as KSL technical director in February 1930. Cyril Fossey, Cope's technical assistant, refused to accept the decision to replace Cope with Mathewson and, as a result, was asked to resign his KSL position. He soon joined the KDYL technical staff.[1]

After the LDS Church gained majority interest in KSL, Glade had a new boss, who would prove to be perfect for the entrepreneurial KSL manager. Presiding Bishop Sylvester Q. Cannon, who dealt with the temporal affairs of the LDS Church, was elected RSC president, a position he held for 12 years beginning in 1926. With an engineering degree, Cannon was previously employed in the mining industry and was the Salt Lake City engineer.

Cannon was not closely involved with KSL's daily operations, and the RSC presidency was only one of several offices he simultaneously held in a variety of organizations from 1925 to 1938. For example, while RSC president, he served in high profile positions for Dr. Groves LDS Hospital in Salt Lake City, the Dee Hospital in Ogden and the Idaho Falls Hospital, all of which were owned by the LDS Church. Cannon's presence was everywhere: president of the LDS Business College, Zion's Aid Society, Deseret Gym, McCune School of Music and Art and the *Deseret News.* In addition, he was treasurer of the Uintah Basin Construction Company, supervisor of Salt Lake County Draining District #2, and a director of ZCMI, Zions Securities Corporation, Utah Hotel Company, Amalgamated Sugar Company and U.S. Fuel. He also was appointed by state office holders to serve on many committees and councils.[2]

This litany of responsibilities for hotels, bags of sugar, buildings, a college, some hospitals and a gymnasium shows how little time Cannon could realistically dedicate to a fledgling radio station. As such, he gave Glade nearly complete freedom to manage and develop KSL, as he saw fit. Beginning in 1926 and for more than a decade after, Glade, who exercised that freedom with creativity and zeal, certainly put KSL on the map, truly making it the "The Voice of the West" during his managerial tenure.

Although clearly a company man, even before Cannon became RSC president, Glade already had expanded his entrepreneurial role at KSL. He parlayed his position as a sales agent for John Cope's KFPT into forming his own company, Radio Broadcasters, Inc. (RBI), a company within a company at KSL. Over the next decade he fostered the KSL Artists Bureau and Public Address Service. These two operations, financially separate from KSL and not under RSC's purview, evolved under Glade's RBI to provide significant compensation to him and additional money to various KSL employees.

Glade's Radio Broadcasters, Inc. brokered time-blocks from KSL, produced programming, and sold advertising, sharing remuneration with KSL. RBI came to own much of the office equipment used at the station and to employ several of those who worked at KSL. For instance, KSL had several announcers, including Richard L. Evans, Roscoe Grover, Lynn McKinlay, Ted Kimball and Ted Rogers, with Kimball and Rogers working for Glade and paid through RBI. In addition, RBI paid Dan Vincent, accountant and office manager, as well as Earl Glade, Jr., who, beginning in 1933, signed RBI payroll checks while also writing continuity and preparing newscasts, among other responsibilities at KSL.

Originally, the LDS Church it seems was skeptical of the new radio medium and may have even feared it as an evil force. Thus, the RSC board was willing to let Glade continue to operate RBI, a company within a company, in order to insulate itself from possible criticism and financial risk. But as KSL prospered, Glade's RBI became problematic for RSC board members. In late 1928, Fitzpatrick expressed concern that the accounts of Glade's RBI and those of RSC's KSL should be separated and that each should have a different bookkeeper.[3]

Glade drew a small salary from KSL, but his major income source came from the sale of blocks of KSL time to RBI. The RSC board of directors was contemplating whether KSL should take over all of the periods and pay "Mr. Glade" a salary, or if KSL should continue to sell Glade the time according to the following settlement:

> *Mr. Glade used the hours from eight to ten a.m. for which he*
> *paid $14.00 per day or approximately $378.00 per month; the*
> *Children's Hour from four to five p.m., $5.00 per day or*

*$150.00 per month; two hours from four to six p.m., $15.00
per day or $450.00 per month. [RSB president Cannon] also
advised that Mr. Glade proposed that he take the Morning
Watch period, three hours, more or less from 6:30 a.m. to 10
a.m., less one-half hour for setting-up exercises, --for which he
would pay $600.00 per month, also the Town Cryer Period
from four to six p.m., more or less, each day for which he
would compensate the station at the rate of $600.00 per
month. If the foregoing arrangement was adopted it would
mean that Mr. Glade would pay $1200.00 [$16,160 in modern
equivalence] instead of $825.00 for the morning and evening
periods.[4]*

Later that year, concerns over the intra-company structure again arose.

*The President was authorized to appoint a committee to
carefully study the contracts entered into with Earl J. Glade
and their effect upon the station, and to consider such matters
to the cost of broadcasting, the rates for time sold, etc ... this
committee to report back at the next meeting.[5]*

Glade's economic and financial muscles had been strengthened and toned for maximum impact, a fact not lost upon the RSC directors. These were the first mentions, of many, in the years to come, expressing RSC's concerns over Glade's business-within-a-business (RBI) arrangement at KSL. Glade's perceived conflict of interest was at the center of the debate. On one hand, Glade bought blocks of time from KSL, selling ads in those blocks on behalf of RBI, his solely owned company, while at the same time also selling non-brokered KSL time to advertisers. Was Glade favoring RBI in his ad sales and would it be financially advantageous for RSC to make Glade a salaried KSL employee rather than paying him on a commission basis? This question cropped up regularly during Glade's tenure as station manager.

Glade was getting a salary of $25 per month and a 20 percent commission on all net sales, exclusive of commissions for blocks of time brokered by RBI for resale. At the July 26 and November 26, 1929, RSC board meetings, contracts with Glade were studied for their effect on the station. This resulted in

Glade's payment schedule being adjusted but not significantly changed, and the company-within-a-company organizational structure was not altered.[6]

In the 1930s, after Glade became involved with KLO radio in Ogden, the RSC Board again questioned his entrepreneurial practices and his capacities to dedicate the time to be an effective KSL general manager.

> *The question was raised by the Board as to the relations of our manager, Earl J. Glade, with station KLO and with Station KSL, and also to the purchase of time on Station KSL [by RBI], and the thought was expressed that it is not good business practice to sell time which affords an opportunity of competition with himself as manager, which it was thought Mr. Glade was endeavoring to avoid.[7]*

Again, nothing came of this, and Glade continued with RBI and KSL and at the same time invested in and became manager and, essentially, owner of KLO. Glade's involvement in Ogden's KLO was as significant as what he had achieved in Salt Lake City. But the stations seemingly didn't greatly compete for audiences, advertising or programming. KSL was, to use a metaphor, the "Cadillac" and KLO the "Ford" for radio advertisers. For a time Glade was listed as the manager of both stations before giving up on KLO for lack of interest from Ogden advertisers. With Cannon in ultimate control, Glade and any apparent conflict of interest went unnoticed or seriously challenged. After all, KSL was making a profit and the parent LDS Church was being well served. Glade's evolutionary involvement in KLO explains his entrepreneurial efforts to expand radio beyond Salt Lake City, while also likely trying to find a way to distance himself from RSC's oversight, and build his personal wealth and status in so doing. A brief accounting of KLO's beginnings is helpful in understanding Glade's involvement.

In June 1924, Peery and Redfield obtained an FCC license for a radio station in Ogden and hired amateur radio operator W. Glen Garner to design and help construct KFUR, later to become KLO, Utah's third enduring radio broadcasting station after KSL and KDYL in Salt Lake City. Peery and the Redfield Electric Company, which supplied many of the parts for the new radio station, financed its construction. The Peerys wanted the station so they could broadcast from their White City Gardens Dance Hall and advertise their two theaters. Garner constructed KFUR, which later became KLO, in the Peery's Ogden Theater, at 420 25th Street. He put the transmitting antenna on the roof of the same building.

The Peery brothers reportedly were "elated" with KFUR when it went on–the–air. The KFUR signal was heard throughout the west and in Hawaii. However, with the passage of the Radio Act of 1927, KFUR was threatened with extinction. The Act required every station in the country to show how its continuance would be in the "public interest, convenience or necessity." Because of interference, especially in rural areas, the Federal Radio Commission intended to eliminate many stations nationwide. Thus, within sixty days of the Act's passage, every station had to justify its continued existence by reapplying for a new license. The Peerys did several things to ensure KFUR's continued license security, but, primarily, they emphasized KFUR's uniqueness as the only privately supported station, as opposed to commercially supported, in the area providing dependable daytime service for the goodwill of the people of Ogden. In his renewal reapplication, Peery emphasized that an increase in signal power would be in the public interest of the KFUR coverage area:

> *There are but three broadcast stations including this one in the*
> *State of Utah, and due to the fact that our nearest other*
> *entertainment by radio is over 600 miles air line distant, and*
> *this is too far for reliable reception during summer months,*
> *and also due to freak conditions in this intermountain country*
> *making it hard to receive outside stations.*[11]

KFUR survived the FRC's station closings, and, on June 15, the date the FRC implemented frequency changes nationwide, KFUR was allowed to continue operations using 50 watts at 1330kc. By November KFUR was broadcasting on 1370 kilocycles from the Hotel Bigelow with 500 watts of power.

In 1928, as KFUR moved to the Hotel Bigelow, its owners unofficially changed its call letters to KLO. In official correspondence with the FCC, KFUR continued to be used, but on station letterhead and program schedules and in local public promotions, the KLO signature was used to identify the station. The 'L–O' in KLO possibly came from Bigelow, which was owned by Archie Bigelow, an Ogden banker. Interestingly, when the stock market crashed in 1929 and Bigelow's bank failed, the name of the hotel was changed to the Ben Lomond Hotel because it was not thought wise to have a hotel named after a failed bank. Fortunately, the KLO call letters remained meaningful, housed at the Lomond Hotel. KFUR, still informally KLO, was on the air about 10 hours a day, six days a week, and an additional hour on Sunday was aired from the Elks Lodge.

Later in 1928, Glade proposed to the Peerys to tie KFUR to KSL for certain portions of the broadcast day. As such, KFUR would carry some NBC programming and, for the first time, would sell advertising time to Ogden businesses other than those owned by the Peerys. KSL would also provide needed business and technical expertise to KFUR.

Glade formed the Interstate Broadcasting Corporation (IBC) as the parent to KFUR. He then became Interstate's President and Managing Director. KSL's John Cope became technical director, and his brother Frank was made station manager. Cope, newly resigned from KSL involvement, designed a new transmitter and later installed it at a site four miles southwest of Ogden, approximately one mile west of the municipal airport. Upon officially taking over KLO --still KFUR in FRC official records-- in January 1929, Glade printed new letterhead, promoting Ogden as "Utah's Railroad and Industrial Center," and KLO as "The Voice of the Great New West." In addition, he issued IBC capital stock in the amount of $100,000, of which $75,000 represented the value of the KFUR Federal Radio Commission license. In putting value on the license and issuing stock against it to raise capital, Glade followed Sidney Fox's innovative asset-promoting lead at Salt Lake's KDYL several years before.

On February 7, 1929, the Peery Building Company executed a conveyance transferring all of its "right, title and interest" in the KFUR equipment to Glade and Cope. On April 11, 1929, the FRC officially approved the change from KFUR to KLO, and finally the practice of using those call letters was proper. The KFUR designation was no more.[13]

Although Glade did not actually represent himself to the FRC as KFUR's licensed "attorney," he had signed his request for the call letter change with: "By Earl J. Glade on behalf of the Peery Building Company." That was the typical way lawyers signed for clients in correspondence before the FRC.

On July 22, 1929, Glade and Cope also assigned all their interests in KLO equipment to IBC. Simultaneously, the Peery Building Company, by now with only a 10 percent interest in KLO, filed an application to assign the license to IBC as well. Because Glade and Cope had invested a large sum of money for KLO's construction and equipment, and now as they effectively owned the station, it was appropriate also to transfer the license to the Interstate Broadcasting Company. FRC's approval came in 1931.

Glade continued to manage KSL while he also owned and operated KLO, with the Peery's as minority owners. Glade's major challenge was to make KLO successful and profitable without competing against KSL. When Glade assumed control of KLO, it still was programmed mostly with entertainment originating from the Peerys' amusement holdings. For instance, the popular Gene Halladay was playing nightly organ concerts from the Peerys' Egyptian Theater.

By 1934, IBC shares were 41 percent owned by Glade and RBI, 19 percent owned by the Columbia Trust Company and Attorney H. L. Milliner of Salt Lake, and 10 percent by Louis Peery. The Interstate officers included Glade as president, Vice president and Attorney Samuel C. Powell, Secretary Oliver G. Ellis, and Auditor Dan H. Vincent. KLO's staff included Gene Halladay, by then studio manager and program director, Production Manager F.W. Stanbrough, and Chief Engineer Eugene G. Pack, who was borrowed from KSL.

Although KLO was selling commercial time, it generated little income and continued, mostly supported by Glade along with the Peerys and their "amusement" businesses. By March, 1934, still only 18 percent of KLO's programs were commercially sponsored and, although there was programming 12 hours a day, a schedule which rebroadcast many network programs via KSL, Glade could not attract Ogden advertisers. As can be discerned from his testimony before the FCC in 1934 transcribed below, Glade also was deeply discouraged that his considerable investments of time, personal financial resources, and KSL assistance had not generated advertiser or community interest in KLO:

> *All I wanted ... was to try to arouse the people of Ogden to the value of that institution [KLO] and I had done more than my part in that regard. I had made over 700 trips to Ogden, there and back, in an endeavor to help that situation, and KSL had big–brothered it all down the line. It ran remote controls and did everything that could be done. We have often run, with the permission of the Columbia System [CBS], as many as ten national programs over KLO, to see if we could not enliven the interest of the people of Ogden; but I have never seen such apathy in my life. KSL is doing a lot of work for that city [Ogden] right now[14]*

By 1935, Glade reluctantly had allowed much of IBC capital stock to be acquired by the *Ogden Standard Examiner's* A. L. Glasmann. Through Harry Anderson, an intermediary, Glasmann quietly took control of IBC and KLO. Glade soon completely gave up his financial interest in KLO and went back to his full time job managing only KSL. It is not known why Glade was unable to make KLO a commercial success. Possibly it was the lingering effects of the Great Depression. Or the sheer volume of what surely was an extraordinarily busy schedule may have overwhelmed him. The station also had significant competition for listeners and advertisers from the mighty 50kW KSL and from west coast stations at night.

But even before his involvement in KLO, Glade acknowledged localism's impact. As early as 1925, Glade recognized the then-still-new KSL served a wider audience in Utah beyond Salt Lake City. His years of advertising and promotion work along with his teaching experience underscored just how customer service could drive the bottom line. KSL's "customers" extended well beyond Salt Lake City, throughout Utah and in parts of surrounding states. An example came in a letter to a Northern Utah listener that ended up in the local paper. It exemplifies the entrepreneurial Glade relating business decisions to individual listeners, while taking a moment to offer a nice word about a town in the KSL listening area.

Glade also instinctively knew radio drew a crowd on every remote, and listeners would tell others about seeing radio production live in front of them. He further knew newspapers within the KSL listening area would give him lots of free publicity when he did radio on location.

In 1927, for example, the *Ogden Standard Examiner* gave Glade's KSL a banner headline:

OGDEN DANCE MUSIC, CALLS PUT ON RADIO

*Thursday night was Ogden night over radio station KSL of
Salt Lake. With Earl J. Glade, directing, a program was
broadcast by remote control from the Berthana. The old-timer
dance music provided a novelty, the microphone being
arranged so that both the music and the calls from the dancers
were sent out. In the intermissions, Mr. Glade gave a lecture
on Ogden and its resources, basing his radio talk upon
condensed information compiled by the Ogden Chamber of
Commerce.*[16]

Not all remote broadcasts reportedly went so smoothly. The nature of live broadcasts combined with the technology of the times and the perfected art of story-telling have fabricated some colorful urban legends that don't completely satisfy the authors' criteria for believability. There is a tendency for apocryphal stories to be passed down through generations. One example credited to KSL under Glade's watch concerned the first weekend in October 1927 or 1928 when both the LDS General Conference and the World Series were carried on KSL.

The World Series game was set to start at 11:45 a.m., and Glade had arranged to cut away from LDS Conference proceedings to carry it. Glade was said to be in front of the Tribune Building where he had coordinated for KSL's "play-by-play" reenactment to be demonstrated with magnetic players on "Old Ironsides," the large baseball diamond sign outside the Tribune Building on Main Street. Other accounts had him in the KSL studio reenacting the baseball game. Up until this broadcast, the Tribune had always recreated the game from the dots and dashes of code for the many people gathered outside the Tribune Building who didn't have home radio receivers. When the hour came to switch from the LDS Conference to the World Series on KSL, the baseball play-by-play signal was fed to the Tribune Building, but the baseball signal supposedly was not simultaneously turned off in the Tabernacle.

Earl Jr. related the following:

> *President [Heber J.] Grant immediately stood up and shouted, "Turn it [the World Series broadcast] off! Turn it off!" But no one at KSL could hear him. Bishop [Sylvester Q.] Cannon, feeling responsible for KSL ran out of the Tabernacle, out of Temple Square to the northwest door of the Union Pacific Building ... and ran up six flights of stairs to get to the control room to 'urge' the operator to shut off the World Series into the Tabernacle. ... Dad [Earl J. Sr.] was at the Tribune [Building] and wasn't aware of this catastrophic happening until later in the day and then to wonder if he would still have a job when he arrived at work on Monday morning. It seemed that President Grant had played baseball as a youth and was forgiving.* [17]

Again, this story is probably exaggerated somewhat and may have only involved crossed wires for those listening at home, but not in the Tabernacle; or it may have involved an LDS Church authority wishing to preempt the World

Series, and not bat second to Babe Ruth. The tale has been repeated and shared extensively over decades, but it begs the question: Why would KSL programming be aired in the Tabernacle where live sessions were outgoing? Granted, both the LDS General Conference and the World Series were sequentially aired on KSL, but both were meant for a listening audience outside the Tabernacle and not for the one inside the building. The switch to the World Series may have interrupted the radio listeners' General Conference proceedings but likely not the proceedings within the Tabernacle. Glade was responsible for creating KSL's "Voice" through a variety of program innovations, both locally and nationally. A topic of the next chapter.

CHAPTER 5

CRAFTING KSL'S PROGRAMMING VOICE

Nowhere was Glade's commitment to representing the programming desires and requirements of KSL's audience and its owners more energetic than in the station's religious and cultural programming. Although nearly every cultural entity and church denomination gained access on KSL during the Glade years, the most well-known cultural/religious program remained (and has remained) the national network broadcast of the Mormon Tabernacle Choir from Temple Square in Salt Lake City. As the narrative goes, the first coast-to-coast choir broadcast resulted from a Glade visit in the summer of 1929 to NBC in New York to negotiate the contract for the broadcast. A 1939 *Improvement Era* article written by William Mulder, likely a University of Utah student at the time, later a U English professor and global scholar and visionary, relates events surrounding the initial broadcast:

> *At three o'clock on Monday, July 15, 1929, the National Broadcasting Company released the initial program on its thirty-station network ... The Choir continued to be presented on various week days including Monday, Tuesday, and Friday – from July 1929 to September 1932 [when KSL switched its network affiliation from NBC to CBS] and since that time it has appeared as a weekly CBS Sunday feature. ... In the summer of 1929, when Earl J. Glade ... conceived the idea of a nationwide Choir broadcast and went to New York to promote the vision with NBC, he realized that scrupulous attention [by the network] was being paid program material and production by leaders in the field. ... The field was ready for programs intrinsically cultural and with an uplifting influence. ... It's a matter of history that the Tabernacle Choir, since its first coast-to-coast concert, has continued to travel [that] highway."[1]*

Being ready for "intrinsically cultural programs of an uplifting nature" was how Mulder described the radio network field of 1929 in his 1939 article, but

Merlin Hall Aylesworth, president of NBC in 1929, had a somewhat different take on why the network was formed and broadcasting's purpose.

In the October 1929 *Popular Science Monthly*, Frank Parker Stockbridge interviewed Aylesworth about NBC's daily task of feeding thirteen-million radio sets. According to Aylesworth:

> *The main purpose of broadcasting is not to make money. It is to give the public such increasingly better programs that people will continue to buy and use radio sets and tubes, reflecting the joint ownership of the [NBC] network by General Electric, Westinghouse and the Radio Corporation of America, all of which sold radio equipment to the general public. Briefly, what we have done by chain broadcasting ... is to bring the best programs of New York stations within reach of all. By eliminating the element of distance, we have made it possible for anybody, anywhere, with any type of good radio receiver, to hear the best features on the air. Previously, only a few independent stations could afford to broadcast such features and only a fraction of the radio audience could hope to pick them up. We have changed all this by connecting some sixty stations, all over the country, with leased telephone wires.*[2]

Aylesworth may have spoken the truth when he said that anybody, anywhere, with a good radio receiver could hear the best programs emanating on the network from New York City. But this possibly would be true only at night on AM stations across the country. It certainly was not true of the daytime signal propagation, which was and is significantly narrower in coverage. The first Choir broadcast that aired at 3 p.m. reached larger cities but that did not include "anybody, anywhere" coast-to-coast, especially those in rural areas of the nation and those west of Denver. Nevertheless, tens-of-thousands of people would have been able to hear that first Choir broadcast, and hundreds upon hundreds of millions have heard it in the more than eight decades since its inception.

However, like so many stories involving Glade that have endured over the decades, the narratives about the beginning of the Mormon Tabernacle Choir NBC Network broadcasts in July 1929 are a blend of fact, legend, and fond and sometimes faulty memory. Accounts such as Mulder's relating aspects of the first network broadcast are enlightening, but the significance of this event can be better understood with some additional clarification, including when the idea of the broadcast was initially conceived, how and with what quality the first Choir program reached New York from KSL, and what constituted the number of NBC network affiliates on which the program was released "coast-to-coast?"

When was the vision of the Choir network broadcast conceived? No mention of what would become a landmark broadcast in decades to come could be found in any of the Salt Lake City newspapers on the days surrounding that first Choir broadcast. But Glade reported to the Radio Service Corporation (RSC) directors on July 26, 1929, eleven days after the broadcast, that he had been in New York where he had "charge" of the program over the National Broadcasting Chain consisting of forty-four stations.[3] In reality, Glade seemingly didn't go to New York in the summer of 1929, as related by Mulder, to "promote his vision" of a nationwide Choir broadcast, he related he went to represent KSL for the actual broadcast.

The Mormon Tabernacle Choir nationwide broadcast "vision" actually was conceived and publicly known in early May 1929, when Don E. Gillman, an NBC vice president in charge of NBC's Western Division, visited KSL to negotiate with Cannon for the network broadcast of programs by the Tabernacle organ and choir. Originally, it was primarily the organ that NBC was interested in featuring.[4]

In addition, negotiations between Gillman and Cannon for the Choir and organ broadcasts initially may have involved airing only on NBC's Pacific Network, which was under Gillman's control. West coast affiliates included KPO and KGO in the San Francisco Bay Area, KFI Los Angeles, KFOA Seattle, KGW Portland, and KHQ Spokane. In his spring visit to Salt Lake, Gillman spoke highly of KSL, saying that as an NBC affiliate, the station was one of the most effective "units" in the entire NBC chain. Glade in the early May meeting said the organ and Choir broadcasts over the network would be of a diversified nature, consisting mostly of classical and semi-classical music, and would give the Choir and the "great" organ, under the direction of Prof. A.C. Lund, an opportunity to be heard by millions of Americans. The NBC contract with KSL as finally adopted eventually included broadcast of the organ and choir across the nation on the NBC network, not just to stations on the Pacific Network.[5]

Another intriguing question concerns the quality of the first Choir broadcast. Heber G. Wolsey picks up the story in his 1967 Ph.D. dissertation covering the history of early KSL radio programming:

> *For the first few minutes of the initial program everything went well. Reception was described as "perfect" by Eastern representatives of NBC. Then shortly after the first organ selection, an annoying line hum became so bad that a number of Eastern stations were obliged to cut away from the network and fill with local programming. However, by the time of the second scheduled broadcast a week later, the technical difficulties had been corrected, and many favorable comments concerning the broadcast were received.[6]*

To answer the broadcast-quality question, it's helpful to put the first July 1929 Choir broadcast in context by further examining the NBC network structure in its early years of existence. NBC began programming on November 15, 1926, with a 19-station hookup. At the time, NBC was "national" in name only. Its coverage reached only as far as Denver, and it did not have a coast-to-coast hookup, as AT&T did not have broadcast-quality telephone lines that spanned the Rocky Mountains in the beginning. To serve the West Coast with a broadcast quality signal, NBC started the Pacific Network on April 5, 1927.

The Pacific Network, dubbed the "Orange" Network, the one Gillman oversaw, complemented NBC's two other networks, the NBC Red and NBC Blue Networks. All three NBC-owned networks were said to be so named by the colors of the lines and push-pins on AT&T's maps showing the path each took across the states to deliver radio programming to their respective NBC affiliates. Because broadcast-quality telephone lines reached to only Denver in the first two years, NBC recreated the same programs for the Orange (Pacific) Network previously heard only east of Denver. As such, after a program ran in the East on NBC's Red Network, all of the program scripts, musical scores and continuity were shipped to San Francisco, where it was rehearsed for performance a week later on the Pacific Network.[7]

There was no such thing as a weekly "coast-to-coast" network program at that time. Making a normal long-distance telephone call connected Denver and San Francisco. (Los Angeles would only later become the terminal for West Coast AT&T telephone lines.) When AT&T completed a broadcast-quality telephone circuit from Denver to the West Coast in December 1928, only then could the programs originating in the East be heard over the Orange Network affiliates without delay or duplication in the West. The Orange Network then mostly carried Red Network programming to NBC affiliates on the West Coast.[8]

However, sending a broadcast-quality signal from East to West in December 1928 was not the same as sending one from West to East. A broadcast-quality signal from West to East, coast-to-coast, was not possible at the time.

> *The first nationwide broadcast from the West Coast had been the Rose Bowl Game from Pasadena on New Year's Day, 1927, with Graham McNamee at the microphone. But, this had been accomplished on a temporary hookup over normal phone lines. The first regular coast-to-coast broadcast from the West over high-quality lines took place in April of 1930, [well after the July 1929 Mormon Tabernacle Choir broadcast] with the broadcast of the "Del Monte Program" sponsored by the California Packing Company.[9]*

So, even though NBC President Merlin Aylesworth bragged in 1929 that programs offered by any one of the NBC Network affiliates, which would include KSL, could be carried by all of them, it was possible only on normal long distance telephone lines when the Choir broadcast aired, not on broadcast-quality lines.[10]

The fact there existed no "broadcast-quality" lines carrying programs West to East in 1929 raises the question if it was possible even initially --sans the hum after a few minutes-- to broadcast a "perfect" Choir and organ program signal emanating in July 1929 from Salt Lake City to New York City. An additional situation speaking to the quality of the broadcast deals with the fact that a single microphone, likely a telephone receiver, hanging above the Choir and monitored by KSL announcer Ted Kimball positioned on a ladder, captured the signal for the first broadcast and reportedly for subsequent ones for years to come.

Mulder relates that when a Columbia Broadcasting System chief engineer later discovered the broadcast was handled for years by remote control on a "one-mike" pickup, and on a single line with no provision for an emergency, he was amazed. "That's impossible!" he protested.[11] The CBS chief engineer's statement might have gone beyond an astonished "impossible" to a professional assessment. The broadcast might have truly been "impossible" over the years with a one-mike system on a single line; "possibly" an apocryphal story perpetuated over the years.

A third question concerns what constituted the NBC network of affiliated stations in 1929 when the broadcast occurred. Mulder relates that at 3 p.m. on Monday, July 15, 1929, the National Broadcasting Company released the initial Choir program on its thirty-station network – Glade said in his report to RSC directors it was forty-four stations – but NBC President Aylesworth in late 1929 tallies an even larger number of total NBC Network stations:

> *If all the [affiliated] stations take a sponsored program, the advertiser must pay the price of nation-wide publicity. This means $9,230 an hour with the Red Network of forty-two cities connected with WEAF [the Red Network flagship station in New York], or $7,960 an hour [over $126,000 and $109,000 respectfully in modern equivalence] with the Blue Network of thirty-three cities connected with WJZ [the Blue Network flagship station also in New York, moved there from New Jersey] ... The programs put on for advertisers are almost entirely entertainment.[12]*

The Red Network was tagged to carry commercially sponsored music and entertainment programs, while the Blue Network carried sustained and non-sponsored music, news, and cultural programming. There is no evidence the first Choir broadcast was commercially sponsored on the Red Network, or that KSL paid the $7,960 hourly rate to reach the thirty-three Blue Network affiliates. The logical conclusion is the first Mormon Tabernacle Choir broadcast sent from Salt Lake City emanated coast-to-coast from WJZ without sponsorship on most of the Blue Network's stations in thirty-three cities across the nation, and possibly on some independent eastern state stations that tapped into the network feed.

This, seemingly to satisfy NBC's desire to carry, in Mulder's words, "intrinsically cultural programs of an uplifting nature." Further support for tapping only the Blue Network for the broadcast lies in the fact that in 1929 coast-to-coast programs as stated earlier could not be carried live simultaneously on the Red and Blue Networks beyond Denver to the West Coast.

The evidence leads to the conclusion the first Mormon Tabernacle Choir NBC Blue Network broadcast, captured using a single microphone, was transmitted from Salt Lake City to New York City using normal, not broadcast-quality, long distance telephone lines meant for the speaking voice. The first broadcast likely was described as "perfect," not because of its superior sound quality, but because it was a remarkable undertaking achieved by a fledgling three-year-old NBC radio network in cooperation with an overachieving KSL engineering and announcing staff at the NBC affiliated station in Salt Lake City headed by Glade.

Glade and Cannon can be historically associated with conceiving the Choir broadcasts, but Richard L. Evans likely is the best-known figure partnered with the historic weekly broadcast. During his lifetime, he was associated with the Mormon Tabernacle Choir network broadcast for all but the first ten months of its existence. At first he was the announcer, but after a while he introduced the *Spoken Word* instead of just announcing the hymns being sung. Evans' weekly broadcasts spanned more than forty years from 1930 until his death in 1971.[13]

As mentioned by Mulder, the Choir broadcast later aired weekly on the nationwide CBS Network when KSL shifted its network affiliation in 1932 and transcontinental lines were installed. After more than eighty-five years, the Mormon Tabernacle Choir broadcasts, still called *Music and the Spoken Word*, remain as Glade and Cannon's programming legacy long after their deaths. It is American radio's longest running network program, now said to be carried on over 2,000 radio and television stations worldwide.

In addition to the Mormon Tabernacle Choir broadcasts, for other programs, Glade surrounded himself with writers, musicians, actors, announcers, technicians and all the other persons and facilities he could obtain on a limited budget. Just a few of the quite remarkable programs and people are mentioned below to show the depth and dedication Glade gave to developing KSL's local

"Voices" during his years managing the station. Ralph W. Hardy, KSL's Public Service Director in 1946, parroted very well KSL's programming philosophy as the station matured decades before:

> *The KSL staff is told that since KSL's radio audience represents a cross-section of the population of the Intermountain area, programs should be designed to meet the desires and requirements of as great a representative part of the audience as possible.[14]*

Glade shepherded a number of original local programs and nurtured some extraordinary local talent. Irma Bitner – later to become Mayor Glade's Salt Lake City recorder – and Josephine (Josie) Goff and their B & G Studios designed programs, scouted performers, and directed and produced several programs on KSL. One especially popular program "Mary and John," called *KSL's Sweethearts of the Air*, was a locally produced daytime serial, featuring Phyllis Greenwood and Gordon Owen as Mary and John, with Leora Thatcher, Mary McPhie, Sherman Nichols, and Dave Elton in supporting roles. Bitner directed the series, Goff produced it, and Gladys Wagstaff Pinney authored every program for what was supposed to be a twenty-six-week series.

Typical of Glade's commercial advertising sagacity, *Mary and John* was a romantic serial created as part of a model home advertising

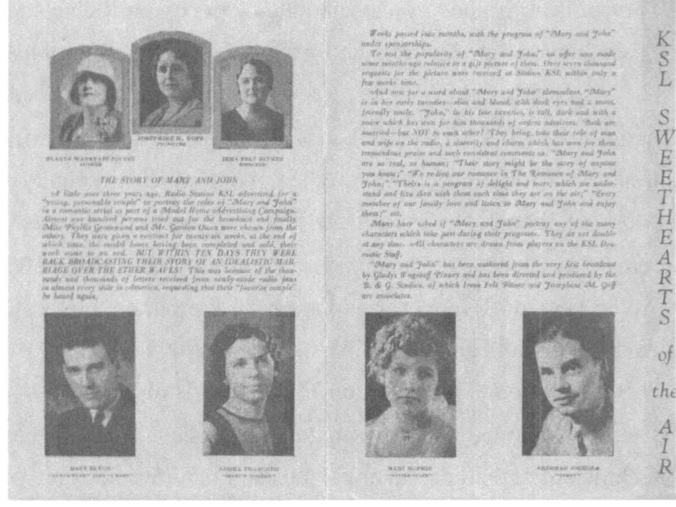

THE STORY OF MARY AND JOHN

A little over three years ago, Radio Station KSL advertised for a "young, personable couple" to portray the roles of "Mary" and "John" in a romantic serial as part of a Model Home Advertising Campaign. Almost one hundred persons tried out for the broadcast and finally Miss Phyllis Greenwood and Mr. Gordon Owen were chosen from the others. They were given a contract for twenty-six weeks, at the end of which time, the model home having been completed and sold, their work came to an end. BUT WITHIN TEN DAYS THEY WERE BACK BROADCASTING THEIR STORY OF AN IDEALISTIC MARRIAGE OVER THE ETHER WAVES! This was because of the thousands and thousands of letters received from newly-made radio fans in almost every state in America, requesting that their "favorite couple" be heard again.

Weeks passed into months, with the program of "Mary and John" under sponsorships.

To test the popularity of "Mary and John," an offer was made some months ago relative to a gift picture of them. Over seven thousand requests for the picture were received at Station KSL within only a few weeks' time.

And now for a word about "Mary and John" themselves. "Mary" is in her early twenties—slim and blond, with dark eyes and a sweet, friendly smile. "John," in his late twenties, is tall, dark and with a voice which has won for him thousands of ardent admirers. Both are married—but NOT to each other! They bring into their role of man and wife on the radio, a sincerity and charm which has won for them tremendous praise and such consistent comments as: "Mary and John are so real, so human; "Their story might be the story of anyone you know;" "We re-live our romance in The Romance of Mary and John;" "Theirs is a program of delight and tears, which we understand and live them with them each time they are on the air;" "Every member of our family love and listen to Mary and John and enjoy them;" etc.

Many have asked if "Mary and John" portray any of the many characters which take part during their programs. They do not double at any time. All characters are drawn from players on the KSL Dramatic Staff.

"Mary and John" has been authored from the very first broadcast by Gladys Wagstaff Pinney and has been directed and produced by the B. & G. Studios, of which Irma Felt Bitner and Josephine M. Goff are associates.

K
S
L

S
W
E
E
T
H
E
A
R
T
S

of

the

A
I
R

John and Mary, "Sweethearts of the Air",
(J. Willard Marriott Library)

campaign. Owen and Greenwood were given contracts for twenty-six weeks, at the end of which time, the model home having been completed and sold, their work came to an end. "But within ten days they were back broadcasting their story of an idealistic marriage over KSL." Thousands of letters received at KSL from radio fans in almost every region in America, requested that their "favorite couple" be heard beyond the twenty-six weeks.

As such, *Mary and John* was extended for weeks and months under sponsorship after its original run.[15] Indeed, Glade's idea has been replicated by the LDS Church in many ways since then, including the more recent 'I Am A Mormon' video campaign featured internationally on YouTube and which has spread to other social media channels.

In 1932, Bitner and Goff of B & G Studios asked Louise Hill Howe, a local actress, to do a short dramatic piece for *Observatory Hour*. Howe adapted a play with women characters and played all three parts. Glade and KSL's program director, Shipley Burton, liked Howe's talent and asked her to do a weekly drama. Glade hired Joe Kearns – later, Mr. Wilson on the *Dennis the Menace* television show – and Pinney, the talented and prolific writer at KSL, to write the shows and help Howe with her radio plays. This group became known as the "KSL Players:"

> *Outstanding dramatic presentations of modern radio are
> assured Intermountain listeners with the signing of the
> Paramount bakers, makers of Holsom Bread, as sponsors of
> the KSL Players. These broadcasts will be heard each
> Wednesday from 9:00 to 9:30 p.m. The series will feature
> realistic dramas, written especially for radio by Gladys
> Wagstaff Pinney, KSL playwright, who is winning Western and
> National recognition for her radio presentations. Louise Hill
> Howe, will continue as director and romantic lead, and Joe
> Kearns, KSL announcer will go on testing his versatility in
> various leading roles. Other members of this staff of widely-
> acclaimed professional staff include: Leora Thatcher, Eleanor
> Silver, J.F. Smith, Ed Broman and others. James Eaken will be
> in charge of the sound effects for the dramatic broadcasts.[16]*

In the next sixteen years, many other talented men and women participated in the KSL Players, including Lynn McKinlay, Francis Urry, Dick Keddington, Wayne Richards, Albert Eccles, Leonard Strong, Parley Baer, Laverne Stallings, Donna Jones, Ethel Baker Callis, Mitzi Poulton, Mary Ethel Eccles and Pauline Strong. Begun under Glade in 1932, the "KSL Players"
continued until 1948, when Howe left to teach radio performance in the Speech Department at the University of Utah.

A charming story involves the young Louise Hill Howe attempting to accommodate a KSL Players' appliance advertiser by going to Park City to demonstrate a washing machine. Howe, the consummate, properly mannered professional, related in a 1990s interview that she had never used a washing machine and didn't know how to operate one at the time. Nonetheless, she reported she was well received as a radio "star" by those gathered for the affected demonstration.[17]

A testament to the popularity of the KSL Players came with a 1936 listener survey conducted by the Logan Garment Company. In a thirteen-week period, 49,600 requests for

KSL News, October 8, 1933
(J. Willard Marriott Library)

pictures of the KSL players came in from forty states as well as Alaska, South America, Hawaii and Mexico. Beginning in 1932 and spanning more than a decade under Glade and his successor, hundreds of dramatic radio plays were written and produced for the KSL Playhouse.

Parley Baer and Francis Urry, known on-the-air as brothers Gerald and Edwin Bates were another popular Glade find. The "Bates Boys" became two well-known comedic characters that had a three-night-a-week run on KSL in the late 1930s and after the war. In addition to on-the-air work, they made more than 300 personal appearances on behalf of local charities as KSL representatives. Urry, while concurrently filling KSL announcing, acting and producing

Louise Hill Howe Directing KSL Players Francis Urry, Parley Baer and another actor. (J. Willard Marriott Library)

assignments, played freelance radio characters on WGN, NBC, CBS and MBS out of Chicago. He appeared on such programs as "Guiding Light," "America on the Air," and "Chicago Theatre of the Air."

Baer left KSL in the 1940s to go to Hollywood, starring in more than 200 productions, including a run as "Chester" on radio's *Gunsmoke*, and as the Mayor of Mayberry on TV's *Andy Griffith Show*.

KSL under Glade cultivated a far-reaching corps of popular personalities and highly talented engineers and technicians. Uncle Roscoe Grover was an artist and a favorite of children for the way he read stories and of adults for his travel items. He later managed KSUB radio in Cedar City, UT, for RSC. Meanwhile, C. Richard Evans was a self-taught KSL radio technician extraordinaire. During WWII, he was called East to Princeton to help with the program of electronic submarine detection. Cyril Fawcee, another KSL technician, received his training as a radio operator on board ship. Foster Cope

*Logan Garment Co. Sponsors the KSL Players and the
KSL Orchestra (J. Willard Marriott Library)*

The Bates Boys Look Over a Script with Glade.
(J. Willard Marriott Library)

and Lowell Durham were principals in the operation and performances of the KSL Orchestra.

A blip in time but a unique addition to KSL's broadcast day occurred on January 1, 1934, when the KSL "beep-tone" was inaugurated. Glade and KSL engineers found the need for an absolutely accurate time signal to efficiently program the station, so it was arranged to have a beep-tone tripped on the hour by a Western Union circuit direct from the U.S. Naval Observatory at Arlington, Virginia. After adjusting to a one-ninth of a second delay and reducing the frequency of the signal from 25kHz to 12kHz cycles – for example, the average listener couldn't hear a signal broadcast higher than 20kHz – the time signal became an important feature

Parley Baer and Francis Urry, known on-the-air as brothers Gerald and Edwin Bates, "The Bates Boys"
(J. Willard Marriott Library)

for the residents in the KSL listening area and to others.

Captains of ships at sea in the Pacific wrote KSL to tell how they used KSL's time signal to check chronometers used in navigation. The signal reportedly also was used to check various airplane instruments at military installations in the Salt Lake area. This early beep-tone was transformed in 1961 using the electrical impulse from the Naval Observatory to activate the Nauvoo Temple bell, which was resurrected from storage in the Visitors Center on Temple Square in Salt Lake City. The hourly bong of the Nauvoo LDS Temple bell, now on display in Salt Lake's Temple Square, was carried on KSL radio until recently. The bong now is synchronized with the U.S. Bureau of Time Synchronization whose signal is used by virtually everybody by which to set clocks.

KSL under Glade also maintained a good balance of all types of music in its schedule. The station sought to develop a public taste for good music while also being cognizant of audience preferences for some types of "old time music." Hillbilly music, popular in some regions, was not a popular draw for KSL listeners, but familiar old ballads, quartets, and standard western cowboy music were favorites. KSL boasted that it pioneered the first live talent groups in the West, achieving success with the "Utah Buckaroos" and "Western Roundup" programs as well as others aired in the morning and evening hours. KSL's transcribed programs also generously included "western" music evoking the region's geography and topography.

One music personality that few people today remember was on KSL for more than twenty years beginning in 1927. Harry Clarke, who came to KSL from the English theater circuit, was the singing star of several popular western homey-type programs over the years, and Glade joined him in singing duets from time to time. Clarke was said to have had a rich, mellow, baritone voice. Early on he had a program called "Saturday Nite in Sheepfold" in which he joined his singing voice with the salty philosophy of "Peter Spraynozzle," an act that proved popular for radio listeners. Employed early on by Glade, Clarke, as late as 1946, was heard on KSL in the "Songs of Harry Clarke," Monday through Saturdays 7:15 to 7:30 a.m., and as featured soloist in the "Little Chapel of the Wasatch," a program of non-denominational hymns heard on the station each Wednesday evening at 10:15 p.m.

Another performer encouraged by Glade but often overlooked in KSL's early programming history is Annette Richardson Dinwoody. She was a staff artist at KSL and a regular on the station beginning in the early 1930s. The importance of KSL to the CBS Network was demonstrated by the network's airing of Dinwoody live across America. Bill Paley, the founder and owner of CBS, reportedly asked Dinwoody to sing "Smoke Gets in Your Eyes" over-and-over from Salt Lake City supposedly so he could hear it on the CBS station in New York City. Dinwoody also supported community performing arts groups such as the Utah Oratorio Society. According to its press pieces, the choral group and Dinwoody have enjoyed a rich history of national and international broadcasts, being heard on NBC, CBS, PBS and other radio and television networks.

Locally produced children's shows also became popular on KSL. Each year beginning in 1936 and continuing for ten years, KSL in cooperation with the Salt Lake City Junior League, of which Glade was president, presented a series of Saturday morning dramatizations focusing on children's stories. Beginning in 1939 Luacine Clark Fox, daughter of J. Reuben Clark, first counselor to LDS President Heber J. Grant in 1936, and announcer Parley Baer started the "Story Telling Time," which ran for three seasons while Glade was still employed by the station in a public relations capacity. Fox played "Miss Anna," Baer played "King Bowler," Russell Stewart announced, and Scott Clawson was the sound technician. It aired five days a week beginning in the late 1930s, with Baer producing and Fox writing. Lynn McKinlay later produced the show. Kids and their parents were invited to the studio to watch the live broadcasts.[18]

KSL under Glade also provided coverage of many events of interests to people in the Intermountain West and around the world. For instance, Glade aired several of President Calvin Coolidge's speeches to the nation, and, in 1927, aired by direct wire from Washington a "welcome home" celebration for Charles Lindberg, carried in the Tabernacle, reportedly, but likely an embellished fact, with the largest single audience in the country. Also, KSL in the late 1920s carried several Utah native Jack Dempsey's heavyweight-champion fights, including the forever remembered and argued "long-count" fight against Gene Tunney. Dempsey failed to regain his heavyweight crown after knocking down Tunney and not immediately going to a neutral corner of the ring, causing the referee's extraordinarily delayed ten-count, allowing Tunney extra time to recover and go on to win over Dempsey and retain the heavyweight crown.

Some events involved locally produced remote broadcast from distant places. KSL remotely aired Utah State Aggie football from Hawaii, the opening of the westward connecting Moffet Tunnel from Denver, and the Indianapolis 500 Speedway classic. In 1935, Sir Malcom Campbell took his automobile to the Bonneville Salt Flats, 120 miles west of Salt Lake, to establish a new record

Announcer Alvin G. Pack on the Bonneville Salt Flats
(J. Willard Marriott Library)

for the measured mile. Campbell became the first person to drive a car amore than 300 miles an hour, and KSL was there. In August and September 1938, George E.T.Eyston and John R. Cobb each made runs over the Bonneville measured mile. For these events KSL fed broadcasts by wire to New York and across the Atlantic to the British Broadcasting Corporation (BBC) for release.

Wally Sandack, Alvin Pack, and Gene Shaw, all KSL announcers, originated coverage for the record runs. From a 1938 KSL script, we can glean the following report from announcer Wally Sandack about Eyston's pending Bonneville run:

*John R. Cobb on the Bonneville Salt Flats
(J. Willard Marriott Library)*

> *Good afternoon Great Britain...good morning America...Here in the sober gray dawn of a late August morning the Columbia network thru its Salt Lake City affiliate, KSL, presents an exclusive international broadcast...from coast to coast and relayed across the Atlantic to England. Here on the world's fastest speedway...the salt flats of prehistoric Lake Bonneville...125 miles from Salt Lake City, Utah, the eyes and ears of a speed conscious world have been magnetically attracted at ...minutes past 6 a.m. Pacific Time this morning a mild mannered and intrepid Briton gave the contact signal that sent his 7 ton racing land speedster hurtling down the 13 mile long course in an effort to better the recognized land speed mark of 311.42 mph held by him and set on this course Nov 19th, 1937. Again this morning after a heartbreaking earlier attempt this week. Capt George E.T. Eyston seeks to boost his claims as the fastest traveled man on earth...Our position at present is 14 miles from the desert town of Wendover on the fringe of Utah's western border.*

KSL was nimble in its efforts to capture consistently mile-marking events in many venues. In August 1939 John R. Cobb bested Eyston's record and set a world's record of 368.8 miles per hour, and again KSL was on site.

As indicated earlier, on September 1, 1932, KSL changed network affiliation from NBC to CBS and switched the weekly Mormon Tabernacle Choir national broadcast to that network. But the Choir made many performances over KSL on other occasions. For instance, on Memorial Day, 1937, the Mormon Tabernacle Choir was featured on KSL from the foot of the Great White Throne in Zion National Park. There was a question about whether the Choir's performances were dubbed religious broadcast requiring time for other religions, but its appearances on KSL were determined to be sustaining programs of cultural value, not requiring KSL to provide on-air opportunities for other religions, although Glade did have the good sense to provide programming on KSL from many other religions to avoid any favoritism perceptions.

That likely wouldn't have been a problem anyway because KSL programming under Glade included participation from churches of many faiths in its coverage area. KSL especially cooperated with the LDS Church by providing facilities and services essential to the broadcasting of LDS semi-annual conferences, among other LDS church sessions. Also, KSL carried the Catholic Church broadcast of what the station logged as "Christian Mass" and other special events for that church. It also joined with the Masonic Lodge to broadcast Easter morning services. In fact, KSL boasted that a large majority of the ministers representing different faiths in Salt Lake City had been in the KSL studios over the years, and they appreciated the exposure that contributed to forming an effective ecumenical community among church officials.

In other programming firsts, as indicated above, Alvin Pack, brother of Eugene Pack, KSL's talented early engineer under Glade, was tagged by Glade to work as an announcer at KLO in the evenings in the 1930s. Alvin and his wife, Lena Marie, were later called by Glade to KSL to do original daily fifteen-minute family and child raising oriented programs written and produced by the couple. Lena Marie's radio name was Maria Fontaine, and Glade said she had a radio voice as "clear as a bell." The Packs also worked at KDYL during their radio careers, and Alvin Pack was KALL radio's first station manager when it went on the air in 1945.[19]

Glade spent a lifetime on the banquet circuit. His voice echoed through hotel ballrooms, dinners, church cultural halls, campaign and fund raising stops, and in reception centers. A longtime waitress told the authors that after each banquet, they would always find a tip under Glade's plate after he left his table. They had never had anyone besides Glade leave a tip.

Earl J. Glade Spoke at Hundreds of Gatherings Over The Years. (J. Willard Marriott Library)

Newspaper accounts discussed his messages, and often relayed his ubiquitous personal message of developing mental, physical, and spiritual attributes along with the acquisition of knowledge and the pursuit of growth. In fact, Glade became so well known as a speaker, that newspapers often just assumed the KSL manager would have a terrific message. For instance, the *Murray Eagle* offered the following on April 20,1933, without even announcing the topic of his message.

EARL J. GLADE TO SPEAK

Earl J. Glade, managing director for KSL, will be the speaker Sunday night, April 23 at 6:30 in the Murray First ward. That Mr. Glade will have a message that will be of interest, and importance to those who attend the service is understood. Mr. Glade has been associated with KSL for a number of years and is well known as a public speaker in the state.[20]

It's not readily known what money Glade garnered, if any, from his many speeches, but he generated significant income for himself in the more than twelve years he operated his wholly owned Radio Broadcasters, Inc. (RBI), through which he brokered important time periods on the KSL schedule, purchased daily at a per-hour rate. As indicated above, Glade resold the time, collected advertising revenue and programmed the station, paying talent and operating personnel from his RBI collections.

In the years from 1925 to 1927 when Glade essentially assumed management control over KSL on behalf of the RSC, he reportedly was accountable for most every function at the station from sweeping floors, announcing, and singing, to producing programming content and handling sales and administration tasks. His wife, Sarah Elizabeth –"Sadie," as she was known growing up-- Rasband Glade, whose on-air radio name was Beverly Snow, also served gratis as piano accompanist to KSL vocalists. And when live performers didn't show, she became a show's entertainment.

Radio by the late 1920s still had not fully developed or had been accepted as a viable commercial advertising medium by station owners, listeners or, more importantly, business owners. In the February 9, 1927 RSC directors meeting, Glade reported it still was difficult to convince certain advertisers and "businessmen" of KSL's real value as an advertising medium.

> *[Glade] stated that, as a demonstration, he had made arrangements with the Scowcroft Brothers of Ogden for a four-hour broadcast of musical program, to be given on Monday next, the charges for this broadcast to be $25.00.*[21]

Typical of Glade's quest for parsimony, program variety, and his unique personal identification with the station, he featured his family live on KSL Christmas morning in 1927. Fifty years after the broadcast, Earl Jr. nostalgically related the story of that broadcast, remembering a gift his dad gave to his soon-to-be wife after returning from his mission in Germany:

*The broadcast opened with Mother playing, the family singing,
and then Dad greeted everyone listening with some of the
words of Dicken's "Christmas Carol," and brought each of us
[children] in turn to the microphone to mention, with
appreciation, what we had received for Christmas and to give
our greetings. ... And would you guess? We wound up the
broadcast with all of us singing, "Silent Night," with Mother
playing the music from the original sheet music Dad had
brought home to her after his Mission in Germany. In our
home then, as it does now [circa 1977] on Mother's piano, the
title of the sheet music reads, "Still Nacht, Heilig Nacht," and
Dad's closing greeting, the words of Tiny Tim, "God bless
everyone."[22]*

After a few lean years, Glade developed a profitable program schedule and for nearly a decade after reaped monetary benefits from RBI, Radio Broadcasters, Inc., his solely owned company-within-a-company at KSL. In 1929, the net income to Glade from KSL was only $62.48, but from his proprietary RBI, he netted an additional $12,858, for a total of $12,920 for that year. His net income nearly doubled in 1930 to $23,827, representing $7,050 from KSL and nearly $16,777 from RBI. Glade's $23,827 net income for 1930 calculated in modern equivalence would have been more than a quarter-million dollars. Glade's annual salary in 1931 and 1932 dropped to $19,499 and $13,889 respectively, and dipped even lower in 1933 to $9,252, as the nationwide economic depression firmly took hold. Glade's gross income decreased while his cost to conduct the RBI business increased significantly, as during hard times, he reportedly often paid station employees from his personal resources.

These annual salaries, on the high-end of the salary scale for the times, showed the radio business to be nearly depression-proof, in that, after an initial listener investment, albeit significant at the time, radio was a free source of entertainment for financially strapped listeners mired in a devastating depression. As a result of industry wide success, conspicuously shared by KSL, Glade's net salary in 1935 rebounded and reached more than $35,000, and by 1937, the year before his Radio Broadcasters, Inc. (RBI) was dissolved, rose to $41,671, representing an income switch in favor of KSL: $24,151 from KSL and

$17,520 from RBI. His 1937 salary calculated in modern equivalence would have been more than $666,000 (one dollar in 1937 had the same buying power as about $17 today).

As mentioned above, it was not all take-home pay for Glade. Besides supporting some employees during hard times, and paying considerable RBI expenses, he sometimes incurred other expenses that decreased the amount he claimed for himself during the flush RBI days of the middle 1930s. For example, besides considerable resources devoted to unsuccessfully nurturing KLO, expenses attributable to the otherwise fully occupied Cannon during his tenure as RSC president helps explain why he had little concern about the existence of RBI, Glade's intra-organization company at KSL:

> *From what I [J. Reuben Clark] can learn, he [Earl J. Glade] and Bishop [Sylvester Q.] Cannon fixed the terms of his [Glade's 1930s] employment, which came from three sources – a very small salary payment direct from KSL ($25.00 per month), next a commission on the sale of KSL time, and then a lease of KSL time [to RBI] (for which he paid a certain sum), KSL furnishing the air and he getting what he could for the sale of his time, he bearing his own expense, other than the cost of the air, which (I repeat) KSL bore. Obviously, this put him [Glade] in the unfortunate position of personally competing for business against the company of which he was the Manager and the facilities of which he was using. His net from operations was not wholly clear to himself. From investigations made at the time, he, to some relatively small extent, shared his net with the Bishop [Cannon], and also gifts of trips for the Bishop and his wife (Brother Glade personally paying all the expenses), the gift of automobiles (3) to the Bishop, the upkeep and servicing of these automobiles, including payment for gas, oil, tires, etc., and it may be other things. These gifts amounted to the following figures, in the years 1934-1938 (to August): $19,769.[23]*

The "relatively small" $19,769 amount Glade provided Cannon in the form of net sharing, cars, gifts and travel in the mid-1930s calculated in modern equivalence would be about $305,000, still a significant sum today. As Clark pointed out, Glade paid for these gifts from his RBI funds –that is, his personal funds – not from money in the KSL/Radio Service Corporation treasury. Also, some of these funds could have gone to Cannon for upkeep and mileage expenses, as he and Glade over the years used their personal cars for company business, sometimes involving long trips.[24]

Clark, in the above note to LDS President David O. McKay, twice brought up what he thought was a significant issue: KSL solely bore the cost of airing Glade's RBI brokered programs. This may reflect some truth, but it does not take into account that some of the programming talent and other personnel were employed by Glade's RBI at no cost to KSL. And, part of the payments made to KSL by Glade beyond the programs' content value, factored into the expenses of airing the brokered programs.

In summary, in the ten years from January 1, 1929, through September 30, 1938, KSL and RBI combined returned to Glade a total net compensation of $296,919 – more than $4 million in today's dollars – representing an average net per year return to Glade of nearly $27,000 after expenses (or adjusted to about a modern equivalence of $378,000 annually). This would not be an excessive income for a highly productive radio executive today, but it is a significant sum given the tenuous economic times of the 1930s, and further proof of radio's ability to provide ample incomes for its practitioners during a depression when other businesses were failing in great numbers.[25]

It is understandable the RSC directors wanted to share in RBI's windfall returns to the benefit of all of its other corporate stockholders, not just Glade. On the other hand, these returns above all were a result of Glade's programming innovations and proven salesmanship, so it's also understandable that Glade would have wanted to continue his intra-company enterprises that so ably nurtured KSL to profitability over the years. But that was not to be, as a high LDS official deemed otherwise. Sweeping changes at KSL were approaching, when J. Reuben Clark, in an earlier time a prominent attorney who served as undersecretary in the U.S. Department of State during the Coolidge Administration and later as ambassador to Mexico in the Franklin Roosevelt Administration, took over the RSC executive mantle.

CHAPTER 6
TRANSITION AND CHANGE OF FORTUNES

Although the LDS church owned KSL through RSC, its parent company, in the station's early years the Church did not assign management and operational duties to its top senior theological officials. This changed on August 12, 1938, when J. Reuben Clark Jr., second counselor in the First Presidency of the LDS Church since 1933, took over RSC presidential reins from Cannon.

However, this most likely was not a theological decision but one of business practicality, as the Salt Lake Tribune Company also endorsed the move. As explained earlier, the LDS Church, through the Corporation of the presiding bishop, and the Salt Lake Tribune Company, under John Fitzpatrick, *Tribune* publisher and a prominent Catholic in the community, were the two major RSC stockholders. Clark and Fitzpatrick long had been bothered by management practices at the station they thought had fostered multiple companies-within-companies, resulting in economic inefficiencies that ultimately siphoned profits from RSC. They wanted to institute what they observed as more generally accepted management and business practices of the industry at KSL.

J. Reuben Clark became Radio Service Corporation (RSC) President in August 1938 (Deseret News)

Albeit, not directly related, this shakeup at KSL may have been extracted from another issue ongoing at about the same time where Clark and Cannon opposed each other. The debate, simmering since 1933, centered on the propriety of the LDS faithful accepting supplemental funding from federal and local governments during the devastating economic depression. Cannon's view coincided with the *Presiding Bishopric's Handbook of Instructions* that LDS members seek county relief before turning to the church. Cannon also supported President Franklin Roosevelt's New Deal while Clark vehemently opposed the New Deal initiative of government relief for the LDS unemployed. In 1933, it was reported that 70 percent of the families receiving public assistance in Salt Lake County were LDS.[1] As the issue evolved, Clark said LDS people should shun federal and local governmental assistance

John F. Fitzpatrick, The Salt Lake Tribune Publisher from 1924 to 1960.
(Salt Lake Tribune)

and depend instead on LDS Church relief to survive. Clark's stance was ideological, in that he viewed the New Deal as a "breeding ground for some of the most destructive political doctrines that have ever found any hold in this country of ours:"[2]

> *I [Clark] am unalterably opposed to the continuance of the greed, graft, and corruption which has [sic] characterized the use of [government] relief funds among us during the last two years. It is destroying our morale as a people and is seriously undermining our moral and spiritual stamina. If continued, it will make professional paupers of very many of us and our spiritual welfare will be equally threatened.[3]*

This issue involving LDS Church policy and its relief program certainly was more complex than can be covered here, but over a three-year period, documents for and against Cannon's and Clark's respective positions on "relief" were considered by LDS General Authorities, and on April 7, 1936, the LDS Church launched its Church Security Program, dubbed by one LDS Apostle as a "tactical revelation." It didn't include some of the more strident points that Clark aspired to, but it certainly favored his position, and he believed the plan was inspired by God; "a revelation if you wish."[4]

In 1937, after years in conflict with Presiding Bishop Cannon over the welfare plan, Clark offered the following assessment: "For four years he [Cannon] has either fought the [Church Security Plan] the Presidency then proposed or has willfully failed to support it. [Cannon should decide] … "to get in line or to get out of the way." LDS President Grant agreed, and responding to Clark's belief that some in the presiding bishopric were against the plan warned the Welfare Committee that the First Presidency would not allow "one of the Presiding Bishopric … to hinder what we are doing and what apparently is a success."[5]

Clark was an intelligent, persuasive and influential, sometimes willful, counselor to three LDS First Presidents who had ultimate jurisdiction over KSL, beginning in 1933 with Grant. It was widely expected that some changes would be immediate when Clark assumed RSC leadership in 1938, but certainly no one could have imagined the extent of those changes and their subsequent effect on Cannon, Glade, the KSL "family" and Clark's own family.

Cannon's arms-length reign over KSL since 1926 ended with his "release" from his position as presiding bishop of the LDS church and subsequent surrender of the RSC presidency to Clark. Clark's appointment did not bode well for Glade, KSL's longtime manager, who had enjoyed a hands-off approach to management, courtesy of Cannon. As discussed earlier, Bishop Cannon had administrative responsibilities over nearly every LDS Church business from sugar to insurance and saw KSL under Glade's watch as a growing business without need to babysit.

Upon taking over, Clark "made it known" he and Glade "were in agreement" that multiple intra-organizational companies at KSL were no longer desirable. As such, Glade's RBI group, formed in 1929, was discontinued on September 30, 1938, after producing a profitable decade-long run for him and KSL. The next day, after "praising" Glade for his pioneer work at KSL, Clark and the RSC board directed that RBI "will write no more time" after October 1.[6]

In addition to dictating that RBI would "write no more time," the agreement covering Glade's employment readjustment after September 30 provided him an annual $9,000 salary ($138,000, in modern equivalence) and a 6 percent commission on the absolute net of KSL's collections. Further, all his commissions on CBS and national programs would cease, RBI contracts for broadcasting would be taken over by KSL, employees of RBI would be continued temporarily by KSL, and KSL would buy all RBI furniture and office equipment.[7]

Just as John Cope had a fall at KSL as Glade took over KSL management in 1925, so did Glade in 1938. "Because of the peculiar nature of the radio business, President Clark felt the necessity of relieving Mr. Glade of the burden of accounting and detail management at KSL, leaving him free for promotional work."[8] But Clark still had a problem. Replacing Glade as station manager would have tremendous repercussions for the station. Radio was a very public business, and Glade was extremely popular among KSL employees and in his on-air and community activities. Nevertheless, Clark believed he needed to replace Glade with somebody that could carry out his new management directives – one who was unquestionably loyal, and over whom he would have multiple controls, significant persuasive powers and ultimate dominion. That is, someone who also could insulate him from the soon-to-be controversial changes he was about to make at KSL. Clark didn't have to look farther than at the family portraits on the wall to find such a person.

Early in September 1938, the new RSC president called Ivor Sharp, his son-in-law, who was working for AT&T in New York City, to tell him there was much to be done at KSL. "I believe you [Sharp] have the qualifications necessary to do the work."[9]

Sharp later recollected this phone call and Clark's summons to work at KSL:

> *Mechanically I replaced the telephone receiver and stared blankly at the papers on my desk. I was worried; my spirits were so depressed that I found it difficult to do even the most perfunctory work. I did not see how I could refuse President Clark, yet I was so reluctant [originally Sharp used "loath " in place of "reluctant"] to accept the offer. For sixteen years I had been employed by the American Telephone and Telegraph Company, Long Lines Department. ... I also understood full*

*well that the assignment ahead [at KSL)] would be unpleasant
in many respects; every reorganization is distasteful in many
ways and I understood that conditions at KSL were
considerably involved. Indeed, the whole view presented a
most discouraging prospect for me to ponder.[10]*

His seniority would also be at risk. But,
when on September 15, 1938, Clark arrived in
New York with the KSL job offer, Sharp
accepted and became Clark's assistant. Sharp's
wife, Marianne, and his children moved to Salt
Lake within a few days and Sharp followed on
October 28.

Normally, Clark visited Grant, 82, the
ailing LDS Church President, at home several
times each week to keep him informed of his
activities:

Ivor Sharp (J. Williard Marriott Library)

> *[If Clark] conducted any major
> business without advance approval by
> President Grant, he quickly
> announced the fact to the President.
> Therefore, after Clark hired Sharp, he
> apologized to Grant ... for not
> consulting him before a K.S.L.
> stockholders meeting [and he] told him about putting Ivor
> Sharp on [the] board of Directors; told him [the] condition of
> [the] company.[11]*

The decision's ramifications have reverberated to modern times. It has
been over eight decades since Clark summoned Ivor Sharp to KSL, and decades
have passed since the deaths of Clark, Sharp and Glade, but over the years
broadcasting veterans, even those who never worked with Glade, have privately
held-fast to the opinion that Clark's choice of his son-in-law was a pure act of
nepotism and that Glade was precipitously cast aside after well managing KSL
for 16 years, making it the thriving station it became in his time. Some wags, as

well as some in-the-know, have even attributed Sharp's appointment not totally to Clark only wanting more effective KSL management, but also to his desire to return his daughter to Salt Lake City, for whom he purchased a home.

The depth of emotion on the matter is profound. Even Glade's son, who worked for RBI and held other positions at KSL, never publicly talked about the circumstances surrounding his dad's strategic removal from station management. He may not even have known about the details. It's possible Earl Sr. never discussed it with other family members either. In addition, people reluctantly have made only off-the-record comments when asked about this transitional time at KSL beginning in 1938. This speaks to the high regard people have had for Glade over the years and to the resolve of people associated with the LDS Church not to speak disapprovingly of their leaders' decisions. This has often been a part of the unique Utah culture when it comes to matters involving the LDS church leadership.

By all accounts Glade and Sharp were men of integrity, albeit with greatly different talents and styles, and it is not the intent here to argue against their abundant and significant respective virtues and intelligence. The intent here is to put Clark's choice of Sharp to replace Glade at KSL in context and to publicly relate for the first time happenings from a timely management and business perspective involving KSL and the Radio Service Corporation (RSC).

To replace Glade and reorganize KSL without enraging his advocates – mortally wounding KSL internally, or offending KSL listeners – Clark had to employ an incremental strategy. Late in 1938, after RBI was dissolved, Glade was appointed second vice-president of RSC and was continued as KSL's general manager "until his replacement could be named." Although the RSC Articles of Incorporation provided for a second vice president, the position had never been filled until Glade was appointed to it.

Sharp had worked for AT&T in New York in finance before being brought to KSL by Clark, but he had no background in broadcasting. On his first day on the job at KSL on November 4, 1938, Sharp met with Glade, engineer Eugene Pack, auditor Dan H. Vincent, and others, and, over the next few days, began reviewing KSL financial records, accounting procedures, reports and other operating statements. Sharp concluded the station's business methods were unduly involved, obsolete, inadequate, without real direction, and unworthy of an important station like KSL. The only effective way to correct conditions, he thought, was to start reorganizing, a position supported by his superiors but certainly not by long-time KSL employees loyal to Glade.

The RSC Board, at its January 25, 1939, meeting, moved again to further separate Glade from KSL day-to-day operations. It authorized Vincent (auditor), Sharp (assistant to the president) and Glade to sign checks and draw money from all corporation accounts to pay bills. However, only two of the three signatures were required to make a transaction legal. This was a way of gradually taking financial responsibility from Glade. Sharp could obtain Vincent's approval on business matters, politely review decisions with Glade, and then consult with Clark to formulate actual plans.

The separation strategy further was implemented when, at its May 10, 1939, meeting, six months after Sharp arrived, the RSC board, on Fitzpatrick's recommendation, changed Glade's title to executive vice president and added to Sharp's titles director of station operations and third vice president, while continuing his status as assistant to the RSC president, his father-in-law. By the next monthly meeting on June 9 and from that time on, Sharp was mostly referred to only as director of station operations. The replacement of Glade as KSL manager and decision maker was effectively complete.

There clearly was tacit collusion in support of Clark's plan to reorganize KSL and replace Glade from the outset. All involved knew the meaning and consequence of Sharp's arrival and subsequent appointments. However, it seems that all parties also kept their heads in the sand, metaphorically, pretending not to know what was happening, in the hope that Glade's removal would not result in a firestorm of protests. Sharp certainly had an accurate read on his role in the matter.

Not knowing him well, Sharp was initially perplexed by Glade's seemingly passive-aggressive display of cooperation:

> *During this early period, Mr. Glade was very congenial with*
> *me and solicitous of my welfare. He expressed himself to*
> *President Clark to the effect that I was an 'answer to his*
> *prayer.' ... Always he was pleasant and seemingly very*

*appreciative of my efforts to work with him, but I never knew
whether he agreed with me or disagreed. ... In respect to
accounting matters or in operating procedures he offered no
constructive help or criticism. He gave me the impression that
such items were details with which he was not personally
concerned. ... In more general matters, he maintained a
friendly but non-committal attitude. He would agree with
whatever I said without objection but I was never fully
satisfied that he did so with conviction. In answer to a
question of mine for advice or counsel, I invariably received a
reply such as, 'I think that should work out satisfactorily.' or
'You ought to be able to work that out all right.' or 'Whatever
you think best, etc.' ... He seemed to be satisfied to let me
correct the procedures within the station that were obviously
out of order.[12]*

Being a gentleman, loyal to the LDS Church, owners of KSL, and likely
knowing that things would happen as Clark dictated, Glade accepted with grace
what certainly was a demotion and replacement. The late Patricia Curtis, Glade's
youngest child, recounted in a 2012 visit with one of the authors that her father
and mother were cordial to the Sharps, citing instances where the couples went
on road trips together and shared time at the Glade's Utah mountain lodge.

Other employees, however, may not have accepted the change so quietly or
tolerably, as did Glade:

*His [Glade's] friends –with or without his knowledge (I [Ivor
Sharp] do not know which) –were doing what they could to
injure the KSL management by spreading false statements
about his treatment at the hands of KSL.[13]*

By all accounting, Glade served KSL well during his tenure at the station,
and clearly his remuneration discussed above testified to that. He brought the
station from meager billings in 1925 to about $390,000 in 1938 --$5.8-million,
in today's equivalent dollars -- and, through RBI and associated companies, had
for years enhanced employee salaries at his personal expense and at little cost to
KSL. He also ushered KSL through numerous technical changes, including

several efforts that resulted in KSL becoming a powerful 50,000-watt, clear-channel station in 1932.

In addition, in 1938 alone, the year his RBI company within-a-company at KSL was dissolved and Glade was essentially replaced, the station aired 7,173 hours of programming, with the station off-the-air only 6 hours and 15 minutes the entire year due to storms and other circumstances.[14]

But just as important as the bottom line, Glade's accomplishments include telling events not reported in RSC board meeting minutes; the little things that led to KSL's reputation as the community service giant it still is noted for today. One of those took place April 29, 1937, when Richard Stringham, who lived in Bountiful just north of Salt Lake City, died and his family held the funeral in a Bountiful LDS ward house. An account of that funeral concludes with the mention that the widow was bedfast and could not attend. However, it says Glade supplied a telephone and amplifier hook-up so she could hear the service. Those stories are as important to the day-to-day cultural history of KSL under Glade as are its financial ledgers.[15]

Removed from day-to-day station operations, Glade soon got involved in national broadcasting matters on behalf of KSL and the broader radio industry. One important assignment was with the National Association of Broadcasters (NAB), where Glade was appointed chairman of the NAB Code Committee and, during March and April 1939, spent time

The NAB Code was adopted on July 11, 1939, and went into effect on October 1.

in Washington, D.C., and on the phone discussing program policies and codes of conduct for radio stations nationwide. Glade was also part of the important "Committee of Audience Relations" which immediately acted to interpret and administrate the NAB Code for those not clear about the new industry self-regulatory code-of-conduct that now presided in the highly government regulated business. The *New York Times* noted Glade's appointment and heralded the new Code rules as "…a yardstick of good taste and decent regard for social sensibilities."[16]

Not all at KSL, however, were favorably decisive in their judgment of the new NAB Code.

> *Vice-President Earl J. Glade gave a brief report of the trip that he and Mr. Sharp had made to Washington, relative to the new [NAB] code, pointing out some of the advantages and disadvantages of it. President Clark made some comments relative to it, pointing out that a code of this type could lead to more restrictions in the radio industry which would increase said censorship prerogatives now exercised by the Federal Radio Commission.*[17]

The NAB Radio Code was a landmark document hammered out by Glade and other committee members. Meant to preempt future Federal Communications Commission (FCC) regulations, it was immensely successful in deflecting government regulation and in bringing stations around the country together with the radio networks, (Mutual, NBC, CBS, and later ABC) to develop program standards. In addition, the NAB code elevated broadcasting from merely the status of a trade organization to one bestowing a sense of professionalism for the first time in its history. Later, Glade told the U.S. Senate Interstate Commerce Committee the radio industry was making steady progress in its efforts to "elevate broadcasting standards." He said the NAB code had been instrumental in reducing the amount of advertising copy per program and removing "unpleasant types" of advertising from the air. At the same time, Glade testified favorably on the Wheeler-White bill to limit the FCC's power to regulate the radio industry. He thought the American system of free enterprise should be "permitted to function" and the industry "be allowed every opportunity to improve its standards" through self-regulation.[18]

After focusing on national concerns for several months, Glade's interests again turned to Utah and the Intermountain West. In November 1939, in a letter to RSC President Clark, Glade proposed an entrepreneurial challenge to the RSC Board:

In extension of the brief luncheon discussion we recently had at Hotel Utah, I should like respectfully to submit the following proposal for your kind consideration: In addition to my present assignment with our company to which I shall continue to devote my best effort, I should like permission to do some exploratory work in the development of a small network in connection with some of the local and possibly regional stations in this section, with a small key station located somewhere, if possible, in the metropolitan area of Salt Lake City; and to foster the local development of smaller stations in areas not immediately contiguous to KSL. I realize that our efforts in the proposed network activity may be fruitless as there are several promoters already in the field and they may beat us to it. However, it is my desire, if possible, to develop such a system which will be friendly to our company's interests.[19]

Glade's proposal visualized a regional network with an anchor station that he personally would control. After discussing Glade's proposal, the RSC board members later concluded that it would not be in KSL's best interest to undertake these ventures in conjunction with Glade. However, the Board kept open for discussion the question of RSC becoming involved in fostering and financing such efforts on its own, separate from Glade. A committee was formed to investigate the possibility of building a 100-watt station in Murray, Utah, a Salt Lake City suburb, but nothing came of it, and neither a station nor a regional radio network was officially developed by RSC at that time.

As KSL evolved under Clark and Sharp's tutelage, Glade assumed control of the KSL Artists Bureau and took on another entrepreneurial endeavor, which involved an application for a radio station, which would compete with KSL for listeners, the topics of the next chapter.

CHAPTER 7
THE KSL ARTISTS BUREAU: RISK AND DISAPPOINTMENT

In March 1940, the RSC board assumed control of the KSL Artists Bureau, which continued to operate throughout the year without much profit, and reportedly with low morale among its employees. Subsequently, the other booking agencies in Salt Lake City complained of KSL's competition, and the American Federation of Musicians advised KSL that no "booking" license would be issued to any radio station. Facing problems with an important trade union, KSL decided to withdraw from the artists bureau business.

Also in March 1940, recognizing that he was not a "program-man" and could not himself fill the void left in programming by the removal of Glade's expertise, Sharp hired a consultant to give KSL some "real help" in its programming department.[1]

Edmund B. Abbott, in transition from senior announcer and assistant production manager at WCCO in Minneapolis to responsibilities at KNX in Los Angeles, came to KSL to learn its listener requirements, and to work with KSL's sales department. He also was tasked with assisting in the actual mechanics of program production, doing limited on-the-air work in order to illustrate good network practices, and making recommendations for change and improvement at KSL.[2]

It is not clear what qualifications Abbott had to undertake these tasks by virtue of his prior experience at WCCO, but on May 15, after nine weeks at KSL evaluating programming and production operations, Abbott gave Sharp his report. He applauded KSL's efforts to produce quality dramatic programs, but panned its efforts to produce and integrate musical programming into its schedule. Without specific names, Abbott also was highly critical of KSL's announcers as a collective, intimating the announcers were not sufficiently professional.

Also in his report, Abbott reluctantly gave his impression of what he called the Glade Artists Bureau:

*I have kept my hands scrupulously clean of the artists bureau
because of the factions represented in its make-up. On one
side Mr. Glade and Mrs. Bitner; on the other side is Mr.
Kimball. Junius Tribe [Bitner's replacement] is somewhere in
the middle. The net result is rampant jealousy, wasted time,
duplicated work, business that could be made more profitable,
lost business, sloppy shows. Each side blames the other, and
the amusing part of it is that, in its present state of
disorganization, no one is to blame. ... I should strongly
recommend that someone from the outside who knows all the
answers be brought in to put the business on its feet. After that
has been accomplished, you may then determine whether any
of our own people have the qualifications to carry on with it,
or whether someone from the outside should be brought in on
a permanent basis.*[3]

Abbott's impression actually had merit, under KSL's direct supervision the Artists Bureau was not faring well. Although clearly not "from the outside," Glade proposed to take over the Artists Bureau and operate it independently from KSL. Clark and Sharp agreed, and on December 11, 1940, the Glade Artists Bureau's, so named to highlight Glade, who probably should have known from past accounting that an artists bureau would be difficult to make profitable. That is, it was questionable to the extent that it could pay him his sought-after $400 per month salary and generate enough revenue to make the payments on a $12,000 start-up loan he obtained from RSC.

On December 23, Glade, unenthusiastically it seems, resigned as RSC vice president and director, and the next day at the KSL employees' Christmas party bid a sad farewell to all those present. Some attending the party related that Glade was quite subdued, and, uncharacteristically for him, made only brief, impromptu comments. He then left the station and, for the first time in 16 years was not employed by RSC/KSL as he prepared to operate a business enterprise separate from KSL.[4]

The fledgling Glade Artists Bureau floundered within three months. It had serious problems and was close to failing when Glade asked to return to KSL. On March 21, 1941, Glade wrote to Clark asking to be rehired at KSL: "As developed in our conversation of Wednesday last, I should like to resume full time duties at KSL."[5]

French novelist and playwright Balzac is credited with having said that most people cannot appreciate that a debt is an act of imagination. He said debt is a gesture of faith, of confidence in the future, a reaching forward to make use of wealth not yet acquired. The imaginative qualities and confidence in the future that made Glade such a legendary man of broadcasting also contributed to his mire of debt. Glade asked that his compensation at KSL again be fixed at $9,000 ($148,000 in today's equivalence) and that his $12,000 ($197,000 today) artists bureau loan be adjusted so he could pay it off without undue hardship. The executive committee agreed to discuss Glade's requests, but a decision was not forthcoming and Glade expressed concern over the delay. On May 4, Glade again wrote to Clark:

> *In fairness, may I say that it is now upwards of sixty days since the movement to effect this settlement [Glade's return to KSL] was begun. As far as I am aware, I have done everything I was personally asked to do to facilitate matters.*[6]

Even after this plea for action, Clark waited almost three weeks to reply, taking exception to Glade's concluding comments:

> *We are not sure that we understand just what you have in mind by the statements of the final paragraph of your letter under acknowledgement [May 4, 1941]. You will, of course, remember that the establishment of the [Glade] Artists Bureau was entirely your own conception, undertaken upon your own initiative, after you had suggested that K.S.L. undertake the enterprise and the Executive Committee had decided not to do so because, among other reasons, it would probably not be profitable. However, we decided that because of your past work for K.S.L., we would help you if you wished us so to do, and accordingly, K.S.L. lent you $12,000 and you gave K.S.L. your note for $12,000 which was dated December 13, 1940. ...Thus the matter has moved steadily forward as rapidly as it would seem its importance demanded, because the officers of K.S.L. felt that you should have time and opportunity carefully*

to consider the whole situation in as much as you had
undertaken such a heavy investment.[7]

With this "I-told-you-so" response, Clark relegated Glade to take up matters with KSL's Gordon Affleck and Ivor Sharp. Glade did so and subsequently resumed full time duties at KSL on June 5, under new employment and a munificent loan agreement, after being just six months away. On the same day he gave the following memorandum to Vincent:

*Delivered to you [RSC] herewith is my promissory note…in
the amount of $5,000. Said note, together with my payment of
$7,000 December 13, 1940, is the amount of $12,000 and
made to your favor. I hereby authorize you to deduct from my
salary, as it becomes due me from the Radio Service
Corporation of Utah, the sum of $100 [$1,500 today] per
month commencing January 1, 1942, and like amount each
succeeding month thereafter, such deduction to be applied in
payment of this new note in accordance with the terms
thereof.*[8]

Upon returning to KSL after his Glade Artists Bureau failed, Glade performed mostly public relations and announcing functions and was removed from daily KSL operations. In this capacity, he represented KSL in the planning and broadcast of important public affairs programs and worked on national matters of concern to KSL, like the NAB Code Committee. He also consulted with advisory, governmental and citizen groups regarding problems at KSL, and engaged special assignments, like negotiations with the Salt Lake City Airport to determine the proper location of KSL's transmitter and antenna away from flight paths. In short, Glade was given the broad charge of coordinating the activities of the public relations department with other KSL broadcast activities to enhance the station's general welfare.[9]

In the same March letter to Clark, referred to above, asking to be rehired at KSL, Glade *implicitly* conveyed he had decided not to proceed with a new Salt Lake City radio station application he had helped prepare during his six-months away from KSL, about which Clark and Sharp at the time knew nothing:

Tacit in his promise not to engage in any activity hostile to KSL interests
was Glade's business dissolution from Junius Tribe, a former KSL employee
with whom he had worked to put a new radio station on the air. Tribe, who had
successfully sold utility appliances, had no radio experience, but with Glade's
strong endorsement had come to work at KSL in March 1940 to sell the
entertainments and generally supervise the business transactions of the KSL
Artists Bureau while it still was under KSL supervision. It appears Tribe had left
KSL and the Artists Bureau to enter the real estate business while he and Glade
prepared the new station application.

Even though Glade had ceased to be involved in the new station application,
Tribe filed it with the FCC on August 8, 1941, under the name Continental
Broadcasting Company. The Continental application ordinarily would not have
been a problem for Glade because his signature was not on it, but Tribe filed it
without changing the programming portions prepared months earlier by Glade
while he had been on hiatus from KSL. For his part, Glade had criticized KSL's
program performance record under Sharp. The RSC Board met on September 8
to review Continental's FCC application, especially the programming part
containing the unfavorable statements about KSL. Glade attended the meeting
and must have been vexed when the application was examined and he
discovered his negative assessment of KSL programming was intact mostly as
he earlier had written.

Glade's chagrin over the Artists Bureau failure must have paled compared to him being mortified as a result of his earlier involvement in the application for the new Salt Lake City radio station. In a dreadful twist of events, Clark, Sharp and the other RSC board members, who were not aware that Glade had written the programming statements critical of KSL, appointed him to file an objection to it with the FCC. Glade now was in the ironic position of protesting the accuracy of a document critical of KSL that he had written. On September 30, he filed KSL's official objection to Continental's application with the FCC.

His introduction read:

> *An examination of [the Continental Broadcasting Company] application by the undersigned [Earl J. Glade] reveals inaccurate and misleading statements therein with respect to the services now being rendered by Radio Station KSL. Therefore, in order that your Commission may be informed as to the accuracy of the statements in the said application, we have prepared and are attaching hereto a memorandum which contains brief comments with reference to a few quotations selected as being typical of many incorrect statements made by the applicant.[12]*

In particular, Glade objected to a "completely misleading statement" in the Continental application that made reference to an "artists' bureau," once even called the Glade Artist Bureau in the application. This likely was a further embarrassment to Glade. The objectionable statement read:

> *The proposed station will serve as the primary outlet for the local professional and amateur talent of the Artist Bureau, an organization established for the purpose of providing work opportunities for people with artistic talents.[13]*

Glade, on behalf of KSL, rightly pointed out that this statement was misleading because the artists' bureau, or the Glade Artist Bureau, had been dissolved in May 1941, fully three months before Continental filed its application, and should have been removed.

Although Clark, Sharp and members of the RSC board of directors at this time had little reason to suspect that Glade had been involved in the application or had written the parts critical of KSL, there were others affiliated with KSL who suspected that not only had he been involved but that he had continued to be involved. One was Ernest L. Wilkinson, KSL's Washington, D.C. attorney, later president of Brigham Young University in Provo. Wilkinson represented KSL in legal matters before the FCC, but he also was KSL's eyes-and-ears in all Washington matters related to broadcasting. When the Continental application was filed and Wilkinson thought he recognized Glade's hand in it, he tapped his sources for information.

Wilkinson found that Glade, when operating the artists bureau away from KSL in early 1941, had hired the Washington, D.C law firm of McNary & Chambers to prepare the legal documents for the Continental application. McNary, in turn, employed engineering consultant Grant Wrathall, part owner of Frank Carman's Salt Lake's KUTA, to prepare the technical parts of the application. On September 3, 1941, before Glade filed his FCC response, Wilkinson told Sharp of his discussions with Wrathall about the Continental application:

> *Wrathall is certain in his own mind that Tribe is merely a dummy for Glade. He says he is sure that Glade is still interested in the new application. He doesn't have any definite information, however, which would permit us to prove that. ... The more I delve into the situation the more I am inclined to believe that Glade may be interested in the present application and that he is merely concealing his identity for the present in order that he may continue to draw his present salary [from KSL] until the application is granted and the new station possibly gets on its feet.[14]*

A week later, on September 10, Wilkinson again wrote to Sharp referring to Glade's possible continued involvement in the Continental Broadcasting application. His accusations became more strident and showed the depth of his distrust of Glade:

> *If any new evidences of subversive activity appear, and
> possibly without new evidence, I think it may be advisable for
> you to consider whether it would not be desirable to expose
> certain facts. Righteous indignation should sometimes prevail
> over patience.*[15]

This likely was a depressing period for Glade. He had significant debt as a result of the failed Glade Artists Bureau and other matters, was essentially removed from any significant responsibilities at KSL, and in the eyes of the three most influential people in his future at KSL – Clark, Sharp and Wilkinson – was persona non grata and his probity was questioned on the basis of unsubstantiated rumors and suspicions:

> *I have a feeling that you [Sharp] should investigate very
> carefully to ascertain his [Glade's] exact relationship to the
> new proposed venture [Continental application] for if
> misrepresentations are being made to the Commission [FCC]
> as to the true ownership, that would probably be a basis for
> having the application denied, and may also prevent Glade
> from competing with [KSL] in the future.*[16]

No evidence was found indicating that Glade continued to be involved with Junius Tribe in the Continental application or ownership of the proposed station after he returned to KSL in June 1941. But indicative of the depth of despair Glade must have been experiencing at the time, he went to KUTA to see if Frank Carman, the station's owner, could employ him. Carman had enormous respect for Glade and saw him as the grandfather of Utah radio. To have Glade come, almost hat-in-hand, looking for a job made a lasting impression. Carman had joined the ranks in Utah broadcasting that felt that Glade had been poorly treated, even cheated out of a job, as a result of Clark's perceived nepotism in hiring Sharp at KSL. Unfortunately, Carman didn't have a job opening for Glade.[17]

Glade's legacy at KSL continued to diminish after the Glade Artists Bureau failure and the unwarranted suspicion that he was still secretly involved in the Continental application. Despite his personal beliefs and the need to please LDS

Church officials while managing KSL, Glade had instituted quite a liberal programming policy during his KSL tenure that likely was necessary to retain KSL's CBS network affiliation. He accepted ads for cigarettes and beer, and encouraged humorous on-air antics from such as Parley Baer and Francis Urry, *The Bates Boys*. He ran a competitive Sunday schedule on KSL, and carried what might be described at times as an overload of ads on the station. On the other hand, Sharp progressively moved KSL to a much more conservative programming policy.

The evidence of a programming shift comes in a comparison of KSL's schedule in 1938 before Glade's RBI was dissolved and 1942 after Sharp had been manager for nearly four years.

	October 1938	1942
Five-minute commercial breaks	33	0
Two or more announcements during one break	129	0 - such business refused

	# of Spots	1938	1942
Number of spots run in any given 15-minute period:	1	1	51
	2	0	43
	3	14	33
	4	28	29
	5	7	9
	6	28	0
	7	30	0
	8	14	0
	9	5	0
	10	0	0
	11	0	0
	12	1	0
Average per period		6+	2+

In addition, the following changes likely met the approval of many of the LDS faithful served by KSL:

	1938 under Glade	1942 under Sharp
Number of beer announcements	55	0 -business refused
Number of dance programs on Sunday	32	0 –appropriate music played
Number of tobacco programs on Sunday	10	0 –tobacco ads refused on Sunday [18]

The differences were stark and the impact was noticeable in the company's financial statements as well. In RSC income statements for the years 1937, 1938, 1943 and 1947, which were retrieved by the authors from the National Record Center in Suitland, Maryland, the short-term results of the changes at KSL are apparent. Net income for KSL in 1937 when Glade still was in charge was $77,945 ($1,300,000 in today's equivalence). It dropped to $49,394 in 1938, the decrease not necessarily directly accountable to Sharp, more likely was a result of expenses commensurate with closing Glade's RBI in October of that year.

Meanwhile, in 1943, net income rose to $108,185, but precipitously dropped to a low of $19,553 by 1947, very likely a result of increased programming and talent expenses and, possibly, initial technical expenses incident to preparations for the impending inaugural of KSL television services two years down the line. Starting in 1949, the onset of KSL television with its huge burdensome expenses, plus competing stations, caused consternation with KSL stockholders and LDS authorities, prompting some to wonder if television should be abandoned. It wasn't, but the continued financial straits of the KSL radio and television operations were a catalyst for significant changes by the late 1950s. Sharpe's programming changes and the resulting personnel changes are discussed in the closing paragraphs of this chapter.

Sharp most earnestly endeavored to reconcile commercial broadcasts with LDS Church doctrine and standards. Accordingly, he stood resolute against large KSL local productions on Sunday, which, if permitted, would have made Sunday the heaviest workday at the station. He also was against radio audience shows on

Sunday evening which would interfere with attendance at church services and against programs that Sharp viewed as verging on lotteries but which other radio stations aired. He also refused to cooperate with local theater owners to promote questionable movies and vetoed dance programs on Sunday.

As a matter of general policy, Sharp was against many of the programs that under Glade had generated a good deal of KSL listener satisfaction and financial success. Sharp was against "jazzy" musical programs; the "undignified" Man-On-The-Street type of broadcast; the "ill-prepared" and "ill-advised" special event broadcasts, such as circus parades and hastily prepared interviews; and station participation in events, such as theater lobby broadcasts during the opening night of a movie premiere, and similar crowd-gathering events. Likewise, he frowned upon unrestrained publicity for performers appearing on KSL when the performers were given greater attention than KSL itself.

Additionally, Sharp pointed out that in October 1938, under Glade's legacy, two of the broadcast periods of the LDS conference were cut short by fifteen minutes each in order to permit the station to carry the World Series baseball game. Such interruptions were no longer permitted under Sharp, likely gathering much righteous anger from baseball fans when KSL took the World Series games in-progress, albeit slightly delayed while announcers such as Wally Sandach created "play-by-play" voice and sound effects —for example, tapping the mic with a pencil to recreate a hit —from wire copy streaming into the KSL control room. In addition, also in 1938 under Glade, the LDS Sunday evening programs over KSL were immediately preceded by tobacco-sponsored programs, an incongruous juxtaposition that Sharp felt compelled to correct. Sharp also pointed out that care was being taken to limit the verbiage in advertisements to fit the time paid for by the advertisers. He said in 1938 the commercials sometimes ran twice as long as scheduled. Prankish and playful habits on the part of the announcing and technical staff, so frequently associated with the more "open" Glade days at KSL, also were corrected. As a consequence of doing Clark's bidding , Sharp's stand against perceived objectionable programming, was variously interpreted as being stuffy, ultra conservative, and negative.

Comments were heard from many quarters to the effect that KSL was now "stifling showmanship," that its artists and performers were being de-personalized, that community affairs were being ignored, and that good program ideas were given no encouragement.

Changes from Glade's more moderate programming policy for the times, to Sharp's conservative one were not well received. Sharp summarized the situation in profound self-awareness:

> *The activities of KSL seem to be such an intimate part of so many people's affairs that each move here has been met with criticism and viewed with apprehension. While I [Sharp] have not been concerned about criticism directed toward me personally, I have, at times, wondered whether or not the barrage of criticism which inadvertently followed each change outweighed for ill, the benefit that resulted from an increase in operating efficiency. Thus, while many adjustments have been made during the reorganization period, it has not seemed wise to proceed with all of the changes that must eventually be made before the station gets under full headway. ...There has been a reluctance on the part of many to support the move toward a conservative program policy, and this situation has been aggravated by lack of trained personnel for the type of operations being placed in effect.[19]*

So, while Glade enjoyed the support of the station staff, the listening audience, and KSL advertisers for his programming policies, he lost favor with Clark who marginalized him from station operations and income. But it was not necessarily different for Sharp in some ways. He faced criticism that largely arose as a result of dissatisfactions within the station itself. The KSL employees were reluctant to accept his policies and authority, and the RSC directors weren't united in endorsing his reorganization plan. They also didn't entirely support him because it became a matter of sacrificing revenue in the interest of supposedly improving programming standards. The directors and other stockholders enjoyed the annuity-like revenue stream that Glade generated even if it resulted from programs that by LDS Church values and conservative broadcast standards were sometimes perceived as not in good taste or well produced. In addition, even though he was doing Clark's bidding, Sharp accepted full responsibility in connection with unpopular changes at KSL so as to keep Clark, his foremost and commanding business, church and family leader, free from criticism as much as possible.

Unlike under Glade, KSL under Sharp did not accept beer ads after he assumed control, but, in 1951, when Mayor Glade was far removed from his 1938 KSL managerial position, this changed for both KSL radio and television. Clark made it known to the RSC directors that the KSL stations could not continue to refuse beer ads if they were to remain financially viable and keep secure their CBS network affiliation. Beer ads were accepted after that, seemingly with little public resistance from the LDS faithful.

Despite his corporate declarations to the contrary, Sharp was by his own admission privately bothered by the criticism he collected. He nonetheless recognized a "higher authority" called him, and even though he wished for a change, knew it was not in the making in the short term:

> *My temperament is such that I have not been able to cast aside, during non-business hours, the difficulties encountered during this period of reorganization, and I foresee no personal satisfaction under present station management responsibilities. I have tried to associate myself closely with the station's programs, the end of all our endeavors here, and one who would enjoy that work, much more than I, would find the responsibilities of management much easier to discharge. I realize the exigencies of the times and much of what I have said will apply only when conditions permit.*

Glade's move from day-to-day KSL operations to focus more on his many civic responsibilities is discussed in the next chapter.

CHAPTER 8
A CHANGE OF CIVIC VENUE AWAY FROM RADIO

For the most part, Glade's work at KSL, from 1941 on, was limited, and he
had little decision-making responsibility except as a Radio Service Corporation
official. This was not the case, however, in his civic involvement outside of
KSL. All during this transitional period, he had important responsibilities in
several organizations nationally and locally, including the National Association
of Broadcasters Code Compliance Committee and the Salt Lake Chamber of
Commerce, where he served as president. He chaired the local draft board and
the Salt Lake Youth Council and served as director of the Salt Lake County
chapter of the American Red Cross. He also served on The University of Utah
Board of Regents as well as the Deseret Sunday School Union and the local
council of the Boy Scouts of America.

The NAB Code Compliance Committee comprised nine members
representing the three major radio networks and the various classes of stations:
clear channel, of which KSL was one, as well as regional and local stations. The
committee met in the East twice a year and conducted work by mail to rule on
stations purported to be in violation of the code.

Glade said that in the administration of the Salt Lake Chamber of
Commerce, he strived to be progressively conservative. He said that much of the
Chamber's work was undercover, especially as it dealt with labor problems.
Most important were matters connected with defense. According to Glade, "We
have the future of our city constantly in mind and are truly bearing down on
values other than the material ones." To achieve this, on behalf of the Chamber,
Glade consulted important media, business, political and church leaders such as
the Salt Lake Tribune's John F. Fitzpatrick, and other banking and business
leaders such as Orval Adams, and E.O. Howard, W. J. O'Connor, and Erick
Ryberg.

As chair of the local Selective Service Board, a post he eventually held for
seventeen years, Glade's responsibilities exponentially increased when the U.S.
entered World War II in December 1941. Glade said that this work had grown to

such proportions that two secretaries were needed to help in handling the exacting work of studying hundreds of confidential reports of Salt Lake military registrants.

The Salt Lake Youth Council represented 111 organizations and covered work involving securing work for young people, attending to educational assignments, and engaging certain health promoting matters. Among this organization's achievements that Glade points to is the establishment of an organization to cope with the distribution of pornographic printed matter, and the cooperation with local, state and federal agencies in setting up a prophylaxis clinic for venereal disease. This latter achievement in hindsight was way ahead of its time and showed Glade's openness to solving problems in practical and doable ways.

His involvement as director of the American Red Cross and as a member of the Salt Lake Chapter of the Boy Scouts of America also consumed his time and resources, but he said he had all his work organized so that it went forward on schedule, although he did admit it involved much nighttime activity for preparation. Presumably, this was his way of lamenting the time all his business, civic and church activities took away from time spent with his family. Even with all these outside commitments, Glade assured Clark:

> *My first obligation is to KSL and I stand ready, earnestly and loyally, to do as best I possibly can, everything the station management [Ivor Sharp] asks of me ... and I try most earnestly to keep KSL's position in mind and to serve the station as well as the public in every helpful way I can.*[1]

In addition to all of the above commitments, Glade continued to be in enormously high demand as a speaker by all sorts of Utah business, civic and church groups, and he often had weeks in which he gave a speech a day, and sometimes made as many as 13 speeches in a week. But even with all his other skills, Glade apparently survived in the early 1940s, not on his business acumen or leadership abilities, but on his warm, gracious, and cordial public persona, his radio performance training and command of the English language, and on his set of beliefs, values, and opinions that shaped his thinking, actions, and understanding of the world, wrapped up in his progressive ideology, parts of which were implicit or explicit in nearly every speech.

Jumping ahead a decade or two, one might ask what eventually resulted from Clark's and Fitzpatrick's shakeup at KSL beginning in 1938. What happened to the influential players in this saga? Well, while still on the RSC/KSL board, Glade continued his community work as outlined above and went on to become a three-term mayor of Salt Lake City, all the time maintaining an enduring friendship with the *Tribune's* Fitzpatrick.[2]

Fitzpatrick, publisher of the *Tribune*, sold the newspaper's 20-year-plus interest in KSL in 1946 and joined with the Abe Glasmann/George Hatch family and the Abrelia (Robert H.) Hinckley family to own KALL radio, which competed with KSL. Clark and Fitzpatrick's close friendship withstood this business parting, and it survived a later 1948 LDS/Catholic brouhaha instigated after Clark brought forth his anti-Catholic views in opposition to a series of Sunday talks on KSL by Monsignor Duane G. Hunt, Utah's Catholic bishop. Hunt, unintentionally, it seems, infuriated Clark by speaking on papal infallibility and defending Rome as the temporal repository of apostolic succession from St. Peter. Clark's own 1948 radio talks on KSL as a result included criticism of papal primacy, and he published a book in 1949 entitled *On the Way to Immortality and Eternal Life*, in which he explicated man's quest for the LDS way of life that gives assurance that personality survives death.

Glade surely would have agreed with Clark's sentiment in the body of the book, but from all we know about him, not with Clark's appendix. Clark added a 220-page appendix about what he perceived as Roman Catholic indulgences, hagiolatry (worship of saints), relics, images, Mariolatry (extreme devotion to Mary, the mother of Jesus Christ), and simony (the buying and selling of sacred things).[3] This sectarian Clark and Hunt fallout resulting from KSL programming continued for six months or more and then moved from public exhibit to private expression in subsequent times.

Continuing with the Clark and Sharp legacy, in 1951 David O. McKay became LDS president and was optimistic about KSL radio and television. At a 1954 special conference session, he spoke of electronic media's potential in carrying the message of Mormonism to the world.

> *Today it is a simple matter for us to reach all nations. The
> Lord has given us the means of whispering through space, of
> annihilating distance. We have the means in our hands of
> reaching the millions of the world.*[4]

But by 1958, it was clear that despite media's potential to proselytize the world, the KSL broadcasting operations were in financial trouble, having barely broken-even the year before. As such, Ivor Sharp's continuance as head of KSL was being questioned. The church's financial advisor, William F. Edwards, issued a KSL status report in 1959 and recommended McKay become chairman of KSL, with his two counselors, one of whom was Clark, as vice-chairmen. In addition, Edwards urged that Sharp be "retired."

President McKay evidently took Edward's advice concerning Sharp seriously. Sharp was "released" as head of the broadcasting company, but Clark was not made a KSL vice chairman as suggested. Instead, McKay also released Clark as president of the RSC and the KSL stations. Prince and Wright in their book *David O. McKay and the Rise of Modern Mormonism* argue, "This may have had no connection to [Clark's] growing dissent over the direction McKay was taking church finances, but it was easy to regard these changes [Sharp's and Clark's release from their respective KSL positions] as a form of punishment."[5]

Interestingly, McKay had been first counselor to President George Albert Smith, and Clark was second counselor. When Smith died and McKay became LDS president in 1951, he chose Clark as his second counselor and Apostle Stephen L. Richards as first counselor, a surprise to some likely aware of McKay and Clark's past relationship and sometimes divergent views on Church and KSL matters. Clark served as second counselor until he died on October 6, 1961. Ivor Sharp was involved in several endeavors after leaving KSL, including mining stock sales, until his death in 1972.

In 1959, when Clark and Sharp were released from their respective RSC/KSL duties, Jay Wright, described as a genius broadcast engineer and employed since 1954 as RSC vice president, was elevated to president and chairman of the RSC board to replace Clark. But after only a year, Wright possibly was deemed not up to the financial challenges facing the KSL broadcast operations. Wright left RSC in 1961 to become the head of engineering for King Broadcasting Co.

in Seattle. He later served as director, vice president and a board member for King, which operated radio and television stations in Seattle and Spokane as well as Portland, Oregon. In an oral history interview three decades after leaving RSC, Wright certainly did not disparage church authorities or KSL management, but his eyes became glassy when discussing that year as RSC president and board chair, seemingly a disappointing time for him in an otherwise brilliant career.[6]

KSL then looked outside the company for a president and chose Arch Madsen, a radioman of longstanding, who proved up to the financial challenges and brought the RSC/KSL combine, later named the Bonneville International Corporation, to secure financial status.   Madsen had worked at KSL early in his career. He knew all about the challenges Glade had confronted, especially the nepotism, and he had great and lifelong respect for Glade. Madsen accepted the job only after McKay gave him assurances that he would report directly to him on RSC/KSL matters and not to the LDS President's counselors, one of whom was Clark. Madsen's first job was to repair relations with CBS, which had threatened to move its affiliation due to KSL TV's low ratings among the Salt Lake TV stations. By raising KSL-TV from number three to number one rated and buying KIRO-TV-AM-FM in Seattle, Madsen satisfied the CBS Network's concerns and did much to improve Bonneville's —formerly RSC— finances. Buying FM stations for very little money before they became the medium of choice for music listeners around the country identified Madsen as one of broadcasting's extraordinary visionaries in the years to come.

Meanwhile, Glade's significant contributions as a member of the University of Utah board of regents, from 1943 to 1949, overlapped with his first term as Salt Lake City mayor. This period is the focus in the next chapters.

SECTION III

GLADE'S NEW CIVIC ROLES: UNIVERSITY REGENT AND MAYOR

CHAPTER 9
THE CIVIC-MINDED UNIVERSITY REGENT

Governor Herbert B. Maw appointed Glade to the University of Utah's Board of Regents on September 3, 1941, some 12 years after Glade left active teaching at the university, more than two years after he had been replaced as KSL general manager, and three years before he became mayor of Salt Lake City. Glade still was an important figure in Salt Lake civic affairs as well as an RSC officer who had continuing public relations and ancillary responsibilities at KSL. At his first meeting as a regent, he was appointed to the school's Building Committee and the Faculty Committee. Glade immediately was put to work. The faculty committee met on September 14 to consider the appointment of a new University president to follow George Thomas who had been president since 1922. Thomas had tendered his resignation, but the Regents would not accept it until they found his successor. The Regents had been searching for a new president in the months before Glade joined the board, and applicants from near and far had applied, but the Regents could not make a choice.

Glade and the other Regents eliminated all but two applicants – one lived in Utah and the other was a Utah native living in another state – but neither could garner majority support of the board members. Finally, in a late night meeting on October 12, 1941, the Regents unanimously agreed on a third person, one who had not even been a candidate and who was unaware he was being considered for the school's top post. It was LeRoy E. Cowles, 61, who had been a teacher in the state since 1903, beginning in the Wasatch County school system and subsequently working at the Weber Academy in Ogden and Carbon High School in Price before joining the faculty at the University of Utah in 1914.

Cowles in his 1949 book *University of Utah and World War II* relates how he learned of his appointment. He was awakened by telephone at 1:30 a.m. and asked by Regents chairman Roy Thatcher to come to the school's board room. He was told that the regent members wanted to ask him some questions about one or more of the candidates being considered for the presidency. After arriving and being ushered in, he was informed the regents had elected him president, and he was asked if he would accept. As the story goes, after Cowles gained his composure and was assured it was not a practical joke, he accepted the call and promised most sincerely to do his best to serve intelligently and faithfully the University and the people of Utah. Cowles officially assumed office on November 15.[1]

Shortly after Cowles was appointed, Glade's business expertise and mediation skills were tested in his newfound role as regent. At the November Regents meeting, a letter from the Utah Retail Grocers Association was read, which vigorously protested the proposed appointment of Dr. Dilworth Walker as dean of the U's Business School. The protest arose from a report published by Walker that apparently disparaged the interests of individual enterprise – more specifically, independent grocers – in Utah. At a later Board meeting, Glade was asked by fellow regents to confer with Walker and the Grocers Association and to provide assurances that should Walker be appointed dean, his appointment would not result in "any unmerited accusation or benefit to the chain store [supermarkets] organization."[2]

Besides being one of the regents largely responsible for Cowles appointment as University president, Glade, in his two terms of service as a regent, also was especially helpful in transforming the medical school from a two to a four-year program, for providing housing on campus and in Salt Lake City for returning veterans, and for playing a leading role in acquiring Fort Douglas land for the University and for Salt Lake City after World War II ended.[3]

Glade was on the committee appointed to study in depth any problems and concerns with expanding the medical school. The committee's work was broadly defined, assisting as advisers in selecting a dean and faculty members, and informing and influencing state legislators about the medical school's budget needs. Glade took special note of Dr. L E. Viko, who was a member of the Salt Lake County Medical Society, for his contributions as a Regent committee member. Glade pointed out that during the early period of the four-year medical school, the school's executive direction called for great administrative skill and discretion and tact, largely because of interagency disagreements as to how responsibilities would be localized. President Cowles, Glade and the other regents were said to have provided excellent administrative guidance.

It took many months of hard work to navigate the many difficult issues surrounding the formation of a four-year medical school, but the University of Utah regents approved the program in May 1942 and appointed Dr. A. Cyril Callister as dean in July of that year. An agreement was made with Salt Lake County to use the County Hospital on 2100 South and State Street for teaching in exchange for care of county patients at no cost to the county. Medical students were accepted that September for their third year and subsequently a fourth year.

While a regent, Glade also served on the draft board and coordinated with several committees to assist in meeting war emergencies. After Roosevelt declared war in his *Day of Infamy* speech on December 8, 1941, a great many students enlisted, as did nineteen faculty members. And Fort Douglas took over acres of campus property to house and train military personnel and to hold prisoners of war on a site on the southeast part of campus near where the Huntsman Center now stands. Meanwhile, the University's enrollment dropped during World War II from 4,632 (1940-41) to 3,418 (1943-44).[4]

The military services drew heavily on the school's student body, as hundreds of men were called into action. Glade later said as mayor he had received numerous personal reports from Army and Navy men applauding the superior character and the stand-out war records of Utah men. As chair of the draft board, Glade said he could personally testify to the "outstanding quality of the young manhood available on the Utah campus."

The question of admitting students of Japanese ancestry to the school also became an issue of importance after Pearl Harbor, especially after the evacuation of Japanese-Americans from the Pacific Coast states, some of whom were moved to the Topaz Relocation site near Delta, Utah. One-hundred and twenty-five "Nisei" -- Glade's choice of words describing first-generation Japanese born in the U.S. who were U.S. citizens -- were registered students at the University. Glade later said that in spite of the delicate situation, these were superior students and their conduct was credible. The 125 were allowed to continue at the U.[5]

Glade and the other regents oversaw the campus being transformed to support war efforts. In 1942, the Army moved in and occupied a substantial part of the Student Union Building, including the entire top floor. The student union at that time was located in what is now Gardner Hall on the President's Circle. In addition, the Field House was converted into a dormitory, providing sleeping and living accommodations for 1,200 men. The school's curriculum also changed to support the war effort. Glade points out the initials A.S.T.P., which stood for Army Specialized Training Program, attained common currency on the campus and included instruction in a wide field of army-oriented subjects, such as all phases of engineering, mathematics, and foreign languages.

Other needs of the University were not neglected during the war. In July 1943, Glade and four other regents were appointed to the "Committee on Gifts," which was requested to bring forth recommendations for a plan for soliciting and collecting gifts and endowments for the University. Subsequently, Glade was involved in the formation of the Alumni-University Development Fund, whose purpose was to raise funds for the school from the private sector. The fund came into being on May 11, 1945, just days after the war was formally declared over, in Europe. The fund raised money from hundreds of small givers but also from such large donors as the LDS Church and Kennecott Corporation. The contributions for the year 1945-46 totaled $481,412 ($5.84 million in today's equivalence). Included in this sum was a $200,000 donation from Kennecott Copper Corporation, to develop a strong mining department at the University.

Glade was instrumental in efforts that would become highly profiled in the post-war period. In the summer of 1944, construction began on the University Health Center, which began offering services in the following year. Funds were supplied by the Federal Works Agency, and the Regent Building Committee, of which Glade was a member and who did considerable work in connection with providing facilities for the health center.

In April of 1945, the regents established programs for the doctoral degree. Also in 1945, the Utah Humanities Research Foundation was established with Dr. Lowell Lees as chairman. The Rockefeller Foundation provided $15,000 of financial aid for the project

The Board of Regents during President Cowles tenure accomplished a great number of things as a group, calling on the individual talents of its members, including Glade who fostered a good relationship first between KSL and the

University, and then as mayor, beginning in January 1944, between Salt Lake City and the University. A. Ray Olpin took office as the University's new president on January 1, 1946, just four months after the end of the war. Meanwhile, Glade was beginning his third year as Salt Lake City mayor and had just begun his second four-year term as a regent. In holding these two positions, Glade was especially valuable because, as never before, the University and Salt Lake City were facing many similar problems, particularly dealing with the housing and employment of returning vets and their families.

With the end of the war, the regents, the city commissioners and the mayor knew there would be an influx of veterans wanting to enter the University after being discharged from the service. The regents gave Olpin great latitude in making new hires in preparation for this enrollment pressure, and Glade, now a seasoned board member as well as mayor of Salt Lake City, was among Olpin's greatest advocates. In preparing for the returning married veterans, 301 dwelling units were provided in the summer of 1946. In the housing of veterans, preference was given to hardship cases and to those students married with children.

Mayor Glade also established a Salt Lake City Housing Committee, which worked closely with the University Faculty Housing Committee, which Glade and the other regents fully supported. In order to coordinate the efforts of both committees and avoid duplication, Glade worked closely with Dean John L. Ballif from the Faculty Housing Committee who also represented the University, Salt Lake City's counterpart committee. Housing units were brought in from Vancouver, Washington, and Portland, Oregon, areas and reassembled in what was then called the Stadium Village, the area immediately northeast of the football stadium, near where the Marriott Library, Social Work and Fine Arts Buildings are now located. Additional buildings, including the bookstore building, the men's hall, and the chemistry, physics, and biology laboratories were acquired from Dugway, the Salt Lake Air Base and other military installations.

The most far-reaching action Glade was involved in as a second-term regent involved the return of Fort Douglas land to the University of Utah after the war. It took over a year, with the University president going to Washington, D.C. to plead the school's case, and a Salt Lake City visit by General Dwight D. Eisenhower who promised to "cut a hole in the fence" and let his University vets through to Fort Douglas. "They're good boys," Ike said, "and I have great affection and respect for them. Let them have everything you can – extra facilities, supplies, and furniture --nothing's too good for them."[6]

Eisenhower delivered on his promise. The major exchange of land was finalized on October 30, 1948, when nearly 300 acres of Fort Douglas land, part of the University's original endowment when the school was founded in 1850, were returned, along with 106 buildings. Fifty years later, juxtaposed with hosting the 2002 Salt Lake City Winter Olympics, another major exchange of Fort Douglas property and buildings was completed, again greatly adding to the U's easterly expansion into the foothills above the main campus.

In conjunction with the University's 1948 application for Fort Douglas land, Mayor Glade requested a parcel of Fort Douglas land and buildings for Salt Lake City. Glade and the Commission were allowed to buy from the United States through the War Assets Administration the acreage now known as the LDS Triangle, land south of South Campus Drive –named Hempstead Road at the time — and west of Wasatch Drive and Mario Capecchi Drive on which presently stands the LDS Institute buildings and surrounding property south from the Huntsman Center. At the time there were many University owned buildings on the property, but the city did not require they be removed, and allowed the school to occupy the buildings and land for a decade or more after. The purchase price was $18,320 ($184,000 in today's equivalence) and the acquisition was approved by the Salt Lake Board of Commission at its meeting on October 28, 1948.[7]

Glade likely expressed the feelings of all involved after the land transfer to the city was completed:

> *I am personally grateful for the friendly working relationship*
> *which Salt Lake City [established] with the University in the*
> *division of the [Fort Douglas] property, a part of which [the*
> *triangle] we were permitted to purchase for Salt Lake City.[8]*

Salt Lake City owned the triangle of land all during Glade's tenure as mayor. In fact, near Glade's last days in office in December 1955, the Salt Lake City Board of Commission with Glade's prompting deeded a parcel of the land to the Boy Scouts of America for its Scout Center. The center remains on the land to date, as does the American Red Cross headquarters, given by the City earlier under Glade's prompting.

As a point of interest, sometime between 1956 and 1964, after Glade was out of the mayor's office, a three-way trade took place that resulted in the LDS Church acquiring the triangle of land from the city. The trade involved the LDS Church deeding to the Federal Government land in downtown Salt Lake City at First South and State Street where the Wallace Bennett Federal Building now stands. The Federal Government in-turn deeded to the city land it owned on Sunnyside and Guardsman's Way where Sunnyside Park now is situated. The city rounded-out the three-way trade by deeding the triangle of land to the LDS Church which allowed the University to occupy the barracks-style buildings on the property for several decades, well into the 1990s, before it developed the expansive LDS Institute on the property.

It is believed that the University was not consulted about or involved in the three-way trade. It was reported that Olpin when he found out was extremely displeased the University was not involved in the transaction. It is a certainty that if Glade had been mayor of Salt Lake City at the time, Olpin would have been informed, and Glade and the city would have taken a hard look at deeding away this strategic land to other than the University, even though Glade's beloved LDS Church was involved.

To celebrate the school's acquisition of Fort Douglas land in 1948, the regents scheduled a handing-over ceremony at the halftime of a university football game, with a federal official scheduled to do the honors.

The University of Utah Board of Regents minutes for October 4, 1948, recorded:

> *On President Olpin's recommendation Regent [Earl J.] Glade*
> *[also Salt Lake City's mayor] therefore made the motion that*
> *the celebration of the acquisition of the Fort Douglas Property*
> *be held in connection with the "Home Coming" October 30th,*

*and that proper recognition and commendation be given to
those who have so graciously helped to acquire the Fort
Douglas property.*[9]

At halftime of the Utah-Colorado game, Olpin and Jesse Larson, representing the United States War Assets Administration, with others, walked to the center of the football field where Olpin introduced Larson.

After speaking on microphone about how important it was to assist in educating returned veterans by providing military land and facilities, Larson in a booming voice announced the gift of Fort Douglas:

*It gives me pleasure to present on behalf of the United States
government this deed of property to the University of Nevada.*

Paul Hodson, in his 1987 book *Crisis on Campus*, describes the scene:

*Disbelief paralyzed the stands –then a roar of laughter
swelled and grew until some of the temporary stands in the
end zones rocked threateningly. Poor Larson attempted to
correct himself, but the 15,000 laughing voices were
merciless.*[10]

Glade, although differing in his estimate of game attendance, echoes Hudson's recollection of the event. showing a flair for hyperbolic prose:

*There is little wonder that on that eventful autumn day in
1948, in the University Stadium with 25,000 excited Utahans
in attendance there was no ordinary apprehension in the air
when a top Washington official, apparently shot-through with
microphone fear, but supposedly reading from large, legible
script, which I myself, saw, gave this priceless property [Fort
Douglas] to the great and sovereign State of Nevada! You may
be assured that those of us standing by, who knew first hand of
the difficulty of getting it, very promptly helped that esteemed
but worried gentleman [Jesse Larson] to get his bearing and
his sense of direction.*[11]

Records show 288 University of Utah students had lost their lives in the war. As a sincere expression of sorrow, the Board of Regents gave each family whose student died an engraved war memorial bearing the signatures of former university president LeRoy E. Cowles and the Regent chairman Roy D. Thatcher.

Glade's term as a two-term regent ended in 1949. Stepping back to 1943, Glade took his significant interpersonal skills, business experience and University connections into the political arena. On September 22, 1943, two years after being appointed to his first term as a University of Utah regent, Glade announced his candidacy for Salt Lake City mayor to run against Ab Jenkins, a popular incumbent. Glade's twelve years as mayor are the subject of the next several chapters.

CHAPTER 10

CAMPAIGN FOR MAYOR

Once more, Glade's on-again-off-again relationship with KSL came into play. On September 15, 1943, a week before he publicly announced his mayoral candidacy, Glade told Sharp at KSL of his political intentions. Sharp talked to Fitzpatrick and Clark about it the next day. Of immediate concern was Glade's continued association with KSL, and whether it would be feasible for him to continue part-time at the station and remain RSC vice president. Of long-term legal and economic concern was the appearance to the public or to the Federal Communications Commission (FCC) that KSL was endorsing a candidate.

On September 16, Clark stated KSL's position:

> *The decision relative to the candidacy for Mayor should rest squarely upon Mr. Glade; that in the event Mr. Glade should decide to stand for election he would have KSL's best wishes in the matter; that in the event Mr. Glade should become a candidate, it should be understood that he would be required by fair play standards to retire from broadcasting over KSL during the pre-election season; and, that if Mr. Glade were elected, the matter of a salary adjustment, would then be considered by the Directors of KSL.*[1]

On September 19, still two days prior to his official filing, Glade said good-bye to the listeners of the *Sunday Evening on Temple Square* program on KSL, the broadcast for which he had been the announcer for 15 years:

> *To my three sons in the United States Army, Captain Frederick R. Glade, Captain James Richard Glade, and Sergeant Keith Glade, who regularly listen to their father, during this hour, and who are now located at remote points, that I am not allowed to mention over the air, may I say that merely a change in my assignment of responsibility makes it necessary for me to leave this well-known program.*[2]

This cryptic statement appeared in public print, indicating to Clark and others at the station some might assume that KSL management had a role in changing Glade's "assignment." At the *Sunday Evening on Temple Square* program on September 26, the following clarifying statement was read in Glade's absence:

> *We know that many have missed tonight the friendly voice and genial personality of Earl J. Glade, who for some 15 years has announced this program. You have felt the absence of a friend at a family party. Mr. Glade's service to KSL over these years has been very great. He has discontinued his broadcast because acting upon the insistence of friends he has entered the mayoralty race in Salt Lake City. He goes into this new field with the good wishes of KSL.*[3]

Yet, the statement did not fully calm concerns about Glade's candidacy and his relationship to KSL.

> *This morning I [Ivor Sharp] received a telephone call from a prominent Salt Lake citizen asking about Mr. Glade's candidacy ... "whether the station wanted to 'get rid' of him," as he put it; that he had heard this comment. I replied that as far as I knew ... that certainly what had been done to date was taken by Mr. Glade on his own initiative, spurred on perhaps by some of his friends; that things were harmonious at the station; that nothing could be further from the truth than the suggestion that Mr. Glade's candidacy was in any way related to KSL. ...We were anxious to have a friendly understand with him [Glade] so that it would be clear to all that any attempt on our part to keep the station free from politics should not be construed by anyone as an unfriendly act towards him.*[4]

While KSL waffled on what to do about his candidacy, Glade was clear about his plans for Salt Lake City. His candidacy was front-page material in *The Salt Lake Tribune*, local news section of May 22, 1943. He promised the fire and police departments would be given every necessary consideration to serve the public. He saw the need to bring in more water to Salt Lake City for safety reasons –presumably for the fire department-- and to anticipate the demand for water with the influx of veterans after the war. He also had the war top-of-mind, even at the local level, and already was front-and-center in national and local war bond and USO funding. In addition, he called for extraordinary efforts for businesses to plan to employ soldiers when they returned from war. He declared: "If private enterprise cannot handle the entire load, I shall favor the city's undertaking such suitable make-work projects for that purpose as it can. These projects should be of a substantial character and provide the city with permanent municipal improvements."[5]

Attending to a subject that would surface several times during his administration, he pledged his personal attention to what he called the serious problem of juvenile delinquency. Glade obviously saw the office one of not only city services, but of morality and moral duty. He would add Sunday closings, his opinions on divorce, and other family issues in his run for mayor. These issues clearly were in adherence to the LDS principle of eternal progression and personal growth Glade had internalized early in life.

During the campaign, Glade revealed his vision for a post-war Salt Lake City. He announced a long-ranged plan of "community building," mentioning plans for a civic center, a municipal auditorium, a community incinerator, Jordan River area improvements, and more improvements in the City Canyon parks. Glade's agenda included smoke reduction – apparently, the 1940s word for "smog," as Salt Lake City's air pollution problem had been exacerbated during a time when most residents burned coal for heat.[6]

The Salt Lake Tribune under Fitzpatrick's guidance paid handsome deference to the new candidate, calling him a nationally known radio authority and civic leader in its stories. It also credited him with his accomplishments in spreading Mormon Tabernacle Choir fame nationwide. All Glade's plans, of course, were looked on favorably by voters who considered Salt Lake City a dynamic place worthy of national attention.

Glade ran against a field of five candidates, led by the well-known incumbent, the popular automobile land-speed-record holder, Ab Jenkins, of "Mormon-Meteor" and Bonneville Salt Flats fame. Glade surprised pundits with a substantial victory in the primary. He captured 8,825 votes while Jenkins finished second with 6,648. The newspapers noted Glade did it practically without any organized support.

In the primary election, Glade led from the start and never looked back, but newspaper reports revealed an intriguing shift in his political affiliation. In the non-partisan mayoral primary, Glade didn't rely on nor could he legally solicit support from the Democratic Party that once counted him as a national youth leader, and voters likely for the most part didn't know of his past efforts in the party or his passionate support of prohibition decades earlier.

The *Tribune* called Glade's primary victory a "kick in the teeth" to the party organizations. Meanwhile, Jenkins generally was identified as a Republican, but he also had to, by law, distance himself from that party. Glade beat the third place finisher, Horace Beck, by a three-to-one margin and I. R. Morrison ran a distant fourth, barely getting enough support to make it into the general election. In reality, it would be a race between Glade and the incumbent Jenkins in the general election.[7]

Glade was viewed as the newcomer against Jenkins who was popular among city workers. Glade's strong early primary victory was not a sure sign of an impending victory in the general election, however. Only 21,000 people, representing a third of all voters, had cast ballots in the primary election. Glade would have to appeal to the silent majority that didn't venture out on that bad weather October primary day, but who would show up for the general election.

The campaign was one of personalities. Glade's public notoriety fostered over years at KSL and on Temple Square, and his decision not to rely on his past political affiliations paid effectively. His strength in the nonpartisan race actually came from the Republican east side stronghold of the city, while he was not as popular in the west side Democratic stronghold. His "get-tough" campaign on youthful troublemakers, appeals for strong police and fire departments, and proposals for civic developments were issues that seemingly attracted those in the more affluent east side Republican districts.

The pundits also were correct in assuming a larger general election vote tally would eclipse the small primary election turnout two weeks prior. The *Salt Lake Tribune* described an election night where Glade and Jenkins traded districts back and forth. After the 36,000 votes were counted, Glade had edged out the one-term incumbent [Jenkins], 19,153 to 16,869.[8]

Of significance, Glade, who never revealed he was a Democrat during his first election, would have a Democrat ally on the Mayor-Commission city governing body. State Senator L. C. Romney would become a close political ally after his election as a commissioner. Salt Lake political historian Dixie S. Huefner wrote in a report that Park Commissioner Romney wielded a great deal of power during the Glade years. Some of that power, no doubt, came from common political agendas, and some probably came from Romney's own political ambitions.[9]

Glade's old KSL colleagues, Clark and Sharp, organized a banquet for Glade at the Hotel Utah after his mayoral victory in 1943, and, as stated above, he was recognized for his years of "leadership" at KSL. Seemingly, forgotten were the previous five contentious years in which Clark and the RSC board had strategically shifted power at KSL from Glade to Sharp. Clark intuitively knew that Glade would be a tremendous asset to KSL as mayor and offered his genuine best wishes at the victory party: "May success follow you, Mr. Mayor." A newspaper account of the banquet mentioned that Glade spoke briefly expressing appreciation.[10]

The mayoral victory publicly closed out Glade's day-to-day association with KSL, but privately he retained a position as consultant to the radio station, and as a member of the RSC board he received a monthly $350 compensation ($4,900 in today's equivalence) while also drawing a salary as mayor. Later in a letter to LDS President McKay, Clark succinctly summarized 22 years of loans and compensation provided by KSL to Earl Glade, including part of his time as mayor.

> *KSL lent Brother Glade $12,000, which he used to try to start*
> *a talent-furnishing company [Glade Artists Bureau] with Mrs.*
> *[Irma] Bitner. This failed. The money still due after his*
> *enterprise ceased operations, he paid back to KSL over a*
> *period, (by $100 per month reductions from the salary of $750*
> *per month which KSL paid him). He had no regular work at*
> *KSL. ... Because he went into the political field, it was deemed*
> *best by the [RSC] Executive Committee to reduce his salary.*

Since he was Mayor [over the last seven years], he has drawn $350 per month. His total receipts from the Company since January 1929, to December 30, 1950 (including fees and dividends), amount to $347,650.00, or at the rate of $15,802 per year, for 22 years.[11]

The $347,650 total "company" (RSC) compensation paid Glade from 1929-1950 inclusive represented $135,000 in salary from 1929 through 1943, and another $29,400 from 1944 through 1950. This was in addition to his mayoral salary during those years. Glade's RBI outfit generated an additional $272,650 in compensation from 1929 until it was dissolved in 1938. Glade's average annual salary ($15,802) over 22 years would average over $130,000 each year in modern equivalence, and the total $347,650 he received over 22 years, would represent upwards of $5 million.

CHAPTER 11

MR. MAYOR

Glade was sworn into office as mayor of Salt Lake City on January 3, 1944, and outgoing Mayor Ab Jenkins warmly welcomed him.

On this, the day of my departure from the office of Mayor, I wish to express to all of the citizens of Salt Lake City, my very best wishes for a new year that will bring peace and prosperity to us all. And to say that I shall always cherish the memory of the honor you accorded me in electing me to serve you as Mayor these past four years.

And to thousands of you whom I consider my personal friends and who have so faithfully supported me in word and action, among whom are the members of the press and radio, the civic and service clubs—both men and women, and the many, many individual friends whom it is impossible for me to thank personally at this time and so I endeavor to so in this manner. I also wish to express my gratitude to the many fine men and women who serve in the Public Safety Departments of our city and who have given such valiant service to us during my period of office. For them I wish happiness in the years ahead.

And lastly, may I say that if mistakes have been made—and who deems himself so great that he would deny making mistakes— that such were of the head and not the heart, for at all times my great desire has been to safeguard your welfare as citizens and friends and to carry and execute to the very best of my ability, and in all honesty, the trust you placed in my hands when you elected me your Mayor four years ago. As a citizen and taxpayer I shall continue to make this fine city my home and I hope and desire to work with you at all times for the general welfare of our city and state.

To my successor Mr. Earl J. Glade, I wish the happiest of administrations and full success in all his undertakings.[1]

As well as mayor, Jenkins also was Commissioner of Public Safety, which included the Police, Fire and Health Departments. He was credited with building up these departments in terms of housing and equipment and increasing total personnel over his four-year tenure from 365 to 438. Two new fire stations were built and the remaining nine fire stations around the city were rebuilt or renovated, with several new trucks purchased, including a 100-foot aerial truck.

To top things off, the departing mayor generously offered to give to the fire department, free of charge, his high-powered racing motor from the Mormon-Meteor. This was estimated to be a $2,000 donation. Unfortunately, the motor could not be fitted into any fire department apparatus, but spare parts and other racing equipment were compatible and were left by Jenkins for the city.[2]

Likewise, Mayor Glade also would give significant attention to the Police and Fire Departments throughout his twelve-year tenure, but initially his main concern was support of the war effort. At his swearing-in ceremony he spoke of his desire to extend his best wishes to the retiring mayor and commissioners and to wish them good fortune in the days ahead, and that he had the utmost faith in the incoming commissioners and felt they'd do everything possible toward the war effort:

> *That sacrifices must be made by all if we are to safeguard our freedom with which we are so richly blessed; that those of us at home cannot equal the sacrifice made by those on the war front but we can all have a spirit of good will and faith in the future.*[3]

The Office of Civilian Defense held a six-state conference in Salt Lake City during Glade's first month in office. Glade met with relevant federal, county and city agencies for the purpose of getting cooperation and a better understanding between these groups with relation to manpower needs regarding Utah's support of the war effort. "All hell is about to break loose on the fighting fronts," said Frank Gaines, chief of war services for the regional office of civilian defense.

It was no coincidence that Salt Lake City became a center for war conferences and the war effort. Various regional and state directors of wartime offices provided some startling deficiencies in Salt Lake City area labor requirements. For instance, an official from the Office of War Services said that he had been working with Gus Backman of the Chamber of Commerce for two and a half years to provide workers for the 13 war plants operating in the Salt Lake-Ogden-Provo area, but there still were shortages. First, 1,700 people had to be made available each day to replace those workers who were absent daily from work. In addition, 33,000 people were required each year –2,250 each month– to be replacements for wartime workers leaving the area.

Mayor Earl J. Glade
(J. Willard Marriott Library)

Workers moved out of the area for several reasons. Transportation to and from work cost too much per day and it required too much time to commute. For instance, it cost 85-cents per day to go from Ogden to the Clearfield war plant. The restaurant accommodations were not adequate, the prices were too high and the service was inadequate. Grocery stores were not cooperating in keeping open at night in order to provide facilities for those who were not able to shop during regular store hours. The laundry situation was unsatisfactory. Military men on leave had no place to stay and hotels and rooming houses charged the same for one man as for two. The housing condition was not adequate: 2,900 houses were needed to take care of the shortage in the area, and 900 homes scheduled to be built were not even started. Local builders were not constructing houses because the housing demand would significantly decrease after the war and they estimated they would be left holding excess housing units.[4]

Mayor Glade could not solve these problems alone but took the lead in addressing them with officials in cities along the Wasatch Front. In addition, he promoted an "I Am An American Day" through the U.S.O., and servicemen and women as well as new citizens were invited to participate in special ceremonies and programs. As a father of three servicemen, Glade never missed an opportunity to recognize, praise, and honor those in uniform.

A local wartime issue that would receive little public attention from the Glade administration was the control of prostitution. Rumors circulated that Salt Lake City was so lax in controlling prostitution that the commander of the Kearns Depot had to threaten to prevent his men from going into town in order to get action on the matter. Tavern owners may have weighed in on the matter, but what action was taken, if any, was not established in press accounts or minutes of official city meetings.

Even with portending weighty issues on the docket, more mundane matters were not neglected as Glade took office. At his first official commission meeting, Glade's first vote as mayor involved a constituent's seemingly insignificant claim to an abandoned bicycle. It was moved that the petitioner be allowed to retain the bicycle until the proper owner claimed it. It was an inauspicious start, but this seemingly inconsequential matter got Glade's full attention as if it was a top priority. It would be typical of the constituent-centric way Glade conducted the city's business over twelve years as mayor. In this instance, the bicycle request easily got aye votes from all five commissioners before they got down to more serious matters.

The new mayor had been a business and civic leader and understood the workings of local government, and he forecasted no major changes in his administration. Within days of taking office, Glade went out of his way to praise city workers. The mayor told the Salt Lake Exchange Club membership that "he did not intend to go about stirring up trouble in his new position." And *The Salt Lake Tribune* of January 18, 1944, quoted the mayor as saying: "I know a number of men working for the city, who could earn twice to three times as much in private industry."[5]

Also, Mayor Glade always had an intense interest in the city's youth, and when elected continued night recreational programs at six centers funded by the commission. In addition, Glade supervised the procurement and renovation of a building and surrounding property near downtown for a boys' and girls' club. The building was left vacant by the National Youth Administration, which had been abolished by Congress seven months before Glade took office. It was in the southwest section of the city, an area Glade agreed was a forgotten part of the city where no park or recreational facilities for youth were available.

But Glade's election did not mean the end of his tireless speaking engagements or of his continued involvement in the issues he held dear, like supporting the war effort. In the middle of his mayoral campaign, he had taken on the job of heading up the state's United War Fund Drive at the request of Governor Herbert Maw. He already was a national director of the United War Fund, along with a group including John D. Rockefeller, Jr, Captain Eddie Rickenbacker and Edsel Ford. Glade was not new to fund drives; he cut his funding teeth during the BYU stadium drive in 1928. He headed that advertising drive in Salt Lake City.

Glade's state committee was an umbrella organization, which meant he now was Utah's chief fundraiser for seventeen war-time-priority organizations that included, among others, the U.S.O, United Seamen's Service, War Prisoners' Aid, Russian War Relief, British War Relief, and the U.S. Committee for the Care of European Children. The largest fund under the umbrella organization was the U.S.O. Fund, which Glade already had chaired for a year. He willingly and dutifully traveled the state trying to raise the $85,000 U.S.O. quota earmarked for that fund. Glade toured the counties of Utah to get each to contribute money at a time most Americans were already financially strapped in the war-time economy. Utah's total share of the national United War Fund was $410,000 ($6.2 million in modern equivalence) and Glade's hand in the fundraising efforts was significant.

Glade, the patriot, appealed to Utah residents to contribute to the "alleviation of distress throughout the war-torn countries, and for welfare and recreational work among our fighting forces." Commissioner Glade, the business person who was about to lead Salt Lake's Finance Department, also appealed to Utah's residents to contribute because the seventeen funds were efficiently administered. He repeated his appeal in county-after-county: "The administrative and campaign expense of the National War Fund is less than two-thirds of one-percent. There is no waste in administering the joint fund."[6]

The mayor had barely pounded the gavel of his new office when he led the city commission to kick off a war fund drive. The commission suspended the city noise ordinance to get the attention of the citizens for the fund drive. Twenty-two cannons would fire from the state capitol, church bells would ring, factory whistles and police sirens would wail, and a simulated invasion would be broadcast from the loudspeaker on top of the downtown Continental Bank Building. The state defense council vetoed the use of the air-raid sirens for the kick-off, but there was no doubt Glade got people's attention nonetheless.[7]

The city created a war services board to coordinate war agencies, with the objective of winning the war. Additionally, Mayor Glade participated in activities that were "of the times." One practice in his administration that was accepted at the time, albeit not acceptable in contemporary context, concerned the city commission holding in abeyance all Japanese American business applications. The American Federation of Labor, the initiators of the resolution, asked the Salt Lake City commissioners to adopt a policy, which would prevent the issuance of city licenses to Japanese people, regardless of citizenship. The mayor and commission backed the resolution. The ostensible reason for adopting the resolution was to protect the jobs of returning veterans and avoid disharmony, which might lead to strife in the city. Later, the mayor praised the city's Japanese-Americans noting, "Not one Japanese American has applied for a new Salt Lake business license since asked not to do so." He further thanked members of the Japanese-American community for their "fine cooperation."[8]

At the time, there were sixty persons of Japanese descent holding business licenses in Salt Lake City. By the fourth month of the new mayor's term, the anti-Japanese-American fervor apparently reached fever pitch among some Salt Lake residents. A letter attributed to Glade was rumored to be circulating around town urging property owners between Fourth and Ninth South and Second West and Third East not to sell their land to those of Japanese ancestry so that the Asian people would have their own restricted area of the city. The mayor quickly reported all such rumors and letters as false and launched a vigorous investigation to find their origins.

Within his first year, the full extent of the horror of the war was front-page news as allies exposed the atrocities found behind enemy lines. Mayor Glade stepped up the need for war fund contributions. He toured the state again and again, stopping in small towns such as in Rich County in September of 1944, with the message that the conquering allies have first-hand information that "needs … may prove to be greater than estimated from reports received from various sources during the German occupation." He went on to say the China and the Balkan areas command the "sympathy of Americans."[9]

Simultaneously, as the war wound down in 1944, Glade returned to his campaign promise of helping vets and making a better postwar America. The mayor challenged Utah residents not to forget the state's veterans. Injured and long-time service vets were returning to Salt Lake, and the mayor directed citizens to let City Hall know when loved-ones returned from the battlefield. In support, Glade planned official ceremonies to recognize Utah vets for their commitment to service and went to each civic organization seeking support for his efforts.

In June of 1944, Glade told an advertising group at a convention in Fresno that Americans in the postwar "must rise to new heights of living, if they are to prove worthy of the sacrifices of their sons on the battlefield." The mayor continued espousing his long held beliefs about the LDS tenets of progression and personal growth: "Mediocrity is not good enough for America. Its citizens definitely must step up the quality of living, if they are to be worthy of the right to live in America."[10]

The mayor saw the Intermountain West as prime real estate in the coming post-war America. He told the Fresno conventioneers "the intermountain empire is the last great area in this country to await development by U.S. capital and U.S. genius."[11] He saw the Army and Navy use of the Intermountain

Utahans flock to Main Street as news of the Japanese surrender crackles through Utah radios. (Salt Lake Tribune)

Region as significant. He would later laud the new Geneva, Utah, steel mill as an example of a new national excitement about the state's potential. During his term, he also would give *The Salt Lake Tribune* a list of the nation's mayors to receive the newspaper's highly promotional annual *Empire Edition*, which lauded the area's progress. Glade never shied from promoting Salt Lake and the Intermountain States.

Glade tirelessly coupled official events to the war effort. He even tied an otherwise passed-over ceremonial "Utah Thrift Week" to the war, suggesting that people should not only save money for their own uses but for the war effort. And he continued his support for the U.S.O. long after the war. Nearly a decade after the war, in his waning days as mayor, Glade dedicated a bus as the "Bond-Bus-Special," as War Bonds became Defense Bonds. The Salt Lake City Line's bus was painted red, white and blue, and the mayor used a bottle of water from the Great Salt Lake to break over its bumper in the dedication ceremonies.[12]

Perhaps, the strangest war and service related story concerning the mayor appeared in the *Vernal Express* of April 3, 1947, in the middle of Utah's Centennial of the Mormon Pioneers trek into the Salt Lake Valley. Five British sailors stationed in Palestine read in an issue of *Pic Magazine* that Utah women were said to be the most beautiful in the world. Utah's state department of publicity and industrial development contributed to the story, and the article carried a photo of Utah's centennial queen to support the claim. Some British sailors wrote Mayor Glade, asking him to supply them with names of attractive Utah women in an attempt to "boost their mail." It is not known if the usually accommodating mayor honored their request for names, but he most likely "boosted" the British sailors' mail with a personal reply, nonetheless.

CHAPTER 12
SALT LAKE CITY'S POSTWAR PERIOD

The mayor was true to his promise of working to get veterans into the workplace. Salt Lake City was in an employment slump at the start of 1946, largely due to a strike at the mines. Winters were always tough, as the Salt Lake area still had a substantial agricultural base that operated with few workers in the winter. Thirty-three hundred veterans were returning to Utah, joining the 18,000 already unemployed. Mayor Glade went back on the speaking circuit asking all employers to list any and all jobs with the U.S. Employment Service in a program that matched veterans to specific job skills. The Armed Forces provided skills training for many of the Utah soldiers, and Glade was forceful in his message that this coordinated program would help both vets and employers.

> *The mayor continued work to get emergency housing for the influx of veterans in the area. He was thrilled to announce on the second anniversary of D-Day, that the U.S. Army engineers cleared 300 housing units for the city's war heroes. There is no doubt the war and its aftermath occupied much of the mayor's time and energy in his first term in office while he simultaneously served as a University of Utah regent. [1]*

The end of World War II did not mean the end to Glade's involvement in global matters. As the late 1940s and the early 1950s saw a nation still jittery from World War II, and at war in Korea, Mayor Glade brought the topic of civil defense front and center in municipal affairs, and later became associated with the Crusade For Freedom movement. This anti-Communist movement signed up 109,000 Utah citizens, or about one in seven of Utah's 696,000 residents, in 1950. Mayor Glade officially opened the 1951 Crusade For Freedom rally at Liberty Park's bandstand and led the enrollment program of music, motion pictures and a community sing-along.[2]

Once again, we can mirror the times through the work of Glade and his contemporaries. The Crusade For Freedom, later discovered to be a CIA front, originally was characterized as a grassroots citizen's group dedicated to expanding the operations of Radio Free Europe, a keystone of the congressionally funded National Committee for a Free Europe. It consisted of rallies and anti-Communist literature, much of it to be sent by helium balloons into Communist countries. A 10-ton bell was cast as the symbol of liberty, along with an inscription on the bell that carried the Abraham Lincoln quotation: "That this world under God shall have a new birth of freedom."[3]

The "Communist scare" had rocked Congressional hearings and now would reach local communities. Two sets of House Un-American Activities Committee (HUAC) Hearings had been held, one in 1947 and another in 1951. Joseph R. McCarthy was in full bloom by 1951 and the blacklist of suspected communists was evolving. Hundreds of people in the motion picture industry, among others, lost jobs when people recklessly began "naming-names."

The freedom bell and motorcade crossed America with a stop in Salt Lake City. The topic of newspaper articles, civic meetings, and a media campaign, Salt Lake City's Crusade was slated to open September 2, 1951. A committee meeting at the Hotel Utah planned the strategy for the event and local businessman Dilworth S. Woolley was elected the chair of the city campaign. He joined Mayor Glade in announcing, "We're a nation of salesmen. We've got a good thing to sell and we're going to help sell it." Mayor Glade further promoted the local cause by tying it to the national effort when he exclaimed that a 135,000-watt radio station is now "piercing the airways in Soviet satellite countries."[4]

The month-long event started with civic flair and flourish, as citizens couldn't help but get caught up in the dramatic presentations. Helium-filled balloons containing information and messages to Soviet-dominated areas were released from Liberty Park in Salt Lake City to be sent aloft on the "Winds of Freedom." The balloons were later found as far away as Heber and Tooele, a distance, perhaps, of forty miles. They were replicas of balloons launched over Europe to land behind the Iron Curtain.

Local personalities, including KDYL newsman Emerson Smith, joined long-time orchestra director Eugene Jelesnik to lead the gathered citizenry in patriotic musical numbers. And as evening fell, a "Freedom Torch" was lit near the block "U" above the University of Utah, which illuminated the giant freedom bell. Mayor Glade joined Commissioners L.C. Romney and Ben E. Lingenfelter to conduct the lighting ceremony. The Crusade's motorcade, which had traveled the state, was also on display along with a radio tower depicting Radio Free Europe beaming a signal behind the Iron Curtain.[5]

The Crusade was designed to do what Glade did best: get names and money. Citizens were asked to step up and be counted. Communism was clearly public enemy number one in 1951, and the country was not going to allow a tyranny as it had seen in Europe and was now fighting in Korea. Civil defense meant an organized and a prepared citizenry in both mind and might, as citizens volunteered to list their names to statements declaring support of the Crusade. University of Utah women students took a Saturday to add 10,000 more names to the list of those joining the Crusade. *Salt Lake Tribune* articles described how students in dorms and sororities would be briefed and then take up posts on thirty Salt Lake street corners to secure enrollment on "Freedom scrolls."[6] *The Tribune* announced teenagers would have an opportunity to "have fun and at the same time do their bit in helping to lift the iron curtain" at a Salt Lake City sponsored dance. The proceeds would be turned over to the Crusade so the teens could "aid their country in tearing aside the Iron Curtain."[7]

As event chairman, Woolley said, "Psychological warfare must be waged skillfully by the nations who have freedom to sell." The city opened up the schools to the Crusade "as a means of sharpening the issues at stake" according to the superintendent of the city schools, Dr. M. Lynn Bennion. He also said the Crusade would show students the great spiritual heritage of democracy.[8]

The balloons, motorcades, and fanfare whipped up emotion throughout the state. Likewise, *The Salt Lake Tribune* editorialized in enthusiastic favor of the "weapon against Communism."

> *Since Soviet communism can thrive only on ignorance and oppression—keeping the truth from the people under the Kremlin's domination—the aim of the drive is all-important. This private organization can do things that governmental agencies cannot do. Operation Winds, the release of message bearing balloons on the edge of the iron curtain, is the latest means of getting messages to the people behind the wall of*

An energetically vocal, dramatic form of patriotism reigned in the Land of Zion. Utahans remember this also was the era they were asked to trust the federal government in its nuclear testing program, recently accelerated to develop bombs to hold the Communists at bay. It was also a time background checks were fanatically being carried out to uncover suspected Communists in academia, the movies, and in public office. Arguments would captivate the country as to what was right or wrong. Whether or not the threat was real, the anti-Communist movement certainly was real. Civil Defense was on the lips of all concerned, and it was the time to definitely be on the Crusade for Freedom Scroll of Freedom and not be found on some governmental list of suspected communists. If the Crusade for Freedom did nothing else, it certainly united the state in the fight against communism. There was no public sign of disagreement with this fight.

Glade represented the view of much of the city's citizenry, the media, and, likely, much of America at the time. His essay advocating government record keeping of all residents was characteristic of a 1950s public mindset that had little reason to suspect political implications or hidden agendas of "trusted" committees who were ferreting out Communists in business, government and charitable organizations.

Glade, an early advocate of civil defense, wrote that his church's ability to collect records about members could be a model for federal record-keeping of the citizens of Utah. Although he wrote his essay ten years prior to the Crusade for Freedom, the logic was resurrected during the 1950s.

> *As is true in all American cities, there is no official
> government registry of Salt Lake citizens. As is also true of
> other American municipalities with respect to themselves, no
> one knows just who the citizens of Salt Lake are. Five
> thousand of them might move away and almost no one would
> know of it. Two or three thousand might move in and the same
> thing would be true. In times of real emergency, these facts*

are important. Possibly, some time in the future, there will be a
system of registry by municipalities for all our citizens.[10]

Based on that argument, the *Deseret News* published Glade's call for federal record keeping in bold type for emphasis.

> **Our Church operates a highly comprehensive and complete record of vital statistics covering all of its members and their families. Our people want their records kept. They want definitely to be citizens of record of the United States of America; furthermore, they want the government to know where they are and what they are doing.**[11]

The then-future mayor described how the LDS church had seventy-five wards in Salt Lake County at the time, and how a family's change of residence is traced throughout the Church system.

> *Thus our Church knows with a high degree of accuracy where its members are residing. It knows the condition of their health; whether the head of the family has work; what the children are doing and where they are. This information is, of course, always available to the government. Would I be within my prerogatives to express the hope that some fine day in the future, our own United States government might have as accurate and as interested a check on its citizenry as does our own great Church on its membership.*[12]

Civil defense remained on the top of many minds throughout the 1950s, although massive anti-Communist rallies died out. While there was no connection between the Crusade for Freedom and the McCarthy hearings, media exposure of fraud and hysteria in the ratting-out of Communists by Senator McCarthy silenced the fever pitch of the anti-Communist movement among millions of Americans. A year after the Crusade for Freedom rally in Liberty Park, Democratic Representative Reva Beck Bosome told a "large gathering" in that same Liberty Park that the anti-Communist movement that was ratcheted up by Senator McCarthy was actually a bigger problem.

<blockquote>
The greatest threat free government has ever had –
McCarthyism, that ranting chanting ritual which has ...
scuttled the program of loyal and constructive opposition
which this nation could otherwise expect from the Republican
Party.[13]
</blockquote>

Years later a substantial, suspicious public looked back at various lists from the era, as well as the years of the Vietnam protests, and in hindsight considered the excesses of government in the collection of personal information extreme, unnecessary, and a violation of basic rights.

Mayor Glade did not let city boundaries get in the way of his efforts to reach his governmental goals. Just as he went county-by-county for the war effort, and continued to speak on national issues such as civil defense, he devoted significant efforts to statewide boards, civic affairs, and "good will" speeches throughout his term all over the state. Glade's efforts extended to many other issues as well in the post-war era, as discussed in the next chapter, including matters of water rights and the appropriate celebration of Utah's centennial as an established territory.

CHAPTER 13
PAST AND PRESENT: THE UTAH CENTENNIAL AND WATER ISSUES

Glade, who ended his first term as mayor in 1947, was appointed to a state finance committee that offered recommendations on spending, such as how the profits from the state-owned liquor industry should be allocated. In addition, he traveled on behalf of the Chamber of Commerce, frequently spoke in Idaho and other states about commerce, and took on responsibilities with the centennial celebration of Utah's founding.

Preparing for the centennial two years earlier, Glade met with LDS Church President George Albert Smith concerning the pioneer trail through Emigration Canyon. The two had driven and hiked in the area in preparation for construction of the "This is the Place Monument" on the acreage at the mouth of the canyon. During the war, he was front and center of a 1945 trek to kick off the Monument campaign. The mayor and President Smith led seventy-five others in an automobile caravan up the old Parley's Canyon Road, and then re-traced the last thirty-six miles of the Mormon pioneer route to the proposed "This is the Place Monument" site. The group frequently stopped to educate people along the way and to gather support.

Glade, who never was shy in publicizing fundraising efforts, was a major supporter of the $250,000 monument ($2.7-million in today's equivalence), which required fundraising, as the state legislature supplied only half of the funds. He spoke at luncheons and dinners and to clubs to help gather funds. One luncheon yielded $3,000 from Sears for the state committee. Glade even used his radio fundraising skills to invite national guests to Utah, including an appeal on the CBS radio show "Cinderella, Inc.," where he told New Yorkers to come to Utah, tacitly implying, with money. The "This Is The Place Monument" was dedicated on July 24, 1947, at a centennial ceremony attended by 50,000 people.

Another memorable centennial promotion had Glade becoming an official judge of the centennial celebration beard-growing contest. The mayor joined Governor Maw, U. of U. President Ray Olpin, and Centennial Queen Colleen

Glade with and without his mustache
(Utah State Historical Society)

Robinson to judge the most unique, darkest, longest, thickest, brightest, and best overall beard.

The mayor did not grow a beard, but sported his familiar mustache, an iconic sight around city hall that even became the subject of a newspaper article when it disappeared one January morning in 1949.

> *Office workers in the city hall are taking "retake" glances at his honor this week ... something seems lacking. The familiar physiognomy of Mayor Earl J. Glade has undergone a disquieting transformation many believe. But it's really nothing. The mayor shrugs, admitting he had a close shave— so close, in fact that it left him minus his familiar mustache.[1]*

As mayor, Glade also produced a weekly radio show for KDYL in the late 1940s. As mentioned earlier, he did not often ad-lib in his public presentations. True to form, he wrote both his and the announcer's parts for his radio shows, managing to include what appeared to sound like ad-libs. As KDYL station owner Sid Fox refused to allow any scripts to leave the station, only a few scripts are in existence today. One surviving script glimpses into the mayor's style as he communicated by radio and in other venues. KDYL announcer Joe

Lee was instructed to make it sound like a candid interview, as indicated in the following script.

KDYL Broadcast, November 1, 1949

Announcer Joe Lee: Now Mayor Glade, what about the pending election?

The Mayor: I believe I would say this, Joe. If Salt Lake City's 90,500 citizens, to whom we have just sent the initiative petitions, would only care enough to take an interest in that phase of our government which is undoubtedly of most importance to them and their families, I personally would not worry. I have implicit faith in the consummate judgment of all our American citizens. But when the 90,500 citizens let about 20,000 do the voting for them and determine all the policies and personnel as they did in the primary election, I wonder seriously if our democracy is really working. You see, Joe, as citizens we cannot say, "Oh well, I won't fool with this election; really it's not important," and think that it will go by the boards, and that, as far as we are concerned, it be passed up. Oh No! That's exactly what certain groups want you to say and to do. The facts are, your apathy and indifference won't be passed up at all. Oh No! Someone else will take care of your citizenship obligations and opportunities for you, and how! Maybe then, after the election is over, you won't like what they do. My experience is that it's a copper-riveted fact that if you don't vote, you'll be sorry. I earnestly ask all of our 90,500 Salt Lake citizen-electors to remember their sacred honor, as Americans, and to vote!

Now, Joe, changing the subject, before we went on the air, we were speaking of football. May I go back to that theme a minute?

Announcer: All right, Mayor Glade, the microphone is yours.

The Mayor: On Saturday, I attended the Homecoming game and the dedicatory exercises of the beautiful new Dane Hansen Stadium at Westminster College. This stadium is a gift of Mr. and Mrs. George T. Hansen of Salt Lake City and represents a magnificent achievement in philanthropy. It fills a great need at Westminster. The appointments and construction features of the stadium are of the finest. It certainly gives real class to the athletic department of this fine school.

Announcer: I am sure, Mayor Glade, if that brave young United States officer, Dane Hansen, can hear your inspiring appreciation of his thoughtful father and his lovely mother, as it goes out on the clear night air, he would approve, with gratitude, what they have done.

The Mayor: Thank you, Joe.

From parades to radio, and from speeches to civic events, Salt Lake residents certainly knew who their mayor was. He never lost his passion for a show. Just as he promised an entertaining season of basketball nearly 45 years prior at BYU, and a rousing rally against prohibition 30 years earlier, he did things in a way the public easily could observe and enjoy. He also used "the show" to bring home opportunities, offer messages, and inform citizens. One such activity took place on a stage in front of the old Sugar House Prison. He had finished efforts to buy land the state no longer needed.

It was also a moment for the get-tough-on-crime mayor to have his own prison, albeit ceremonially, but just for a moment. In 1953, the state department of corrections handed the state prison keys to the crime-fighting mayor, who opened the doors to the old Sugar House Prison that stood on land adjacent to 21st South and 1300 East. The city purchased the 180-acre property to build Highland High School and a massive museum of pioneer history. The museum never was built and the majority of the property became the still-popular open space of Sugarhouse Park.

The mayor didn't stray from his original campaign promises, which included bulking up Salt Lake City's infrastructure. Being mayor in post-war Utah meant the city was modernizing following the stagnation brought on first by the Great Depression and later exacerbated by the war. Often projects were completed with the trademark Glade promotional flair, such as when he threw

the switch
that lit up
new street
lamps,
opened parks
such as the
International
Peace
Gardens, and
enjoyed
seeing the
town prosper.
And he
was mayor
when
decisions
came for the
new
freeways.

Mayor Glade accepts the key to the Sugar House Prison on behalf of Salt Lake City. The state opened a modern facility at Point of the Mountain.
(Salt Lake Tribune, October 21, 1955)

One involved developing a freeway on the west side or making State Street, already a major city thoroughfare, a super-road. The mayor fought against the State Street option, recommending that funds be used to develop the West Side freeway instead. Glade saw freeways as important emergency thoroughfares for interstate traffic, and a much more practical way to spend money than on super-sized local roads such as what was envisioned in the State Street proposal. The overpass at Beck's Hot Springs was another early Glade undertaking that laid the foundation for the Interstate system on the city's west side. The mayor also was a major proponent of petitioning the Denver and Rio Grande Railroad to abandon train tracks east of 13th East in Salt Lake, clearing the way for highway construction in Parley's Canyon that later became I-80.

In October of 1951, Glade announced all the plans were complete for where the west-side freeway would go and that the city and the state would split the costs for the right-of-way. Glade estimated the city would pay a million dollars for its share over the next decades for the project.[2]

All wasn't roses in his third term, however. Water was both his most shining accomplishment and his greatest nemesis as the mayor took on water-and-more-water –notably, city water and flood water. It is notable to revisit Glade's response, as this issue continues to grow in prominence, as local and state officials contend with the increasingly urgent concerns about water demand and usage as well as environmental and climate change issues. Mayor Glade early on said, "Utah's main limiting factor was the lack of water; that goes for Salt Lake City also." Of main concern in 1946 was the anticipated arrival of Deer Creek Reservoir water in the Salt Lake Valley, and the city's obligation to commence paying the federal government $300,000 annually for forty years. This financial burden was especially disturbing when the administration realized the Deer Creek water could not be completely exploited because no adequate provisions had been made for its treatment or distribution to people on the Wasatch Front.

Daring in design, cautious in execution, Glade put Salt Lake City's water problems in perspective.

> *Our citizens will justifiably cry their protest to high heaven [if Deer Creek and other water sources cannot be used] and that cannot be permitted to occur. We want all of our citizens to have ample, high quality water under good pressure. ... The price of this splendid culinary water in Salt Lake City will be less than ½ of the price of the municipal average. ... In the Department of Streets the city administration has secured from the Federal government $60,000.00 to survey and plan for adequate sewage and garbage disposal facilities, that planning will go forth immediately.[3]*

As such, projects that remain today as perhaps Glade's greatest legacy as mayor are connected with water. The United States Public Health Service (USPHS) started a comprehensive examination of Salt Lake City water in 1947, toward the end of Glade's first administration. Salt Lake City chlorinated water, but it wasn't enough to purify water sources such as what flowed from City

Creek. Additionally, all other watersheds needed water treatment plants, and urban reservoirs needed covering.

The USPHS threatened to disallow Salt Lake City water for use by interstate carriers, and a massive investigation was launched into all Salt Lake City water sources and watersheds. Deer

1950's era Chlorination station such as this one in Big Cottonwood Canyon were determined to not be enough for purification, and a massive public works program would start under Mayor Glade. (Salt Lake City Utilities Archive Photo)

Creek, City Creek, Parleys Creek, Mill Creek, Big Cottonwood Creek and Little Cottonwood Creek all had various problems. For instance, Mill Creek water was not being used due to its poor sanitary conditions, but engineers knew it would be needed in the future for a growing city. The15-month study concluded a sanitation program would cost $16 million, a staggering sum at the time ($150 million in today's equivalence). On December 28, 1951, all parties met in Mayor Glade's office and, despite the intimidating dollar figure, emerged with a plan to purify Salt Lake City's water supply. The sedimentation basins that operated in places such as the mouth of Big Cottonwood Canyon were created on paper that day. Electric-eye automatic alarm systems to alert to unsafe water were drawn up, and City Creek Canyon was closed until a treatment facility to provide safe water could be built in the city's northern end.[4]

City officials resisted some of the study findings initially, but ended up embracing its major recommendations. Additionally, Mayor Glade did his share of defending the Metropolitan Water District's study. At one point, the Chamber of Commerce passed a resolution demanding an "impartial" committee to study the matter. The mayor's riposte to the Chamber was the investigations were being done efficiently and decisively and a study was unnecessary.

A prominent and outspoken member of the Council of Twelve Apostles of the Church of Jesus Christ of Latter-day Saints who was a critic of the Salt Lake water plan also attacked Glade. Henry D. Moyle spoke before the Utah Water Users Association and declared: "I have seen the mayor and other city officials up there [at the State Legislature] pitting Salt Lake City's wants against those of the rest of the state." The church official felt Glade represented a powerful municipality whose plan was detrimental to the water rights of smaller places in Utah.

Mayor Glade was upset, and righteously replied to the same group: "I haven't the slighted idea what Mr. Moyle referred to in his address ... when he declared he has seen the mayor and other officials up there pitting Salt Lake City's wants against those of the state."[5]

By then in 1952, the Salt Lake water plans had expanded due to a crisis in the city. Spring rains and a record snowfall flooded more than 400 city blocks and caused $6 million in damages.[6] Mayor Glade saw block after block of damage and asked the Army Corps of Engineers to help alleviate future flooding problems. The answer was the Little Dell Dam in Parley's Canyon, which would take years before it was built and put in operation in conjunction with the already established Mountain Dell Reservoir. However, the 1952

The large City Creek Canyon Water Treatment Plant was the first to be built in the 28 year program. (Salt Lake City Utilities Archive Photo)

The city built temporary dikes to hold the water along
1300 South, in April of 1952.
(Salt Lake City Utilities Photo)

flood and the city's planning put the wheels in motion. The idea had been around for years, but it took the flood and Mayor Glade and his staff to finally move it toward reality. A year prior, the mayor had urged an upgrade of the city's storm sewers, but the flood demonstrated the flood threat was too formidable for Salt Lake City to rely on storm sewers alone.

The flood certainly represented one of the most difficult times for the mayor during his time in office. Three thousand residents were evacuated from 50 blocks as the water kept rising, while the May temperatures soared to 83 degrees and the 150-inch snow-pack poured over the soaked city. The *New York Times* chided the city by writing: "Utah's capital city in particular paid a heavy penalty for poor planning and past engineering errors."[7] However, the same article attributed the fact that there was no loss of life, to Glade's city engineer, Roy McLesse, and his staff who warned the city before the water hit. Volunteers, city workers, and others created a street canal to the Jordan River similar to the one built for the 1983 floods some thirty years later.

The *New York Times* reported Glade did fear the worst was yet to come. The city had spent $50,000 for flood control just a few months prior, to dragline the

Jordan River and Surplus Canal to accommodate more water. The fifty-foot wide river would need to carry the runoff from the canyon creeks as well as the overflow from Utah Lake to the Great Salt Lake. If it failed, more flooding would result. Mayor Glade and the city survived the flood and surmised it had been the most devastating disaster to ever hit the city. Nevertheless, all took comfort that no one was killed.

The awful spring had spoiled what otherwise had been an uplifting winter for the mayor. He had started his third term in 1952, following an election where, as mentioned, the popular mayor had been reelected and was unopposed. That he had made it even to a second term was unprecedented in Salt Lake City history. No mayor, in the forty years since the city had adopted the commission form of government, had ever been reelected. But the filing deadline passed at the close of business on October 3, 1951, and only Glade's name appeared on the books, assuring him a third term in office.

Mayor Glade said he was surprised to be unopposed but was "deeply grateful," again promising to make Salt Lake City the kind of city all wanted it to become. He had shunned political affiliation during his administration, and with no primary or general election, he could easily keep all pundits guessing again as to his political leanings. Even though Salt Lake City elections are touted even today as non-partisan, few mayors truly have been as non-partisan as was Glade.

The Salt Lake Tribune echoed voter opinion about the popular mayor, and had prior to the election editorialized in favor of the sole candidate on the ballot.

Mr. Glade's 2 Good Terms Call for Another

> *Salt Lake City has been fortunate to have Earl J. Glade at the head of its municipal government during the last seven critical years. During this period, the city has "busted at the seams" with population pressures, spilling out into the county. In the wake of the depression, public works were necessarily neglected during the war and now improvements are urgently needed. At the same time, the period is one of economic peril, as the cost of federal government mounts almost beyond the ability of the taxpayers to support it. Mayor Glade stands*

*forthrightly and courageously for municipal public works, but
has wisely refused to go overboard. He favors completion of a
municipal master plan calling for freeways, arterial highways,
parks, recreation facilities and proper zoning, but he opposes
bonding the city beyond a conservative point. Visionary and
expensive municipal public works at this time conceivably
could be the back-breaking straw, while the nation is rearming
and endeavoring to help support the free world.*

*When so much is needed by the thriving growing city, it is
not easy for a city executive to steer a middle course. Mayor
Glade deserves credit for keeping his feet on the ground, but
encouraging progress.*

*The first mayor to be reelected since Salt Lake City
adopted the commission form of government, Earl J. Glade
now bids for a third four-year term. Articulate and personable,
he looks and acts like a mayor of a progressive city, and has
done Salt Lake City credit on many public occasions. Making
speeches and officiating at ceremonies are among a mayor's
duties. Mayor Glade has discharged these public relations
responsibilities with brilliance and discrimination. Assuming
leadership, he has done much to cover the basic weaknesses of
the commission form of government. Mayor Glade stands
fearlessly for clean, progressive government. His honesty
matches his forthrightness and likable personality.*

*Mayor Glade's varied professional background qualifies
him for leadership in Utah's leading city. Well educated, he
taught and administered business education courses at both
Brigham Young University and the University of Utah before
entering the advertising business. Later, he did notable
pioneer work in the field of radio. His civic contributions have
been extensive.*

*The fact that nobody filed for the mayoralty candidacy
before the deadline last night, attests to the strength and
popularity of the incumbent official. While it is possible that a
write-in candidate might emerge from the primaries, it is
highly improbable. Salt Lake City seems assured the
continuous service of its competent mayor.*[8]

While the war efforts were his most public expressions during his first term,
the end of the war allowed him to take on water issues discussed above as well

as another issue close to home which trumped even his flood fighting efforts, namely youthful "hoodlums," which is taken up in the next chapter.

CHAPTER 14

GLADE'S SECOND TERM:
SAFETY, LAW ENFORCEMENT
AND YOUTH CRIMES

Late in 1947, before the flood, the mayor turned his attention toward
fulfilling a campaign promise that he would revisit for years to come – to make
Salt Lake City a safe place for families and not to allow hoodlums to foster
crime in the city, especially youth related crime. In true Glade fashion, he started
at the top. He met in Washington, D.C. with J. Edgar Hoover, the long-time FBI
director.

Hoover told Glade of his enthusiastic support of Boys Clubs, which "next
to good homes, good schools, and churches … contribute most to reducing
juvenile delinquency." Glade immediately sought advice on how to establish
Boys Clubs. He reported Hoover stressed guidance and direction and
"emphasized negative conduct such as rough-housing, improper language and
discourtesy, if condoned in the clubs, will encourage bad habits." The mayor and
Hoover had a long discussion about the clubs. Glade reported there also were
"definite social advantages to be gained by bringing boys and girls together in
the same club, but the need for supervision is greater when that is done." He
further observed: "One of the reasons that cooking is so popular among the
young girls where the clubs are coeducational, is that the boys may be treated
with the results of the girl's kitchen wizardry."[1]

Hoover and Glade concluded their discussions with a chat about radio
programs and if they contributed to delinquency. Hoover warned the mayor that
too many of the programs only explain that crime doesn't pay at the very end of
the program. He did cite the "Lone Ranger," however, as a type of program
which he approved.

The mayor, who championed morality, obviously was impressed. He
announced the next day: "J. Edgar Hoover is my candidate for the president of
the United States." The exchange offers a glimpse into Glade's unbending
pursuit for what he viewed as wholesome values. Earlier, the religious man,

Glade, wrote about the LDS tenet of progression he pursued here on earth that was the reward for good works and wholesome values:

> *Merely to live forever is not something to be desired unless one lives a life that is worthy of being perpetuated. ... Nobody grows old by merely living a number of years; people grow old by deserting their ideals.[2]*

After the war, Glade seemingly was driven to lead the city fueled by long-held personal beliefs. Few seemed to dispute his morality-driven agenda and style, as evidenced by his easy reelection. The mayor had crime battles to win in his fight for youthful morality. Once he committed to an issue, he brought unrelenting concentration to it. Combined with his gift of speech, the results were forceful, colorful, and, to be sure, the mayor made for good newspaper copy on issues where he captured the public's attention in his fight against crime in the city, especially related to juvenile delinquency and youth crimes. One should remember Glade was skilled in publicity and he knew how to craft a persuasive message. For instance, a year after his visit to Hoover, he went after comic books, charging that they taught murder, mayhem, and other crimes. Glade enlisted the support of L. C. Romney, the city's public health commissioner and L. C. Crowther, chief of police, in his anti-comic-book cause.

The Vernal Express in eastern Utah was one newspaper that picked up the campaign and editorialized in favor of the crusading mayor, stopping short of Glade's plan to get the police involved.

IT'S THE PARENTS' PROBLEM

> *A widely discussed subject for editorial comment during the past week or two has been a drive inaugurated by Salt Lake City's Mayor Earl J. Glade against unfunny funny books. "I believe this is a situation that can be remedied in the home, school, church, and by the public," the mayor explained. "I don't mean to butt into a family's business, but a lot of youngsters were bringing into the homes in the guise of entertaining, constructive, and harmless reading, this vile literature." We [Vernal Express] agree that the problem,*

which is an extremely grave one, must be answered by parents.
It is a matter of education, not police supervision. To allow the
sale of millions of such rotten books to the children across the
nation has given youth an education in glorified crime.[3]

Interestingly, anecdotal evidence shows that comic books more than any other reading material were a mainstay in the knapsacks of young American soldiers heading into the war, and were invariably included in care packages sent by parents to their sons stationed at home and abroad. These soldiers were representative of the same young men for whom Glade had uttered unwavering praise for decades.

Glade had always maintained an enormous pride in what he surely believed to be superior Utah youth. Just as he had years earlier compared the intellect of those in states with high alcohol consumption to a largely dry Utah, as a local Selective Service official, he compared the Utah boys to those in Cook County, Illinois, the home of Chicago.

Glade pointed out that Cook County had an unprecedented rejection rate of 47 percent for the draft due to physical unfitness. He proudly stated only 4.24 percent of the young men in Utah were rejected from the draft due to physical health issues. Utah youth, he pointed out, fared much better than other states in the west.

Oregon	13.81-percent draft rejection rate
California	10.10-percent
Washington	11.52-percent
Nevada	6.98-percent
Idaho	8.88-percent
Montana	4.89-percent
Utah	4.24-percent[4]

Glade earlier had noted the superior well-being of those youth associated with his religion. In an earlier address in the Salt Lake LDS Tabernacle, Glade attributed much of Utah youths' physical and spiritual excellence to the LDS Church's many neighborhood buildings where he said recreation facilities helped to foster an exceptional generation of youth:

*I ask this audience to compare the housing facilities in such
distinctly Latter-day Saint communities as Salt Lake, Ogden,
Logan, or Provo for meeting the Church requirements of
young people with those of other American cities of
comparable size. In Salt Lake County with a population of
200,000, there are, I repeat, one-hundred-thirteen Latter-Day
Saint wards having church edifices and recreation centers
operated by the Church.[5]*

Prior to the comic book discussion, and despite objections from wartime workers, Glade had gone after stores that sold goods on Sunday. Again, he knew how to craft a good quote. He declared that Salt Lake City "is a Christian community, and it is characteristic of such a community that stores should be closed on Sunday." During the war, Glade astutely rose above principle and didn't protest Sunday store openings. As discussed earlier, nighttime and Sunday store closings were a significant problem for wartime workers unable to shop during weekday and Saturday hours. But now it was 1946 and the war was over.

While most of the electorate agreed Sunday should be a day of rest, not everyone enjoyed the spillover from the pulpit to City Hall. The *Murray Eagle* was one journalistic voice to draw the line on Glade. Using the mayor's logic, the *Eagle* editorialized that Murray's citizens may, in fact, be accused of being un-Christian under Glade's standards, as the smelting town allowed Sunday openings. It further lampooned Glade and his supporters, who championed free enterprise, as being the same people "who want to tell a businessman whether or not he can do business on a certain day." In another dig at the Salt Lake mayor, the paper reminded its Salt Lake neighbors that under the proposed law, beer can be had on Sunday, but no milk.[6]

A survey of Glade's speeches and proposals shows he had a way of expressing city problems in human terms, often expressing them in top-of-mind moral issues. For example, he addressed a group of homebuilders in Albuquerque, blaming the post-war housing shortage for an increase in divorce and juvenile delinquency. He called the problem "frightening," adding it is a miracle that the social breakdown is not even more serious.

The Mayor, in his familiar center seat at a City Commission meeting.
(Utah State Historical Society)

Even though Glade bestowed most of his efforts on prescribed city business, Glade was sidetracked occasionally by morality issues. For instance, he focused intense efforts on the city's perceived juvenile delinquency problem and championed that cause year after year. Every meeting seemingly was an opportunity for him to get his message out. He addressed groups, including the disparate Ladies Society and the Brotherhood of Locomotive Firemen and Enginemen, telling them there is a tendency to underestimate the mother's role in raising sons.

> *When we realize that juvenile delinquency is largely a matter*
> *of parental delinquency in attending to duties, it is important*
> *to know that every boy needs a close, loving relationship with*
> *his mother to put him in good shape to be a companion to his*
> *father in later years.*[7]

The mayor traveled to New York City to meet with that city's acting mayor, Vincent Impelletteri. He told the New York press to take an interest in our childhood and youth that America has never known before: "Let no man delude himself, that this is a matter to be relegated to a few baby sitters."[8]

Glade's LDS beliefs had informed his position on prohibition in the Bamburger governor's race decades prior, guided his civil defense and emergency planning efforts based on the LDS Church's membership registry model, and directed his promotion of patriotism before and after the war. But the year 1951 was a turning point in his crusade against juvenile delinquency. His LDS channeled moral compass turned from finding *the* solution to juvenile delinquency in more attentive parents to actively involving city government in the effort.

This war against what was referred to as gangland hoodlumism was brought to the forefront the entire year in 1951 by the newspapers concurrently with the anti-Communist "Crusade for Freedom" movement. Perhaps the emotions of the era already were boiling, or perhaps people simply imagined enemies from within and without were compromising their pristine lives. The war on juvenile delinquency captured headline after headline. Clearly, the mayor had other issues that consumed his attention in 1951, but far more public interest and Utah newsprint were devoted to the crusade against "young hoodlums" than was dedicated to stories about the "Crusade for Freedom" or any other Glade public endeavor. As such, the discussion below articulates Glade's considerable, some said unnecessary or misplaced, efforts devoted to counteracting juvenile delinquency throughout the months of 1951.

Salt Lake City Police Capt. E.J. Steinfeldt, youth bureau chief, wasn't as convinced as Glade that the state's youth's morals were getting progressively worse in the years after the war. He took a page out of Glade's previously cited address at the Tabernacle on how every boy needs the love and attention of his mother and how parents are the key to an upstanding youth, to issue a statement that the juvenile crime trend was static even in the years of uncertainty during the Korean War.

Capt. Steinfeldt related: "The [Youth] bureau is alert to the possibility of increased delinquency, should a wartime economy be imposed on the country." He indicated that unless fathers are taken from their homes and mothers leave their housekeeping in favor of war work, the problems should be about the same as those usually encountered, saying there was not enough variation from the leveling off of the past two years [1949 and 1950] for any increased juvenile delinquency trend to have been established.[9]

In January 1951, the actual crime figures hadn't reached the mayor's desk, but the Salt Lake City police captain reported an opinion that must have gotten Glade's attention. At least the attitude behind the opinion would seem to counter Glade's pride in the Utah home life, especially among the high LDS concentrations in established neighborhoods associated with middle-class and two-parent homes.

Captain Steinfeldt said Salt Lake City's absence of a "slum district" is one reason for the low incidence of juvenile crime and vice:

> *Our minority groups have tended to congregate in certain areas ... but they are not giving us the trouble we are getting from the better residential areas. It's the boy with a car and a little money to spend who is keeping our bureau busy. That is a problem of home control over the young people, and one in which the police department can play only a corrective part, rather than a preventive role.[10]*

Interestingly, Captain Steinfeldt's observation: "It's the boy with a car and a little money to spend who is keeping our bureau busy." predated by several years the youth crime problems enabled by President Eisenhower's 1956 National System of Interstate Highways, where young people with cars nationally began to roam more freely and greater distances from direct family supervision.

Despite Captain Steinfeldt's observations based on factual data about the city's juvenile delinquency problem, or lack thereof, Glade, with encouragement from the *Salt Lake Tribune,* continued his efforts. There is no doubt that any perceived threat to or by Utah's youth pushed the wrong buttons in the mayor's office and in much of Utah at the time. However, the tone was sometimes light and feature-styled in the reporting of juvenile crime early on in the year:

> *A gang of juveniles went to school over the weekend, but it wasn't because they were intent of getting in some extra*

Other articles, starting in January 1951, included some matter-of-fact acknowledgments of a delinquency problem. The year opened with two youths confessing to seven burglaries over ninety days. Three of the burglaries yielded about $25 in total. Another at the New Pacific Inn on West South Temple resulted in two dollars being lifted. Later in the month, a fifteen-year-old boy was arrested on shoplifting a card of shirt buttons from Grand Central market on 900 South. [12]

Then newspaper headlines over the year steadily escalated in calling increased attention to what was perceived to be a ferocious juvenile delinquency problem. A community never ignores such activities, but there was no real evidence in support of a ferocious "crime wave" consuming the city. Nevertheless, on the heels of what could be considered news accounts of rather innocuous youth crimes in the *Salt Lake Tribune* in January 1951, Mayor Glade sounded an alarm, calling for a "probe" into the juvenile crime problem. In the coming months, he would hold town meetings, make speeches vowing stern action, beef up police patrols, call for "right minded" students to be the eyes and ears for the cops in high schools, and by fall of 1951 pronounced that mothers and girlfriends were no longer safe.

Glade's views reflected the times, not all that different from the anxieties and fears captured decades later in the 1998 film of *Pleasantville*, when people seemingly felt threatened. Utah and the country were gasping at a "Red Scare" reported to have infiltrated American institutions such as the military, the motion picture industry, government, and education, eating away the fiber of freedom. The country was fighting Communists in Korea a mere half dozen years after fighting tyranny in World War II, and now, youth, the hope of the world, were ostensibly being dragged into the dark world of crime.

"Rockabilly" music was infiltrating record stores and gaining access to radio airwaves, although Elvis and his hips were still a few years away. Kids aimlessly cruised the streets, driving up Salt Lake City's State Street to the drive-in on 9th South, drag racing and picking up other teens. The term "Hot Rod" became common, even organized, as the National Hot Rod Association started that year. Bikinis were showing up at the Great Salt Lake by 1951, and kids at Utah drive-in theaters with names such as the Romanic Motor-Vu, were thought to be doing everything but watching the movies. A Utah television campaign against Daylight Savings Time even suggested extended daylight meant extra trouble time for teens.

The *Salt Lake Tribune* didn't report a single story on juvenile delinquency in the month of March. But as the weather got warmer, delinquents caused incidents similar to those unfortunately expected in a city, especially when one mixes, as Captain Steinfeldt said, boys with a car and "a little money to spend."

Glade championed scouting, church events, and "outdoor" activities at the same time he put the kibosh on more rebellious night activities with a citywide youth curfew. The curfew more than anything showed how dire Glade perceived the youth crime and morality problems in the city. City commission members also perceived an out-of-control juvenile crime wave was upon them by mid-1951. The mayor's probe continued, and the *Tribune,* which frequently supported the mayor when reporting on this issue, gradually developed a harder edge in its stories. Headlines in May offered a sampling.

> *Bicycle Riding Teenager Abducts, Tortures Boy*
> *10 Teenagers Hurl Bottles at Trio in Car*
> *Brick Damages Auto of J. W. Smith*
> *Youths Admit Hitting Car with Bottles*[13]

The newspapers now more than ever seemed to side with Glade. The *Tribune* suggested the police would get more action if they dropped the attitude of "boys will be boys."[14]

The word "gang" was common in newspaper stories and gangs became listed as, "gangs of hoodlums" or as a "gang of teen-age marksmen," as reported in this *Tribune* article.

> *Police are after a gang of teen-age marksmen who prowled around town Saturday in an old-model automobile, expertly knocking out windows with slingshots and rocks. The toll was seven windows before the vandals went into hiding.* [15]

The *Tribune* editorialized "No one will gainsay that 'boys will be boys, but do boys have to be hoodlums?"[16]

By August, according to newspaper accounts, the city was under siege. However, no one could accuse the *Tribune* of understating juvenile delinquency in this front-page story.

Hoodlum Gang Attacks Youth

> *Another incident of apparently unprovoked hoodlumism in which a defenseless youth was attacked by a gang of "tough guys" was reported to the police Saturday. The second beating victim within three days was 18-year-old Donald Yohn, son of Mrs. J. W. Wooston Jr. 405 North 6th West, who was attacked and slugged Saturday about 1:30 a.m. as he was walking toward his home. Five youths, riding in a coupe, three of them aged 12-14 years and two aged 18-19 years, pulled up along side of Donald, officers were told, and one of the quintet got out of the car and pushed the victim over backwards. "Get out of the way," the first assailant reportedly said. The other four then left the auto and beat the Yohn youth leaving no marks. He said he suffered pains in the stomach, however.* [17]

The journalist did not question why the victim was violating curfew at 1:30 a.m. or that Police Captain Steinfeldt repeatedly discounted the beatings as gang-related. He waited a week before stating that only one beating in the "crime wave" was unprovoked or not part of an argument. Nevertheless, a week later, the *Tribune* continued: "Gang Beatings Break out Anew in S. L. in Beating of Two." Mayor Glade had already commanded a closed door meeting the day before the 1:30 a.m. beating on the city's west side and was developing a corrective strategy. He said he and law enforcement officers were discussing means of coping with gang beatings and vandalism "in a wholesome and positive manner."[18]

Ten days later, with capital letters over the lead article in the *Tribune* entitled MUST BE STOPPED! Mayor Glade upped the tactics in his get-tough plan. The mayor recommended that Salt Lake would pay a bounty of a $100 reward for the arrest of street gang members. "It is vitally important that citizens of the city realize that their assistance is needed in bringing a halt to these unprovoked beatings."[19]

The mayor promised if his reward system didn't round up the delinquents, he would try another approach. He said, "We'll bring an end to it one way or another." The mayor urged all to check on the whereabouts and activities of their children and to enforce the curfew. Ironically, he told citizens not to let the "crime frenzy" get to them and to be calm and take care of the children at home. "We urge this, because of the fear we have that this terrorizing and attendant attacks may provoke our citizens to a point where some of these youngsters may be injured seriously."[20]

Even though Mayor Glade generally was getting tough, he still promoted recreational facilities as fruitful deterrents. As he dedicated the Dilworth School Park on 21st East, he gazed out over the facility and remarked: "There isn't an antidote comparable to wholesome play when it comes to solving present youth problems."[21]

Youth crime was front-page material all of August 1951. The *Tribune* greeted its morning readers with: "New S. L. Hoodlum Gang Goes Into Action, Pursues Couple." The couple reported that someone had removed the throttle and choke knobs from its car in a theater parking lot. The wife reported that the perpetrators followed them for blocks after the movie and tried to force them off the road. "My husband kept the car in the middle lane of traffic and reached speeds up to 60 miles per hour."[22]

Headlines now blared out: "There'll be no Leniency," as judges promised to send hoodlums to the State Industrial School. Mayor Glade wanted more than a term in the reform school. He called for jail sentences from six months to several years for those using abusive language and beating up other kids. He lashed out at four youths who attempted to assault a carload of adults. "Such crimes as upsetting automobiles seem like more than misdemeanors. They seem like attempted manslaughter to me."[23]

Glade fanned the fire. While his own police department was downplaying the chance for random attacks, the usually low-key mayor surprised many with his stern warning that the alternative "will be a community of citizens forced to carry blackjacks for their own protection against unwarranted attack."[24]

In October 1951, the issue came to a head. If Glade fanned the fire, the newspapers threw in the gasoline. On October 6, the *Salt Lake Tribune* headlined: "Fight at Game Hurts East Cheerleader." The lead used the words "Outbursts of hoodlumism" in which contingents of police were involved. Further down in the article we find the cheerleader had a cut lip. The only arrests were for curfew violations hours later. On October 19th, the *Tribune* editorialized that hoodlumism had continued and pointed to the recent "riot" at the East-West football game.[25]

The next day, in an extraordinary act, Glade proposed enlisting student leaders at city high schools as auxiliary police in juvenile crime detection. He said: "We are certain, that right-minded youth are in the overwhelming majority in our schools." He revealed a plan where city officials would visit the schools to offer assistance in establishing and training the "monitors" along with the police who were instructed to thoroughly investigate juvenile violations. The mayor toughened his message: "We are not going to tolerate viciousness. If necessary, parents will follow the youngsters' reports through with police aid." He did warn untrained citizens not to take up the hoodlum problem without police assistance.[26]

At this point, the war on hoodlumism became a day-by-day account of verbal bombs and bombshells. If the citizens were scared before, they seemingly now were in a fearful frenzy. Crimes had turned from beatings into sex attacks. Reports circulated that a man had attempted to lure a fourteen-year-old child into his car. The suspects weren't necessarily juveniles, but all of these accounts were all lumped together to portray a city under siege.

The *Deseret News* greeted its readers on October 20, 1951, with a scathing open letter to the mayor, expressing the outrage and fears articulated by readers in a barrage of calls flooding the paper. "What are the police, what is the city commission, what is the mayor going to do about it?" The paper clearly pointed out the "IT" was what the paper saw as a continuous series of sexual attacks.

The paper left out any mention of "reports of" or "alleged" sexual attacks, and sans objectivity wrote:

> *[The] attacks reached a peak of brutal horror this week when, first, a 19-year-old victim was seized, mauled, slashed, and cut, threatened with worse, and robbed by three sadistic young thugs in the heart of the residential district that surrounds East High School; and then an even younger girl was dragged into an automobile by a man who stripped her stark, beat her cruelly, attempted her violation, and threw her semi-conscious body into a gutter in the avenues.*[27]

A week later, the police department reported that an earlier report of a major case of attempted sexual molestation receiving widespread coverage turned out to be a hoax. It did not identify the crime, but the only case of attempted molestation in the news was the young girl allegedly dragged into the automobile.

The *Deseret News* continued in its open letter of October 20th.

> *The police books show that since the beginning of June, this city's young girls and mature womanhood had suffered almost 200 sadistic and sexual attacks, assaults, attempted assaults and attacks, molestations and the suffering experience of indecent exposures and peeping toms.*[28]

The paper continued to take the mayor to task, and then described what it saw happening in the homes of Salt Lake.

> *Salt Lake City women cower in their houses, fearful to venture in the street after dark. Families hesitate to permit their daughters to attend even school functions or meetings of*

*church organizations least some pervert waylays these girls in
the short distance they may be occupied on their way home.
Terror stalks the short distance between a bus stop and the
door of home—every shadow may conceal a lurking sadist.[29]*

The *Deseret News* demanded Mayor Glade, the head of the government,
immediately do something about this. The paper hinted the mayor who was
running unopposed in the upcoming election might want to act quickly for
political reasons "unless the surge of indignation which is now sweeping the city
should mount into a spontaneous write-in campaign."[30]

The mayor responded in the next evening's newspaper. He conceded the
threat had reached the idyllic city he wrote about with such pride a decade prior.
He conceded that those well-behaved youth he earlier respected so much might
have a few bad apples now. He no longer spoke of wholesome church and
recreational activities as the reason Salt Lake City youths were of sound mind
and body.

> *Our citizens must remember that this particular type of
> outlawry — this surge of sadism — is new to Salt Lake City.
> Obviously, we must know the problem before we can
> adequately meet it. Apparently this is one of the penalties of
> our city's becoming a great metropolis, and we as citizens
> must brace ourselves to meet it. That part of this heavy
> assignment lies on the shoulders of parents is revealed by the
> shocking revelation that, in some of these outrages, the girls
> themselves have been important contributors. This is hard for
> me to believe, but some of the parents have voluntarily
> admitted this fact.[31]*

In the statement above, the mayor didn't specifically define what outrages
the youthful girls had brought on themselves, but the *Tribune* clearly expressed
what it thought he meant.

> *Women and girls should be coldly realistic. The brazen attire
> and actions of some girls — they are in the minority of course
> — is conducive to sex activity A stock reply to this kind of*

*criticism is that girls are too young to know that tight
revealing clothes stimulate baser passions in some males. If
this is the case —mothers have a special duty to make it
abundantly clear to them — and if mothers are vague about
the problem, fathers or adult brothers have a responsibility to
explain the facts of life.[32]*

Glade laid out a seven-point plan saying it was time to protect mothers, sisters, and girlfriends:

1. Explore the issue at the City Commission meeting.
2. Enlist students in assisting the city by reporting on other students.
3. Have the police alert themselves as never before.
4. Discuss the acceptance of proposals from the American Legion and the VFW.
5. Have parents chaperone their children.
6. Ask judges to hand out penalties commensurate with sex and sadism crimes.
7. Ask citizens to maintain a calm, earnest and serious-minded appraisal of the situation.

The mayor's critics immediately took issue. William Dawson, the state welfare director, said there was no cause for "hysteria." Glade's call that sex offenders must be hunted down unmercifully, he cautioned, needs to be differentiated from the problems of rape and juvenile delinquency.[33]

If it was Mayor Glade's desire to have the citizens remain calm, this apparently was not the way to do it. Citizens crammed into the next city commission meeting, clearly wanting to honor Glade's charge to "explore" the issue. At the meeting, Mayor Glade said it was time to get the facts out. He cited the *Deseret News* open letter stating there had been 200 attacks of a sexual nature since June 1951 as justification for his seven-point plan, specifically his extraordinary proposal to employ students to spy on other students in the high schools.

Police Captain Steinfeldt jumped in at the meeting, cautioning that many of these 200 reports were not serious at all. He said peeping-tom calls often turn out to be a cat on a fence or kids running around the neighborhood.[34] Steinfeldt's call at the meeting for prudence, however, was seemingly ignored. The next day's *Tribune* (October 23, 1951), reported that at the meeting blame was spread around the city. The police department was blamed for its ineffectiveness, parents were blamed for their neglect, the press was blamed for distorting the facts, and the general public was blamed for "continuing to emphasize sex in various aspects of daily life."

At the same time, with the headline "The Public Must Help," the *Tribune* tempered its support of Glade's ongoing crime busting policy and published a rare four- column editorial warning that "hysteria and vigilantism could be more damaging to the community at large than the isolated sex offenses themselves." Specifically, the paper challenged the mayor not to enlist youngsters as snoops and tattlers; that could make the local situation worse, not better. The paper said that slightly less dangerous than a trigger happy, outraged vigilante is a highly imaginative "stool pigeon."

Also, the *Salt Lake Telegram*, which was owned by the *Salt Lake Tribune* and competed with the *Deseret News* in the afternoon, editorialized against pretty much everyone contributing to the affected frenzy. The *Telegram* headlined its editorial "Let's Not Be Hysterical Old Women." It took readers back to the city commission meeting under Glade's gavel, when the mayor reported two hundred sexual cases and detailed the citizen participation plans.

> *The meeting followed suggestions that the National Guard be called out to deal with the situation, and that citizen vigilante groups be organized to patrol the city. From all this one might think that Salt Lake City was equal to Chicago at its worst, with young gangsters running up and down Main Street with blazing pistols, sexual degenerates battering their way into homes and a regular parade of perverts and exhibitionists through the city's streets. It isn't a pretty picture that all of this commotion and talk presents, either to ourselves or the world at large. And it isn't an accurate picture at all. Most women and girls travel with perfect safety about our streets with never more than an admiring glance or perhaps an occasional complimentary whistle passed their way. Let's not get our sights out of line on this matter. ...Some emotional individuals*

*see gunmen or perverts or hoodlums lurking behind every
bush ... but, whatever we do, lets [sic] not act like hysterical
old women. We're not going to the dogs. And we're not about
to.[35]*

A town whipped into mass emotion wasn't listening to the more moderate voices. Hours after the *Telegram* article hit the porches, as indicated above, hundreds crammed into City Hall waving a petition signed by 1,700 others. A *Salt Lake Tribune* headline reported: "Irate Citizens Call for City Cleanup." Most people wanted police action. The paper quoted as the most vocal, Jordan Park Ward LDS Bishop E. Albert Rosenvall who said the police were inefficient and used what he called fruitless efforts to uncover the man who attacked and clubbed his daughter. He then exclaimed police aren't taking sex offenses seriously and that dope was being peddled at Salt Lake high schools. The head of the Chamber of Commerce reminded parents they, too, had a responsibility in the crisis. Those present booed him. They had come to blame others. Typical of his decency, Mayor Glade apologized for the booing, saying all should participate in city affairs, and not made the butt of impoliteness.[36]

The tribunal of Glade, Park Commissioner Romney, and Police Chief Crowther convinced the city commission to adopt the Mayor's step-by-step plan. And Mayor Glade, not to be deterred, continued with his plan to get the school board to sign off on his program to get "right-minded" students to tell the cops who was doing what in schools.

The Commission also authorized $75,000 to hire twenty-five more police officers, supplementing the current force of 188 officers. Glade told the commission and the city: "We mean business, as we've never meant it before."[37]

It's interesting to note, even after all the above furor, the Salt Lake Commission meeting minutes for October 25, 1951, report that 200-300 people, mostly from Salt Lake's west side, enabled by an LDS bishop and a Chamber of Commerce executive, had gathered to voice displeasure with crime suppression efforts. The Commission minutes in a single paragraph reflect sympathy and cooperation with these "people" but no commission action appears to have officially been vigorously undertaken, except for Glade's individual efforts, ostensibly on behalf of the commission.

The overstated talk of juvenile crime in 1951 suddenly ended. It wasn't because Mayor Glade's extra cops rounded up notorious sex offenders or thwarted gang activity. It wasn't because the Mayor's pointed plan yielded great success. It wasn't because citizen mobs secured their neighborhood boundaries, and it wasn't because of "right minded" student monitors in the high schools. *It was because actual crime statistics were revealed and validated.*

When the actual crime figures were released to the public, they showed there virtually was little justification for concern, let alone hyper reaction, at least when 1951 data were compared to previous post-war years. The last statistical reporting period, January through September 1950, showed juvenile delinquency was declining since the end of World War II. For instance, in the first post war year, 1946, Salt Lake Police arrested 479 teenagers for all crimes excluding traffic offenses. In 1950, the number had fallen to 367.[38]

A panel consisting of police participants and a judge at a November 1951 PTA meeting concluded that crime figures were exaggerated. Judge Rulon Clark of the Second District Juvenile Court said, yes, there had been more youths referred to his jurisdiction in 1951, but chiefly because of intensive police campaigns against juvenile traffic offenders. He said serious cases had actually fallen five percent. The most serious of all sex crimes, rape, totaled eight arrests through October 1951. Public Safety Commissioner Ben Lingenfelter added that Salt Lake City was a "clean city and a place where I'm happy and proud to live."[39]

The *Salt Lake Tribune* printed a graphic, showing three kids each leaning against a light pole with a cigarette dangling from his mouth. The three represented teenager arrests for January to October in various years. Figures for 1946, 1950, and 1951 were compared. The 1946 kid represented the largest number of arrest, the smallest punk in the graph represented 1951, with the 1950 kid in the middle.

The *Salt Lake Tribune* would only have three more stories of Salt Lake City juvenile delinquency for the rest of the year. None were about beatings, sex, gangs, hoodlums, or the like. It was a year of threats, real or created. Mayor

Glade did not knowingly mislead, but apparently let the need to protect his beloved youth substitute anecdotal evidence for fact, and he led like-thinking citizens and accommodating media on a yearlong fast-lane journey that didn't need traveling with such vigor.

In the short-run the war against juvenile delinquency bolstered Glade's popularity among voters. He ran unopposed and was elected to his third term as mayor in November 1951. Clearly, however, vote concern was not Glade's reason for taking on the "hoodlum" issue. Without question, Glade consistently had been heart-deep in youth and morality issues through the years, political ramifications aside, staying true to his convictions and principles. In fact, the stage had been set for Glade to pursue higher political ambitions.

CHAPTER 15

GLADE'S STATEWIDE AMBITIONS

Shortly after Glade took office for his third term as mayor, *The Salt Lake Tribune* reported what most political pundits already knew. The Democratic Party was trying to reclaim the popular mayor as its standard party-bearer for the 1952 governor's race. The mayor wouldn't commit, although by the first week of February, the Democrats were feeling they had at least attracted his ear.

The mayor didn't really announce his candidacy, but instead sent letters to delegates with return cards carrying the message: "Okay, you can count on me, I will help you win the nomination for governor at the Democratic convention."[1]

Finally, in the middle of April, Glade told the state he was a Democrat and a candidate for Governor. He announced a campaign that favored "intelligent economies in government that will build our commonwealth, and that, because of our favorable tax structure, will encourage new industry to come to Utah."[2]

He also pledged a return of "dignity to the state's highest office" and "criticized severely the constant bickering and brawling which has marked the present governor's [J. Bracken Lee] term."[3]

However, the bickering and brawling of the campaign had just begun. The campaign soon was consumed by the clash of personalities. The first hurdle for Glade was a primary race against Heber Bennion, Jr. As secretary of state, Bennion had the dubious task of being the number two person in the state under the colorful persona of Lee. Utah did not have a lieutenant governor at the time, with the secretary of

state holding many of the responsibilities of that office. Bennion was not overly effective in reining in Lee, and Glade knew he could attack that weakness.

Bennion touted his affiliation to the Democratic Party, zeroing in on characterizing Glade's tepid party loyalty. After all, even within city hall, few could positively say if Glade was a Democrat during his then nine years as mayor. *The New York Times* wrote that Glade's Democratic label even surprised some of his closest friends.[4]

Bennion knew the party issue was probably his best shot and waited until late into the primary campaign to unload the charge to loyal Democrats who were about to vote. Bennion believed he had served the party well and could prove it. Glade also unloaded a week before the September 9 primary. He accused Bennion of "bad taste, and bad timing on challenging my Democracy." Glade went on to say, "I was an active Democrat when the Bennion advisers were in swaddling bands." Glade recalled his days on the dusty trail for Woodrow Wilson and Simon Bamberger: "I am an active life-long Democrat and I won't take second spot to Heber Bennion or anyone else in my loyalties to the Democratic Party."[5]

Glade then went on the offensive, accusing Bennion of being weak and not representing the Democrats as Lee's second-in-command. "For want of anything to criticize, Mr Bennion has now opened up his own great weakness that is apparent among Democratic Party people. During Bennion's years as secretary of state, he had countless opportunities to fight Brack Lee's pernicious administration." Glade was just warming up his skills as a captivating orator. He told a Utah County Democratic rally: "Yet Bennion sat up there for four years and allowed Lee to have his way and destroy almost every worthy thing previous Democratic governors had created. Had Bennion voted his controlling vote on the state board oblique of examiners as a loyal Democrat? He did not. Bennion let Lee get away with piece-meal destruction of our party and policies."[6]

Democrats agreed that Glade truly was a Democrat, and the right Democrat to best battle Lee. Of the 68,000 votes cast in the democratic primary for governor, Glade picked up 36,182 to Bennion's 32,603. The only dark spot of that September day was the realization his Republican opponent, Governor Lee, picked up more votes than were cast in total in the democratic primary, while his token opposition, A. Cyril Callister, gathered nearly 15,000 more. Obviously, there were more Republicans than Democrats, and Glade could only hope a number of the Republicans were really Democrats who crossed over due to a wild race for the Republican U.S. Senate spot between Arthur Watkins and Marriner Eccles.

The race was on and Glade didn't mince words. He attacked Lee over the spoils of government and political appointees. He said Governor Lee violated all principles inherent in the state constitution relating to the operation of the commission form of government.

Utah Governor J. Bracken Lee
(Salt Lake Tribune)

He has gone over the heads of his duly appointed and confirmed representatives; he has dictated the personnel they must work with; he has made public commitments of commission policy without consulting the commission involved; and, he has made the posts created by the constitution and law mere clerkships to His Honor the Governor.[7]

The mayor, fresh off his municipal war against crime, also was motivated to go after Lee and problems at the Utah State Prison. Again, he accused Lee of appointing cronies to handle complex jobs, such as in staffing the prison. He told a rally in Heber: "The present Utah State Prison mess, with its escapes, strikes, and administrative blunders, dominated by Gov. J. Bracken Lee, is the most expensive and intolerable scandal in modern state history."

The mayor chided Governor Lee for his domination of all state departments, bureaus, and boards. "It is getting more critical every day. Judging from the sit-

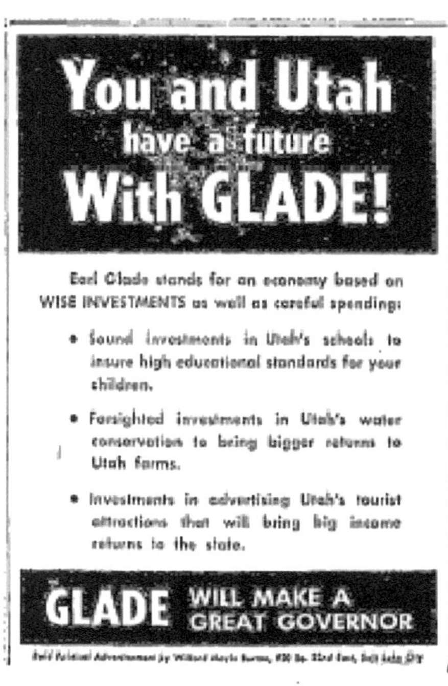

down strike and disappearance of two more inmates, it certainly is Lee's responsibility."[8]

Glade loved to quote Lee, who once said no honest person would want to be governor more than four years. The normally calm Glade no doubt enjoyed using his gift of speech to prickle Lee. Glade had a style that combined emotion and fact to produce an oratorical intensity that moved people to action, albeit not always in the way he intended. He must have felt as he did in the days of his prohibition speeches given to theater crowds.

Here's the Lee record of economy and efficiency: Half a dozen wardens and acting wardens replacing each other; prisoner escapes to the point of humor; convict riots with property destruction running into the thousands of dollars, mounting administrative costs; narcotic and alcohol violations; and now a sit-down strike in a $1-million escape proof prison.[9]

Glade wasn't finished. He continued that Utah spent $798 per inmate per year under Lee, while spending only $178 per year for every school child. Glade knew he had hit a home run with the issue of education, and dogged the governor the entire campaign over schools. The Democratic controlled legislature had appropriated $2 million in emergency funds for schools in 1951, but the Lee administration had not released the funds a year later, and Glade kept demanding that "Lee untie the strings of his parsimonious economy and release these needed funds at once."[10]

The 1952 campaign had a new wrinkle to it. Salt Lake City had two television stations and, for the first time, TV played a role in the election. While less than half of all Salt Lake area residents had TVs, and people were straining their eyes at the fuzzy black-and-white pictures, the candidates did have a live forum on TV and the video-look became part of Utah politics. One such broadcast took place on September 25. Glade was an old pro at broadcasting and combined his ability to speak with being comfortable behind a microphone and in front of a camera. He started on his popular topic of education, stating that Lee is

"against education, against our school, and against our teachers."

Glade spelled out a step-by-step assault on Lee's record similar to the way he earlier had spelled out his Seven-Step Program to stop hoodlums in the city. He accused the governor of failing to recommend or request appropriations for new construction at institutions of higher learning in both the 1949 and 1951 budget sessions. In addition, Glade pointed out that despite Lee's statements of a 40-percent higher education appropriation during his administration, he twice vetoed the appropriations and they only became law without his signature. Glade finished with his favorite, the two-million-dollar emergency building fund that Lee had failed to distribute.[11]

As the election neared, the mayor continued his assault on Lee's education record. Governor Lee was finally forced to answer why the emergency funds weren't distributed as required by law. He said it was because the School Building Commission had not completed its report and now the money would be distributed under the new building commissioner. Glade grabbed the news and ran with it at a rally in the Forest Dale Clubhouse:

*When Gov. Lee said that the funds were not distributed
according to law on Dec. 31, 1951, because the building
commission had not completed his report, he did not confess
that the commission was not able to function because he, the
state's chief executive, had not filled the vacancy created by
the resignation of Howard Baker. Now with the election
nearing, it is understandable that Lee would fill the position
and the commission would be called upon to distribute the
funds, nearly 12-months after the legal deadline.[12]*

As governor, Lee earlier had upset University of Utah regents, including
Glade when he was on the board. The mayor remembered the grudge match
between the Governor and the University of Utah. Glade had once commented
that the state official's constant sniping was damaging the school's morale and
striking at the faculty's "spirit [sic] de corps."[13]

Glade tied the University's squabble with Lee to his neglect of higher
education and reminded people of Utah that the governor had twice vetoed the
U's appropriations, declaring that it had a poorly managed maintenance staff.
Lee also was vulnerable to a charge that he had ordered a $25,000 survey to
snoop into each department at the U. Glade maintained the study was to nose
around to see what professors were doing, among other things. Lee's study
predicted the university would lose enrollment, but Glade contended that
enrollment was up.

*Is there any real economy in denying your youth the
opportunity for higher education? Yes, we've had enough Lee-
way in our state education. We've had enough false economy
in our school program.[14]*

The charges continued. Glade, the "old" advertising man, was upset that
Lee had abolished the Utah State Department of Publicity and Industrial
Development. Lee had said it was because its campaigns weren't working and
the Democrats in the legislature hadn't come up with anything better.

Lee had slashed the state budget by eliminating entire programs. Glade
went through them one-by-one and challenged the wisdom of their being

deleted. The mayor went back to his ubiquitous issue of liquor, challenging the Governor's elimination of the State Liquor Control Commission Enforcement Division. Lee, who was from "wide open" Price, Utah, no doubt wasn't fond of some of the liquor officer's raids on establishments in his hometown. Glade charged that Lee had "cut off the good right arm of the state liquor commission. This was in keeping with Lee's campaign promise to relax liquor law enforcement." Lee claimed he had cut the Division for a two-million- dollar cost savings. Glade countered that the state is deprived of fines and the local governments had to pay for the enforcement.[15]

It was the closest Glade approached a direct appeal for the non-drinking Mormon vote. Lee was not Mormon, nor did he hide the fact he did not follow Mormon traditions of not drinking or smoking. Lee answered most of Glade's challenges, stating he had one purpose, and that was to operate the state government "honestly, efficiently and economically." He said those principles sometimes made him take an unpopular stand on issues.

> *There are those who belittle any attempt toward governmental*
> *economy, but look how much better off we are today because*
> *of the efforts we have made. We have cut out the waste and*
> *graft in the Liquor Control Commission, reduced the overhead*
> *in the Road Commission and made savings in virtually every*
> *department under my [Lee's] control.[16]*

Glade announced his fiscal plan for the state and endorsed federal assistance for the Colorado River Project because of what it could do for development. He also proposed a highway program funded through federal aid; promoted the state's tourist trade; and encouraged harmony among state employees and the legislature. He said the governor's decision to cut budgets in programs such as tourism had hurt the state greatly.

The campaign didn't involve one-sided challenges, however. Lee had found inconsistencies and fault with the mayor's administration. He pretty much echoed the same charges as his opponent had made. Glade answered the challenges with his own rejoinder, stating that he stood on his record, working to improve the city's finances, physical facilities, law enforcement, and the morale of employees.

Glade saw that Lee was ahead in the polls, so he went on the defensive just before Election Day. He spoke out with righteous indignation at his opponent who he said was trying to make people "close their eyes to my years of honest service and to believe that I have suddenly exchanged my cherished principles for treacherous expediency."

He continued defending his record to an Ogden crowd:

> *You have been asked to believe that I am no longer honest, but dishonest, and that I am no longer careful and frugal, but wild and extravagant ... in a wild orgy of vote-getting [promising] everything to everybody with no hope of fulfillment.[17]*

Lee also challenged the Mayor's handling of the flood in Salt Lake City, as soggy city residents were still cleaning up well into the campaign and as the levies weren't removed until June. Glade went to Lee's home territory of Carbon County to announce:

> *While he [Lee] criticizes Salt Lake City for our own flood, he does not remember that there were many floods throughout the state this year. ... We seek to be fair and honorable in not saying that he is responsible for all the floods throughout 17 counties this year, nor do we say that he should have stopped the rushing waters that hit Morgan and Weber counties.[18]*

It was a bitter campaign. It can be summed up with a September 22 speech at the Newhouse Hotel in which Mayor Glade said Lee's "two-headed position as a candidate and governor makes for half-truths and double-talk." Mayor Glade had earlier used the words "double-talk, hogwash, and the big-lie" in another speech. However, he said he was just quoting verbatim Lee's speech of September 26, 1950, over the Intermountain Radio Network. Lee had used those words "double-talk, hogwash, and the big-lie," referring to Democrats.[19]

SAMPLE BALLOT

DEMOCRATIC PARTY ○	REPUBLICAN PARTY ○	○
For President of the United States ADLAI E. STEVENSON	For President of the United States DWIGHT D. EISENHOWER	For President of the United States
For Vice President of the United States JOHN J. SPARKMAN	For Vice President of the United States RICHARD M. NIXON	For Vice President of the United States
For United States Senator WALTER K. GRANGER	For United States Senator ARTHUR V. WATKINS	For United States Senator
For Representative in Congress ERNEST R. McKAY	For Representative in Congress DOUGLAS R. STRINGFELLOW	For Representative in Congress
For Governor EARL J. GLADE	For Governor J. BRACKEN LEE	For Governor
For Secretary of State MILTON B. TAYLOR	For Secretary of State LAMONT F. TORONTO	For Secretary of State
For Attorney General CLINTON D. VERNON	For Attorney General E. R. CALLISTER	For Attorney General
For State Auditor FERRELL H. ADAMS	For State Auditor SHERMAN J. PREECE	For State Auditor
For State Treasurer REESE M. REESE	For State Treasurer SID LAMBOURNE	For State Treasurer
For District Attorney DUANE A. FRANDSEN	For District Attorney STANLEY V. LITIZZETTE	For District Attorney
For State Representative L. FRANK REDD	For State Representative FLOYD W. NIELSON	For State Representative
For County Commissioner (4 Year Term) U. PRINT BLACK	For County Commissioner (4 Year Term) GRANT L. BAYLES	For County Commissioner (4 Year Term)
For County Commissioner (2 Year Term) J. W. NIELSON	For County Commissioner (2 Year Term) J. W. CROWLEY	For County Commissioner (2 Year Term)

The Glade magic didn't prevail in the gubernatorial race. The mayor, who won office without opposition a year earlier, fell to defeat at the hands of Lee. The incumbent governor engendered some antipathy toward Glade, but that is not enough for political pundits to explain how it happened that the governor won reelection. It could have been a combination of many factors, or it simply may have been that the citizens of the state wanted the incumbent Lee returned to office. It might also have been what voters at the end of the century had come to embrace: "It's the economy, stupid." Lee was a "just-say-no" candidate when it came to spending for even what Glade saw as essential services. Also, Dennis Lythgoe in his Lee biography, *Let 'em Holler*, starts his discussion of the 1952 election by first mentioning the immense popularity of Dwight Eisenhower at the top of the Republican ticket and the coattails he provided other Republican candidates throughout the country, including those in Utah. The whole state GOP ticket was elected, the first time that had happened in many elections.

During the 1930s, the Republican Party suffered several major defeats in Utah. Republican Senator Reed Smoot was stunned by Democrat Elbert D. Thomas in 1932. That same year, presidential candidate Franklin D. Roosevelt on his transcontinental tour visited Salt Lake and proved to be very popular among Beehive State voters because of his support of railroads and agriculture. He carried the state and brought local Democrats to power with him. In every national election from 1932 to 1948, Roosevelt's appeal in Utah continued, but Democratic coattails four years later failed Glade in his gubernatorial bid.

There also is considerable evidence the LDS Church supported Lee over Glade, even though Glade was a faithful Mormon and Lee was not. The Church-owned *Deseret News* editorialized in favor of Lee. Also, Lythgoe cites a meeting between LDS Church President David O. McKay and the two candidates following the election. In the presence of both, President McKay told the winning candidate how glad he was that Lee was the victor in the election.[20]

Lee also mentioned, upon reflection, that Glade was a weak candidate. He said Glade was told to say what he said in his speeches and was not just being his familiar persona. Lythgoe goes on to cite a letter Glade later wrote to a political scientist. Glade said he really didn't know politics and had no political contacts. He also admitted in the letter that much of his monetary support came from Republicans.

As an endnote, Lee, after serving two terms as governor (1949-1957), was elected mayor of Salt Lake City for three terms (1960-1971). After the brusque remarks Lee made of Glade in years past when they squared off, one might question the sincerity of his statement expressing sorrow at Glade's passing in 1966:

> *I feel certain I speak for the entire Salt Lake City Commission and a great percentage of the citizens of Salt Lake City when I say Earl J. Glade was a fine man, a gentleman at all times and as mayor of Salt Lake City, he was a credit to our city. He served well and long in his many public capacities.[21]*

CHAPTER 16

BACK TO OFFICE AS MAYOR

Glade returned to his day job as mayor of Salt Lake City after losing in the governor's race. His third term had started with the flood crisis and continued with an emphasis on infrastructure development for the growing city. One political historian, Dixie Huefner, quotes civic leaders as always referring to the mayor as "a nice guy" who was never described as dynamic or aggressive. Huefner argues that civic affairs may have lagged under Glade, and cites an unnamed source as suggesting that not Glade but Commissioner L.C. Romney ran the city during Glade's administration. In Glade's defense, Romney said the "civic lag" charge was untrue, saying the business community was largely at fault for whatever lag there was.[1]

L.C. "Rennie" Romney was correct in at least one assessment he held for Glade. He lauded the mayor for never making monuments to himself. There are few things carrying Glade's name, and research shows he neither asked for nor received many favors while in public office. Even detractors agree Glade unquestionably was honest and diligently scrutinized city spending.

For example, Glade called for a full investigation into what others might consider a minor incident in which a squad car had been in an accident. Originally the damage was thought to require $20 to repair, but the car dealership charged the city $84.45 because the body shop believed there was an additional kink in the car. Glade's full investigation started with the person who took the car to the shop: Why was the preliminary estimate of $20 exceeded? Did the repair shop that also leased the squad car to the city make only the needed and proper repairs? What could be done to keep this from happening in the future?

Glade also called for a full probe of parking ticket procedures when a citizen named Stratford L. Wendelboe of Fourth South St. found what he thought were discrepancies in parking tickets. Mayor Glade praised the whistleblower: "Mr. Wendelboe is to be complimented for his constructive criticism." Glade sat down with Wendelboe for two hours and was incensed that the citizen had paid his tickets, yet still was receiving bills from the city. As a result, Glade hired an outside auditor, and the city subsequently modernized the procedures by which tickets were handled.[2]

In another matter, the Mayor ordered restitution for another citizen, C.L. Reese, who paid two parking tickets and a jaywalking ticket but yet still received a summons. The mayor said: "I have told all those connected with the traffic court to be extremely careful in handling tickets so that our citizens will not be put to any additional trouble or embarrassed in any way."[3]

Glade seemed to take it personally when there was a complaint against the city and viewed the mayor's position not only as one of administration but of counsel. He had no problem in using his bully pulpit to achieve what he thought best for the city. His discussions about divorce, hoodlums, parenting, safety, and moral issues were legendary. When he declared a "no accident" day and a terrible accident happened, he

Traffic, safety, freeways and the infrastructure were among Mayor Glade's passions throughout three terms in office. Shown flanking the Mayor are Commissioners Romney, Stewart, and Gordon. Commissioner Stewart denied Glade a fourth term in the Mayoral 1953 election. (Utah State Historical Society)

mounted his podium and delivered a major address on the subject. Nine persons had been killed and Glade urged Utah drivers to make full stops when seeing flasher lights.

The mayor's third term would be his last. The mayor filed for a fourth term, and in an almost understated announcement said: "If the people of the city desire it, I shall be pleased to devote my energies to their services in another term." This time, the seventy-year-old mayor had substantive opposition. Adiel Stewart, who was the Salt Lake County Commissioner of Health and Charity, was a LDS stake president and a Republican, although the race was non-partisan. That *something* Glade always had previously -- sincerity, charisma, luck -- failed him this time. Stewart squeaked out a narrow victory. The new mayor was quoted in Huefner's book as stating Glade could have won.

*As Mayor, Glade also served as the
Commissioner of Public Affairs and
Finance.
(Salt Lake Tribune)*

*That fellow [Glade] was
very popular. But he had a
funny view that if the
people wanted him, they
would elect him. So he
didn't campaign—wouldn't
even let some of his friends
and backers go out and
work for him. And you
know, after eight [actually
twelve] years of turning
down a few people here
and there, some people
were tired of him. But, he
still could have won easily
if he had worked at it. You*

Glade gave the *Salt Lake Tribune* a long interview three days before he vacated City Hall, looking back twelve years and happy he had received thousands of letters complimenting Salt Lake City about its "cordiality:" The mayor, who also held the position of Finance Commissioner, was proud of his record. He called himself a progressive conservative, easily countering claims by critics that water projects were the only ones he completed during his time in office.

On December 2, 1955, Glade celebrated his 70th birthday, the last one he would spend in office as mayor. He recounted some interesting "episodes" in his 12-year tenure in office. He saw the city transition from a wartime to a peacetime economy, watched the city budget grow from $1 million to nearly $4.5 million, and the population from 150,000 to 200,000, and boasted that the bonded indebtedness of the city had been reduced from $5.1 million to $1.5 million. He led the way in 1947 to end rent controls that had been instituted during the war, nurtured the city through two floods (one of which cost $1million in 1952), invested more than $6 million in water improvements, spent another million for a sewage pumping plant, improved the airport for another million dollars, and pointed out that during his administration the city gained new roads and made sweeping improvements in parks and recreation facilities. As to what the future held for him, he said he didn't know, adding, "I will have to find some way to make a living. I think the future presents a real challenge to me."⁷

In the official minutes of the last board of commission meeting Glade presided over as mayor, on December 29, 1955, there is no mention of Glade's 12 years of service to Salt Lake City nor any kind words wishing him good fortune and health. However, the *Deseret News* on December 29 indicated that at the meeting Commissioner Romney, who took office in 1944 with Glade, on behalf of other fellow commissioners, reviewed the accomplishments of the city administration under the leadership of the mayor. Among other accolades,

Romney told Glade, "You are leaving Salt Lake City in better financial condition than any city of its size in the nation."

Other than that unofficial tribute to Glade, it was business as usual on December 29. The outgoing Mayor's last act of business was to preside over the inauspicious board approval to purchase fifty-four acres of Rose Park area land on the city's west side, which abutted city-owned land used for the sewer pumping station. The acreage was purchased for the purpose of serving as a buffer between the sewage plant and the Rose Park residential district.

On Tuesday January 3, 1956, Stewart was sworn in by Irma F. Bitner, the city recorder, of B & G Studios' early radio fame and a long-time friend and KSL associate of Glade. However, of the 115 guests, Glade was absent for reasons unknown. Unlike when Mayor-elect Glade was officially welcomed to the office by outgoing Mayor Ab Jenkins twelve years before on January 3, 1944, Glade's absence seemed uncharacteristic of the ever gracious and proper man of so many public experiences, as not even an eloquent written statement from Glade was found in the Commission's official minutes, although Glade's good wishes and success for Stewart were liberally reported in newspaper accounts during the transition.

Bitner would stay on as city recorder for four more months. Soon after leaving her position with the city, she was diagnosed with colon cancer, and later heart disease and diabetes. She lived another ten years and died at age seventy-seven on October 10, 1965, a year before Glade died. She had been his friend and colleague for more than thirty-five years in broadcasting, public service and church.

Meanwhile, Glade had overcome the job "challenge" he spoke of on December 2 in the previous year and found a way to make a living. Some speculated that Glade missed the swearing-in ceremony of his successor because he already was on to his next job, which he started on January 3, 1956. Romney, whose Commission responsibilities also included the Salt Lake Municipal Airport, had come to his longtime friend and colleague's aid, selecting Glade to continue his civic service as the Salt Lake City Airport finance and public relations counsel. He would get $400 a month ($3,500 in today's equivalence), which was $10 a month less than the airport manager received, and a seven-cent-per-mile gas allowance. Glade's new job was to finance the new $3.5-million airport building and the additional $1.5-million improvements that went along with it.

Also on that same January day, Glade, alone, and evidently reminiscing about events long past, penned a letter to Ivor Sharp. He clearly showed no outward animosity toward Sharp as a result of heartbreaks nearly two decades earlier at KSL.

> *I can see both of the KSL radio and TV transmitters from my windows, so I feel quite important. Under such remote control surveillance, our engineers should keep an eagle eye on their broadcasting apparatus. Building this proposed big new airport without in any way burdening the people, is a real challenge, but we'll do it! I am so proud of the way you men are managing the station. It is a very heartening experience to observe. Please let me know if there is some bit of service I can be helpful with. I am grateful beyond words for your thoughtful consideration.* [8]

Mayor Glade told *The Tribune* when he left office that he loved the luncheons, the meet-and-greets, and personal contact with citizens, but perhaps the most telling example of Glade's focus on people and things ethical and upright appeared in *Time* magazine August 15, 1955. It is not a story about a monumental city commission decision, about a new city project, or a speech he made. It is a story about a citizen named M.S. McRae who called and asked the Salt Lake City police to remove a dog that had been hit by a car near her home. The police referred her to the city dogcatcher. McRae tried in vain to reach the dogcatcher. Indignant, she called the mayor. A few minutes later, Glade arrived in his Cadillac, stepped out and gingerly lifted the animal into his trunk and drove off to the dog pound. [9]

At a final tribute to Glade, civic dignitaries, including Mayor Stewart and members of fourteen civic clubs and professional groups, 450 people, in cooperation with the Salt Lake City and Junior Chambers of Commerce, sponsored a luncheon for the outgoing mayor on Friday, January 13, 1956. After numerous speeches of congratulation and appreciation from various dignitaries and with some physical tokens in hand, Glade gave a magnanimous valedictory that is the exemplar of civic pride.

> *Day before yesterday, piloted by Joe Bergin, manager of our airport, I had the thrill again of inspecting Salt Lake City, County and the entire valley from an elevation of 2,000 feet above the terrain. As there were no leaves on the trees, the street and avenue contours were clearly evident. It was mid-January, with sunshine and green grass, but no snow!*
>
> *With the back-drop of Black Mountain on the north, and the Wasatch on the east, the settling was nothing short of heavenly. I have never seen the homes in residence clusters and contours so beautiful. The 150,000 automobiles of Salt Lake County were a veritable riot of color whether they were anchored in off-street parking lots, or were being used on the highways. From our vantage, they all appeared to have had a brand new car wash. They were rainbow radiant.*
>
> *And then there was Temple Square, with its unique architecture, in that glorious walled-in setting, inspiring in its impressiveness. Even from the sky, I like to remember that it is the only historic church auditorium enclosure in the world where, at the end of a symphonic concert, wondrous excerpts from those same glorious masterpieces are heard through high fidelity, wide range recording, in incredible night-time echoing over and beyond the entire grounds area. And you all know full well the wondrous choral story and spoken word which flow out of that square to an enthralled nation, each Sunday morning.*
>
> *The downtown financial core presented a bankerish skyline and was busy beyond words. Where in the world could all of those people be going? And what were they doing? Well, we advertising men have a pretty good idea!*
>
> *The State Capitol and the colorful parked cars, surrounding it, from our altitude, were as beautiful and alluring as Walt Disney-Land. The University of Utah buildings were so attractive that even a member of the football squad, in that environment, should be able to pull down a Phi Beta Kappa key.*
>
> *Yes, and the City and County Building did not look at all like it was going to tumble down. In fact, it appeared sound*

*and monumental. The building's dark gray background gave
Mayor Stewart's light green Cadillac, parked on the east side,
a chance to shine, which it surely did.*

*The handsome, young enthusiast whom we could see
directing all southbound traffic into the spacious Sugar House
shopping center parking lot must have been Jim Cannon or
Ray Free. He certainly had Jim's persuasive gesture. Even the
County roads looked magnificent from that elevation. That
was, indeed, something!*

*Yes, and the industrial center with its pastel colored tank
farms and railroad tracks, was an exciting ensemble. It was
lovely! And so, President Hinckley, members of the Board of
Governors, Gus [Backman], and all of your wonderful staff,
and you presidents of our valued civic, advertising and
Chamber of Commerce clubs, we saw realized before our eyes,
the incomparable Salt Lake City we have been telling millions
of tourists about, lo! these many years. And it is even more
beautiful by far, and more colorful than we had ever dared say.*

*So, then, as a parting thank you for today's generosity,
may I suggest that we Salt Lakers count our blessings as well
as our calories. Don't let's wait until we retire to realize that
we like to work. If we have not already done so, let's start
enjoying our jobs today! And thus we shall become exemplary
citizens who might well ask ourselves this challenging
question:*

*What kind of town would Salt Lake be,
If every citizen were just like me?*

Glade took a short leave of absence from raising funds for the airport to
successfully run for the Utah Legislature from Salt Lake County, serving from
1959 to 1961. Three years after retiring as Salt Lake mayor, Glade was elected to
serve in Utah's Thirty-Third Legislature, which began sessions on January 12,
1959, in the House Chamber of the Utah State Capital and convened for 60
sessions ending on March 12. Glade represented Salt Lake County in District 8
with 22 other House Representatives, including one woman. At that time, the Utah
Legislature met in regular session biannually. So, although Glade served for two
years, he attended only one additional regular legislative session and a two-day
special session in 1959. No regular or special sessions were convened in 1960. It

is not readily known what other governing activities, if any, Glade was involved in that second year.

Glade, as could be expected, thoroughly engaged in legislative business, although there were no especially significant achievements or events during his brief tenure in the lower chamber. He attended every one of the 60 sessions in 1959 and voted affirmatively on hundreds of bills, resolutions, family condolences, and other matters. He cast no nays.

As a junior legislator, Glade was appointed to three standing house committees: Revenue and Taxation Committee; the Industry Subcommittee – Tourist Development; and the Political Subdivisions Committee –City Government, which he chaired. The committee appointments reflected Glade's areas of expertise, but the city government committee obviously was a natural for him, given his long tenure as Salt Lake City mayor.

Glade was among the sponsors on several bills that seemed modest at first but potentially targeted the state's greatest long-term potential for its community and economic development. He was among the sponsors for a bill to protect and preserve Utah's scenic beauty by empowering the state and municipalities to enact statutes, ordinances and regulations regulating the creation and maintenance of dump grounds, junk or salvage yards adjacent to state or federal highways.

As chair of the Political Subdivisions Committee, he shepherded a bill permitting cities to prohibit certain games, pinball machines, and dancing that passed with 50 ayes, 10 nays, 4 absent. Glade's committee also dealt with proposed legislation affecting election-day issues, city judicial appointments, and common motor carrier definitions for garbage and waste haulers.
There were two bills that especially mirrored Glade's involvement. In February, his committee reported out unfavorably on a bill to appropriate $50,000 for a summer educational program. It is not known the ayes and nays of this committee vote, but with his enduring devotion to Utah's youth, the unfavorable reporting-out vote was surely a disappointment to Chairman Glade, who likely drafted the bill. Two days later, a joint resolution was sent to the House Rules Committee requesting the U.S. Army Engineers survey the boat harbor at Saltair on the Great Salt Lake and to assess what improvements would be needed to

make the facilities more adequate. The resolution was rejected by the House in regular session but was later reconsidered in Special Session.

Glade was a dutiful, responsible representative never missing any of the sessions. He likely, however, was somewhat disappointed when many of the bills seemingly of importance to him or proposed by the committee he chaired did not pass out of committee or were stricken for consideration by the full house.

Two and a half months after the 1959 regular session ended, Glade returned to the two-day special session called by then Governor George D. Clyde to amend Senate Bill 97, which was intended to provide sufficient funds for continuing operations of the state's Insurance Department. Glade voted for the amended legislation and, on the second day he voted affirmative on bills dealing with school district bonding, correcting the salary of the commissioner of public safety from $6,000 to $7,300 ($59,000, in today's equivalence), grazing and mineral rights, investing idle funds, surveying the Saltair boat harbor, and instituting a tax on margarine. Finally, in one of his last votes as an active member, Glade affirmed an act that essentially prohibited swine from being fed raw garbage and that any garbage given to livestock would require first a permit from the state's Agriculture Department.

Glade's brief tenure in the legislature was not remarkable and likely not very satisfying for him. Unlike the dynamic and prominent role he played in so many issues as mayor of the state's capital and largest city, Glade was, at best, a minor supporting cast member in the state's theater of legislative politics. In fact, the legislative session seems so mundane and routine compared to those of recent years where political battles have been pitched at high tension surrounding social issues that echo the sorts of causes Glade championed as mayor.

In 1960, Glade did not run for reelection, and, instead, in late 1961 he once again returned to KSL, not to radio but to television where, among other things, he anchored a television show featuring high school students who aired their thoughts about freedom and the meaning and obligations of citizenship.

EPILOGUE

CHAPTER 17
GLADE'S FINAL YEARS

When he reached maturity, Glade already had been highly motivated to do good things, possessing a sincere sense of calling in both religion and business, with the LDS Church and capitalism forming the twin pillars of his adult life. Glade's LDS religious convictions were connected to business so as to form an unbroken sequence in time and place. He saw his LDS religion as a means for moral reformation on earth tied to a system of otherworldly rewards by honoring the LDS principle of *eternal progression*. Glade frequently called the principle provocative and motivating. He wrote that it gave him "the urge so to learn, to live, and to work, that one, indeed may be worthy of the continuing life [after death].[1] The LDS principle of *eternal progression,* for Glade, was an essential catalyst for doing good works and reaching his eternal reward.[2]

Glade was an undeterred entrepreneur in his teens and twenties while creating a stable of advertising courses at the University of Utah. And, at 39 in 1924, he was the fearless pioneering speculator in radio broadcasting. Although daring, he also was temperate and reliable and completely devoted to broadcasting, especially when he persuaded the LDS Church to reenter the business, partnering with the then Catholic family owned Salt Lake Tribune Publishing Company.

Glade's Radio Broadcasters, Inc. (RBI) venture was a success in form and in finances. It appears that Glade was not so much a financial expert as he was an accomplished promoter and salesman; his ability to raise funds during wartime and for public policies and projects was unmatched. His disciplined speaking voice – a matter of tone and timbre rather than pitch and volume – and his ubiquitous two-fingered hand gesture used for emphasis showed the self-confidence of one who, although cordial and formal, expected people to treat him right and to engage that which he promoted or held dear.

In his fifteen years as KSL manager, focused on seeking financial independence from the LDS Church owned Radio Service Corporation parent to KSL, Glade promoted ventures and risked large sums of his own Radio

Broadcasters, Inc. (RBI) money, with ominous results on several occasions, as detailed in earlier chapters: primarily, involvement in Ogden's KLO, the Glade Artists Bureau, and the Continental Broadcasting application.

In reality, when Glade's RBI was dissolved in 1939 and he subsequently was replaced as KSL station manager, it likely was time for Glade to change his relationship with the station. RBI, the company-within-a-company that Glade had

Glade in his home library on Highland Avenue in Salt Lake City.
(J. Willard Marriott Library)

used to make KSL a highly profitable business enterprise for both RBI and RSC, had seemingly outlived its revenue generating usefulness for the Radio Service Corporation/Salt Lake Publishing Company partnership, then the majority owners of KSL. Although his replacement choice was ill considered, an examination of the market structure – a company (RBI) within a company (RSC) – under which KSL operated indicates Glade may have reached the pinnacle of his financial contributions and taken KSL as far as he could with the managerial talents he possessed. Glade apparently and wisely knew his limits. Other managerial talents were thought needed to restructure KSL and for station executives to embark on a new business model and move Glade to an RSC directorship. A problem arose primarily because an individual who had no previous radio broadcasting experience marginalized Glade; a replacement who was thought hired because he was the son-in-law of a high LDS official.

Clearly the transition was not handled well and resulted in a great deal of unnecessary discomfiture for the people involved and damage to KSL's image, reputation, bottom-line, and employee morale. While Glade did not start KSL and was pushed out of the station's daily operations after heading it for more than fifteen years, he nevertheless left his mark, demanding that radio help the community it serves. As a corporate officer, he also saw the station as a voice of its owners, namely, The Church of Jesus Christ of Latter-day Saints. Today, KSL AM Radio still is a voice of its ownership, and those who have succeeded Glade still decide many business decisions based on LDS Church structure, beliefs and traditions that he, too, adhered to in his decisions. KSL AM radio at 50-kilowatts of power, the station that "made" the Mormon Tabernacle Choir America's choir, maintains its status as the preeminent broadcast outlet in Utah and the Intermountain West.

Five years after being "released" from KSL operational duties, Glade pursued the opportunity to become mayor of Salt Lake City. He always had firmly believed in private enterprise characterized by a free competitive market and motivated by profits. Seemingly a paradox, however, as Salt Lake City's three-term mayor (1944-1956), he saw a role for government in cultivating the moral aptitude of youth, of the general populace and of business; and he advocated the federal government create a comprehensive registry of wide-ranging information beyond the usual vital statistics on all its citizens, much like the LDS Church maintains a comprehensive registry to keep track of its members.

Civic minded and stirred to action to achieve social justice, as mayor, he also began to see government's role as providing social services, especially as such services benefited returning WWII veterans and the youth of the state. He didn't totally rely on Adam Smith's invisible hand of the marketplace to achieve his goals, but coupled it with government efforts to promote the interests of the people of the state.

Mirroring the times and remaining faithful to his beliefs, as Mayor, Glade tolerated a separate-but-equal law for black Americans, even providing Negro soldiers their own USO meeting place. And he accommodated restrictions on Japanese-American business owners in Salt Lake City during WWII. He also expressed concern with people who had been in the U.S. for many years but made no effort to acquire the language or to become citizens; people who would possibly foster discord in the workplace or in times of war.

Although a cheerful, peaceable man who assiduously avoided quarrels and arguments, Glade, ever the patriot, raised substantial funds for and heartily supported war efforts once the United States was involved. In a Memorial Day speech during the Korean War, however, Mayor Glade's conscientious nature shown through when he called for the prayers that a meeting-of-the-minds of nations may be achieved through a triumph of the human spirit rather than by a resort to arms:

> *I hope my friends, the gallant living veterans, their buddies,*
> *now of sacred memory, we tenderly honor today, will*
> *understand when I humbly say that war has never really*
> *settled anything, and I wonder if it ever will.*[3]

Glade, who achieved three successful terms as Salt Lake City mayor but lost to Adele Stewart in his quest for a fourth term, may have overestimated his competition-proof status because by all accounts, including Stewart's, he hardly campaigned in 1956 for another term. Or, he maybe was tiring of the 24/7 mayoral job and wanted to move on to another adventure. Romney was planning a new airport for the city and needed a proven fund-raiser, so Glade was his choice. After being a three-term mayor, in the subsequent four years, Glade promoted the airport plan, raised the necessary funds and left that position only after confirming the airport would be built.

In his years of public service, Glade strove to produce what he thought was the greatest good for the greatest number of citizens. He was not indifferent to the approval of others, but Glade, for the most part, was inner-directed and did not strive to take credit for each step he took toward reaching his city goals. Nevertheless, in the nearly half century since his death, his place in Salt Lake City history has not been completely lost, and many of those institutions he helped form and lead are as relevant today as they were during his life. Salt Lake Citizens still drink water from the same reservoirs and pipelines that Earl J.

Glade made a priority nearly seventy years ago. The nation's travelers drive over the same Interstate corridors that Glade's administration mapped out in the mid-1950s, 21 million of the world's travelers go through the airport that Earl J. Glade gathered financing for after his terms as mayor of Salt Lake City, and many more millions listen to the Mormon Tabernacle Choir network broadcasts he helped foster each week across the nation and other parts of the world.

Whether by choice or by opportunity, Glade's life, beliefs, and vocational endeavors reflected nearly eighty years of the most formidable years of Utah history. He was raised in and served the LDS church as it became the preeminent force and political influence in Utah, led Utah's largest city in and out of the war years, was a champion against Cold War communism, a protector of popular family values, served the University of Utah as a regent as that institution reached national status, and was in the right place at the right time with the right talents as mass media quickly set the pace of modern life.

Glade received a medal in 1956 for his long service to veterans and was elected president of the Advertising Association of the West, which had more than 6,000 members. In 1958, he received an Honorary Doctor of Law Degree from the University of Utah, as well as numerous other honors. In 1961, he resigned after four years as Public Relations and Finance Counselor at the Salt Lake Municipal Airport.

Throughout the period, the former advertising, civic, broadcast, and mayoral leader stayed active, albeit at progressively less demanding positions. Glade performed some public relations functions for the city parks and public property department, and assumed the chair of the Board for Junior Achievement of Utah, Inc., and Section Manager of the Sugar House Chamber of Commerce.

But, at age seventy-seven, with a badly damaged ankle caused from falling off a curb, Glade was in financial trouble; he had reached a nadir. He had been given a three-piece set of luggage in 1956 after twelve years as mayor, and four years later after finishing city work at the airport, a $9.85 ($86 in today's equivalence) monthly pension to pay for premiums on city insurance. There had been no pension plan in his early time at KSL, and in 1961 he had no substantial source of income. The sizable net income he garnered in the golden age of radio seemingly had been dispersed. Unlike many of today's politicians who find more than comfortable economic circumstances once they leave office, Glade's situation appeared quite needy.

Arch Madsen, who became president of Bonneville International Corporation (BIC), formed out of KSL Inc. and its predecessor, the Radio Service Corporation (RSC), took notice of Glade's circumstances. BIC was the company that consolidated the LDS broadcast holdings, including KSL, KIRO in Seattle, and WRUL in New York. Madsen was charged to give unified leadership to KSL and the other broadcasting entities, mostly FM radio stations acquired by the visionary Madsen and developed for the LDS Church. Madsen had always held Glade in high regard for his pioneering efforts at KSL and for his civic service, but, even after nearly a quarter-century, still was incensed by what he saw as a pure act of nepotism in 1938 when Glade was ousted from KSL management and replaced by the son-in-law of a high LDS Church official. Madsen reports:

> *[Glade's] financial condition had deteriorated to the point where he was about to lose his home. I immediately went to [LDS Church] President McKay and asked for permission to bring Mr. Glade back to KSL as vice president for Community Affairs. President McKay eagerly responded and ... I was authorized to hire Mr. Glade ... with a salary to match his position ... This I did near the end of 1961, and [Glade] gave distinguished service to KSL from then until his death ... in 1966.[4]*

In his seventies, Glade, the KSL radioman, added KSL television to his repertoire in late 1961 when Madsen put him on-the-air after a twenty-three-year hiatus. Besides his other community affairs responsibilities, for several weeks Glade conducted a Saturday noontime television series titled "Let Freedom Ring." On February 10, 1962, the format was changed to "American Heritage." Where he had been interviewing businessmen of Utah about their ideas on freedom, the new series focused on the ideas of high school students of the state.

Glade's new show involved talking to high school students on the general theme of "what my American citizenship means to me." Glade started each show with an interview, and then each guest gave a short talk on the subject. Shows in the series also allowed for discussion with students about how they believe the institutions of homes and schools could guide thinking in changing times.[5]

The show brought Glade back to the omnipresent subject of his intense interest –sharing his worldview, experiences, opinions, values and religious beliefs with impressionable youth. The youth of the state had always been Glade's preeminent concern. Even accounting for his tenure as mayor, he had an unbroken lifetime record as a supporter and defender of Utah's youth.

Remembering Glade's ouster in the late 1930s from KSL, Madsen rigorously enforced nepotism rules when he took charge of LDS broadcast holdings nationwide at Bonneville decades after the event. Even Gordon B. Hinckley, much later to become LDS president, attentive of the policy, inquired of Blaine Whipple, Senior VP of Finance for Bonneville International Corporation officer, if nepotism rules would be violated if his daughter was hired for a one-summer internship at KSL. She was hired, consensus being that such short-term employment was innocuous and not a violation of Madsen's Bonneville nepotism ban.[6]

Madsen may have been justifiably irate at Clark for ousting Glade from KSL management in 1938 in favor of son-in-law Ivor Sharp, but records show that Glade and Sharp seemingly had reconciled their differences and assessed that a higher authority had shaped their relationship. As loyal LDS workers, they dutifully honored the Church "callings" and accommodated accordingly. Earl and Sarah Glade and Ivor and Marianne Sharp after a period of time also apparently developed friendly personal relations to the extent they took a long trip together. Marianne Sharp, J. Reuben Clark's daughter, related: "Earl Glade, his wife, Ivor and I went together on a trip back through Rushmore, through eastern Canada, down to New York, and went to some shows. I guess they [Earl and Ivor] had work to do there. That was a very enjoyable trip which we had with them."[7]

In 1957, a year before Sharp was released from KSL management, Ivor, the decent individual he was, intimated heartfelt thoughts to Glade in recognition of bygones at KSL:

Sometimes I glance back over my shoulder at the yesterdays and linger a bit over the KSL years when we worked together. The memories, for the most part, are happy ones —the KSL spirit radiated around about us and we were anxious to move the station forward. I say "for the most part," because my coming to KSL later occasioned some unhappy days for you.

I wish that this had not been the case, and in retrospect I wish I had done some things differently. I know, however, that under the pressures we did the best we could at the time, and I am confident both of us regret those difficult days.

It is reassuring to know that whatever happened, our respect, our affectionate feelings one for another, and our friendship withstood all the events.

But you have had so many glorious days along with the cloudy ones, and also have numerous achievements to your credit. And after all, that is what counts, and I wish you a continuation of the best in life, as well as well as much happiness in doing the things you like to do, along with good health.[8]

Glade died at age 80 on September 12, 1966, in Salt Lake City. Two months after his death, Glade's widow sent appreciation to Blaine Whipple for the $400 ($3,000 in today's equivalence) monthly checks she received.

Dear Mr. Whipple,

Please Express to President McKay my sincere gratitude for his generosity in sending a check for $200.00 twice each month. I appreciate the checks but feel very humble in accepting them. I want to tell you [Whipple] personally how grateful I am for the many kind things you have done for me and my

*Sarah Rasband Glade
(J. Willard Marriott Library)*

> *Gratefully,*
> *Sarah R. Glade[9]*

Madsen expressed the thoughts of many at Glade's funeral.

> *Earl J. Glade distinguished himself in so many walks of life
> that any comment on his life runs the risk of sounding
> excessive if it is to begin to measure the contribution of the
> man. But we at KSL remember him best for what he was —not
> what he did. He was a man of unfailing gentleness and
> goodwill and it is those qualities in him that we remember. We
> shall miss his counsel and companionship here at KSL. ...We
> can know our grief is tempered by the knowledge that his life
> enriched ours and the entire community immeasurably.
> Indeed, of him it can be said that there is no measuring where
> the influence of his works will end.*

Richard L. Evans, who was the voice of *Music and the Spoken Word* for more than four decades (1930-1971) on KSL's Mormon Tabernacle Choir network broadcasts, picked up Madsen's theme. Evans was president of Rotary International at the time, when he spoke of Earl J. Glade's passing.

> *Earl's every impulse took into consideration its effect upon
> everyone concerned —so considerate was he. He was a
> gentleman in the truest sense. He was respected by all men.
> There were no two Earl Glades. He was unique and shall be
> remembered by all who knew him.*

Madsen and Evans certainly captured Glade's considerate, gentle and engaging nature with their tributes, but Gordon B. Hinckley of the LDS Council of the Twelve at the time perhaps best captured Glade's essence, the fundamental *eternal progression* principle, that gave precise meaning to Glade's life and identified what seemingly drove his every living act.

Earl J. Glade's faith was quiet. It was solid and it was consistent in sunshine and in shadow, both of which he was intimately familiar. He made preparation for [glad reunions which will follow] in the summer of his life, when there was time. By the manner of his living, he planned carefully for eternity.

Earl and Sarah's children produced a personal account of their upbringing and family life. In it they quote Mahatma Gandhi in reference to their father:

My Life is My Message, concluding, [our father] left the message of his life to the benefit and blessing of many more than are able to be known or named.

CONCLUSION

Unlike the wealth of books and research about the American presidency, we have little in relative comparison regarding a comprehensive composite history about the political institution of the American city mayor. One of the best-known books which asked historians to rank the nation's best and worst mayors was Melvin Holli's 1999 work (*The American Mayor: The Best and the Worst Big-City Leaders* by Penn State University Press) which included 679 mayors from the nation's 15 largest cities as well as more than 50 other municipal chief executives, covering nearly 175 years of American history. Although Glade was not referenced, the book was widely acclaimed for its informative depth. It also was noteworthy for its conclusion, one that Glade surely would have agreed with. That is, there are "leaders for situations and situations for leaders, but no universal leader or leadership style that fits all historical situations."

Enter Earl J. Glade who served three terms as Salt Lake City's twenty-fifth mayor, and who history shows was the consummate public servant whose genuine love for the city shaped and guided his civic life and pride. For decades, Glade was among the city's best known figures for his ubiquitous presence in politics, business, broadcasting, education, and church venues. However, in twenty-first century Salt Lake City, there is not one significant monument honoring his work or contributions. As the fiftieth anniversary of his death has passed, Glade is barely remembered except in the closest or most intimate circles of those who are deeply versed in the history of Utah broadcasting and politics.

If one considers the earlier years of Glade's formative history and his entrance into the new field of radio broadcasting, he seemed destined to become one of Utah's most celebrated leaders, both in business and politics. With all of the proper and appropriate credentials and with his work in a high-profile industry, Glade was making all of the correct choices in crafting a political career with a vision that ultimately could extend into statewide and, perhaps, even national office. A skilled orator and an energetic participant in virtually every major type of civic organization, he was cultivating a worthy portfolio that proved his capabilities for leading complex organizations through complicated circumstances.

In many cities, the mayor often is the most dynamic, even most powerful, figure. However, in Salt Lake City, the mayor and the governor are overshadowed by the president and prophet of The Church of Jesus Christ of Latter-day Saints. In Utah's uniquely structured quasi-theocratic framework, the mayors of Salt Lake City (LDS, formerly LDS, or of some other denomination) historically have navigated quite adeptly a narrow channel of independent authority and leadership. No one can ever realistically deny the LDS Church's deeply integrated roots that touch upon such a large portion of the city's infrastructure, economy, and overall community engagement. Even the city's most recent mayors, regardless of political or ideological disagreements and differences, find some wise semblance of accommodation to the LDS Church.

Glade seemed a natural candidate to become a hugely successful figure in the city. He was a committed LDS believer, who relied on core principles of his faith to drive his generally pragmatic agenda. Yet, he also saw value in being independent, especially in nurturing a nascent broadcasting empire that did face several significant crises that could have ended the existence of the state's largest media and entertainment entity of the airwaves. He was fully engaged in his service as a regent for the state's flagship public university, as he was for any and all civic ventures. It would be difficult to name a contemporary figure from the prime period of his life and work who had built a presence or connection in so many of the city's organizations and institutions of his time.

Despite his willingness to be so publicly engaged, Glade, however, also appeared to work strenuously to keep details about his family life and personal friendships private and limited. It is not all that unusual for an individual with an active public profile to be shy, reticent, retiring, or even introverted in more intimate social circles. While we know as much as we can about his professional relationships and affiliations through the work and service he accomplished over many decades, Glade also appeared to keep more personal connections often at more than an arm's distance. Clearly, he was deliberate in separating the public and private spheres of his life, and family members likely only knew what acquaintances or the public knew about his work or life. He was diligent, dutiful, ethical, and honest, which can be fairly assumed given the absence of scandals or disturbing details beyond innocuous, easily reconcilable questions about conflicts of interests in his work as a radio business entrepreneur.

Yet, one wonders if, in that reserved nature, there lies the answer of the somewhat withdrawn, anti-climactic tone that characterized the last years of his professional and personal life. Some of it can be traced to the loss of the gubernatorial election in the early 1950s, and later to his unsuccessful attempt to win a fourth term as mayor. He served just one term in the Utah House of Representatives, leaving a rather unremarkable record. And, it does seem striking, that after a long life of innovative entrepreneurship, productive service as a public official, and as a faithful member of his church community, Glade's final years were marked by extremely modest means, especially financial. It might seem at least curiously odd to today's political observers or students of history that a prominent public figure could not leverage the impact or reputation of his legacy to live out the remainder of his years in more comfort and to enjoy the admiration and gratitude for a public life well served. Ironically, he may have been too scrupulous about balancing the need to be self-effacing even as he was among the most familiar, engaged citizens of Salt Lake City for a long time.

Glade's legacy cannot be dismissed nor should it be forgotten or minimized. It carries historical merit for numerous reasons both for the general realms of his pioneering contributions to Utah's broadcasting industry and to his leadership for a city making a demanding transition from a wartime economy to a post-war period in which city leaders and residents were learning to cope with the growing pains of a maturing Salt Lake City. It also is an enlightening case study of the checks and balances that allowed the city to grow and prosper with a healthy dose of independence even as it acknowledged and paid due respect to the church's major presence. Glade's administration generally avoided the sort of partisan polarization that has come to characterize much of Utah politics today. There might have been an LDS/non-LDS divide in many aspects of community life and interaction but in politics, there seemed to be quite the distinct flair for centrism and moderate ideological stances. Cultural values steeped in faith or conventional morality usually could be expressed without resorting to inflammatory context.

Indeed, Glade managed to temper even strident, hyperbolic, or emotional moments (which were relatively infrequent) with a sobering inflection of maturity, competence, and sensitivity toward the objective of being a responsible public servant who knew the value of serving the entire community. Even today, the citizens of a community would benefit from the modest, even humbling attitude and work ethic Earl J. Glade brought to his civic life. His life and work comprise a worthy testament in every regard.

ENDNOTES

CHAPTER 1: THE EARLY YEARS

1. Mark Twain and Charles Dudley Warner, *The Gilded Age* (Hartford: American Publishing Company, 1874), 69; Also Ron Chernow, *Titan*, (New York: Vintage Books, 1998), 81.

2. John A. McCormick, "Silver in the Beehive State*"Utah History to Go,"* Beehive History 16, http://historytogo.utah.gov/utah_chapters/mining_and_railroads/silverinthebeehivestate.html

3. *Ogden Standard Examiner*, November 30, 1903.

4. Gary James Bergera and Ronald Priddis, *Brigham Young University, A House of Faith.* (Salt Lake City: Signature Books, 1985). One of the more complete accounts of the history of BYU sports of the early 20th Century.

5. Earl J. Glade, letter to his father, James Glade, May 2, 1904.

6. *Park Record*, July 7, 1904.

7. Earl J Glade, letter to his grandmother, December 8, 1904, from Strassburg, Germany.

8. *Accounts of the life* of *Earl Joseph Glade*, an unpublished biography authored by Melba Glade with contributions from his other children.

9. Sadie Rasband, "Dear Earl," letter on a Souvenir Mail Card, Park City, UT, November 17, 1906, to Glade in Germany on his LDS mission.

10. Earl J. Glade, "Ours is a Practical Faith," *Deseret News*, July 12, 1941.

11. *Park Record*, September 14, 1907.

12. Ernest L. Wilkinson, Speech: *Highlights in the Ninety-Nine Year History of BYU*, (Provo: Brigham Young University Press, October 10, 1974).

13. Gary James Bergera. "The 1911 Evolution Controversy at Brigham Young University," A Chapter Gene A. Sessions and Craig J. Oberg, eds. *The Search for Harmony Essays on Science and Mormonism* (Signature Books, Salt Lake City, Utah, 1993.)

14. *University of Utah Catalog*, 1917-1918, 23-24.

15. Earl J. Glade, "Advertising at its Best," *New Improvement Era*, 1937.

16. *University of Utah Catalog*, 1917-1918, 24.

17. *University of Utah Catalog*, 1918-1919, 163.

18. *The Utah Chronicle*, November 19, 1920, 1.

19. Earl J. Glade, "Truly Great Men Recognize Spiritual Power," reprinted by the Church of Jesus Christ of Latter-day Saints, first appearing in the *Deseret News*, July 26, 1941.

CHAPTER 2: THE PERSUASIVE ADVOCATE WHETS HIS POLITICAL AMBITIONS

1. *Box Elder News,* July 18, 1916.

2. *Park Record* July 21, 1916.

3. *Box Elder News*, "Prohibition Discussed Sunday," August 1, 1916, 1.

4. *New York Times*, December 9, 1916.

5. Gene A. Sessions, *"Two Utahs: A Centennial Retrospective,"* *Weber Studies: Voices and Viewpoints of the Contemporary West,* Vol. 13.1, Winter 1996, College of Arts and Humanities, Weber State College, Ogden, Utah.

6. *Vernal Times,* September 15 and 18, 1916.

7. Ibid.

8. The Ancestor Files, "Elizabeth Puglsley Hayward and the Ratification of the Nineteenth Amendment," August 18, 2010, http:// theancestorfiles.blogspot.com/2010/08/elizabeth-pugsley-hayward-and.html

9. W. Paul Reeve, *History Blazer*, February 1995.

10. *The Utah Chronicle*, "Glade Makes Appeal for National Unity," November 12, 1917, 1-2.

CHAPTER 3: GLADE AS RADIO PIONEER AND THE BIRTH OF KSL

1. Lionel B. Cornwell reminisces on audiotape about his early days at KZN/ KFPT, circa 1960s.

2. Ibid.

3. Minutes of the Radio Service Corporation of Utah Board of Directors Meeting, November 17, 1924.

4. Letter to the Bureau of Standards, Department of Commerce, Bureau of Navigation, Washington, D.C. from W. G. Purvis of 715 3rd Ave., Salt Lake City, Utah, February 3, 1925.

5. Earl J. Glade, "Preaching the Gospel Through the Radio," *Improvement Era,* Vol. 28, No. 3, January 1925, 242.

6. Ibid. 245.

7. Heber G. Wolsey, Ph.D. diss., *The History of Radio Station KSL From 1922 to Television*, Michigan State University, 1967, 87; and, Minutes of the Radio Service Corporation of Utah Board of Directors Meeting, April 21, 1925.

8. *The Salt Lake Tribune*, April 19, 1931.

9. *Deseret News*, October 1, 1931, 1.

10. *The Morning Oregonian*, Saturday, October 29, 1932.

11. Tim Larson, interviews with Lawrence W. Lichty, November 16, 2007 and May 5, 2011, in Evanston, IL and on May 27, 2015 in Portland, OR; and Lawrence W. Lichty, *The Nation's Station*, unpublished dissertation, Ohio State University, 1963.

12. Tim Larson, interview with Lawrence W. Lichty, May 5, 2011; and "Engineering Statement and Exhibits, WLW, The Crosley Broadcasting Corporation, Cincinnati, Ohio." Submitted to the Federal Communications Commission, March 1960 in Support of Comments Relative to Third Notice of Further Proposed Rule Making, Docket 6741.

CHAPTER 4: UTAH'S RADIO ENTREPRENEUR

1. Minutes of the Radio Service Corporation of Utah Board of Directors Meeting, February 18, 1930.

2. American Society of Civil Engineers, "Memoirs," prepared by a committee of the Utah Section of the American Society of Civil Engineers. The committee was comprised of Richard R. Lyman, Chairman, R .A. Hart, and R.K. Brown. Memoir obtained from biographical pamphlets in the Church of Jesus Christ of Latter Day Saints Library.

3. Minutes of the Radio Service Corporation of Utah Board of Directors Meeting, December 4, 1928.

4. Minutes of the Radio Service Corporation of Utah Board of Directors Meeting, July 26, 1929.

5. Minutes of the Radio Corporation of Utah Board of Directors Meeting, November 26, 1929.

6. Minutes of the Radio Service Corporation of Utah Board of Directors Meeting, January 25, July 26, and November 26, 1929.

7. Minutes of the Radio Service Corporation of Utah Board of Directors Meeting, November 15, 1932.

8. Elections - Utah History Encyclopedia, *Elections in Utah 1896*, http://www.media.utah.edu/UHE/e/ELECTIONS.html

9. W. Glen Garner, unpublished autobiography, circa 1986, 42.

10. Earl J. Glade "Truly Great Men Recognize Spiritual Power," reprinted by the Church of Jesus Christ of Latter-day Saints, first appearing in the *Deseret News*, July 26, 1941.

11. Federal Radio Commission, Washington, D. C., *Application for Radio Station License, Peery Building Company*, April 1, 1927.

12. Elmer W. Pratt, Federal Radio Commission Assistant General Counsel, "Memorandum to Commissioner Harold LaFount," February 7, 1929.

13. Acting Chief, Radio Division, Federal Radio Commission, "Letter to Peery Building Company, Broadcasting Station KFUR," April 11, 1929.

14. Federal Communications Commission, Testimony of Earl J. Glade before the FCC regarding applications for Utah broadcasting stations, 1934.

15. *Box Elder News*, November 6, 1925.

16. *Ogden Standard Examiner*, February 18, 1927.

17. The Joint Oral History Project, Brigham Young University Archives, Brigham Young University Alumni Association Emeritus Club, Earl Glade [Jr.], Interviewed by Alma Heaton, November 15, 1984, 75-76.

CHAPTER 5: CRAFTING A UTAH VISION OF RADIO PROGRAMMING

1. William Mulder, "Music and the Spoken Word from Temple Square," *Improvement Era*, Vol. 42, No. 7, July, 1939, 440.

2. *Popular Science Monthly*, October, 1929, 40-41, 153-155.

3. Minutes of the Radio Service Corporation of Utah Board of Directors Meeting, July 26, 1929, 3.

4. *Deseret News*, May 4, 1929.

5. *Ibid.*

6. Heber G. Wolsey, Ph.D. diss., *The History of Radio Station KSL From 1922 to Television*, Michigan State University, 1967, 133 and138.

7. John F. Schneider, Seattle, Washington, *The NBC Pacific Coast Network*, 1997, http://www.oldradio.com/archives/ stations/sf/nbc.htm; *Broadcast Weekly Magazine*, August 24, 1929, 6.

8. John F. Schneider, Seattle, Washington, *The NBC Pacific Coast Network*, 1997, http://www.oldradio.com/archives/ stations/sf/nbc.htm; E. P. J. Shurick, *First

Quarter Century of American Broadcasting (Midland Publishing Company, 1946), 163.

9. *Popular Science Monthly*, October, 1929, 40-41, 153-155.

10. William Mulder, "Music and the Spoken Word from Temple Square," *Improvement Era,* Vol. 42, No. 7, July, 1939, 442.

11. *Popular Science Monthly*, October, 1929, 40-41, 153-155. One other scenario needs to be eliminated concerning how the first Choir broadcast reached New York from Salt Lake City. What if KSL, ignoring the propagation limitations of its daytime signal, aired the program and it was picked up and relayed station-to-station over-the-air to New York and then out over the NBC wire connections to affiliates? NBC's Aylesworth in a 1929 interview discussed a reverse of this method. He was asked why wires were used to reach NBC affiliates across the country, and why the power of NBC's WEAF flagship station in New York City was simply not increased to reach affiliates in the chain and relayed over-the-air from station to station. "In the present state of the radio art, it cannot be done. Part of the program would get through. Part would be lost by fading, static, and interference. Because atmospheric disturbances and interference do not affect wires, we [NBC] pay the American Telephone and Telegraph Company $2,000,000 a year to keep our stations connected. Some day engineers may show us how to get reliable communication between stations by radio, and we are experimenting in that direction." The over-the-air method leaping from station to station most certainly was not used to reach New York from Salt Lake for the first Choir broadcast.

12. Albert L. Zobell, Jr., "From the Crossroads of the West, with Music and the Spoken Word," Vol. 49, No 7, July, 1946, 438; and Heber G. Wolsey, Ph.D. dissertation, *The History of Radio Station KSL From 1922 to Television, Michigan State University, 1967, 148.*

13. Ralph W. Hardy, "Testimony in behalf of Radio Station KSL," Federal Communications Commission, Clear Channel Hearing, Docket No. 6741, May 1946, 16.

14. *Mary and John,* a pamphlet presented with the compliments of the Ecker Studio, Salt Lake City, circa 1930s.

15. Tim Larson, interview with Louise Hill Howe Malloneé and Parley Baer, Salt Lake City, Utah, September 27, 1992.

16. *KSL News*, "New Series Promises Outstanding Radio Plays," Vol. XII, No. 41, October 8, From: all-hum-bounces1933, published weekly by KSL.

17. Tim Larson, interview with Louise Hill Howe Malloneé and Parley Baer, Salt Lake City, Utah, September 27, 1992.

18. Tim Larson, interview with Luacine Clark Fox, Salt Lake City, Utah, May 30, 1990; and Tim Larson, interview with Parley Baer, January 19, 1989, Tarzana, California.

19. Tim Larson, interview with Lena Marie and Alvin Pack, Vol. 2, Everett L. Cooley Oral History Project, December 4, 1986 - February 10, 1987, 409-412.

20. *Murray Eagle*, April 20, 1933.

21. Minutes of the Radio Service Corporation of Utah Board of Directors Meeting, February 9, 1927.

22. Earl J. Glade Jr., manuscript "I Remember…Thoughts about the Early Days of KSL," circa 1977.

23. J. Reuben Clark, letter to LDS President David O'McKay, May 22, 1951.

24. Tim Larson, interview with Patricia Glade Curtis, August 2, 2011, Salt Lake City, UT.

25. Ivor Sharp, reported in a Memorandum to President J. Reuben Clark, May 21, 1951, "Compensation calculations for Earl J. Glade," tabulated on September 29, 1945; J. Reuben Clark, reported in a Memorandum to LDS President David G. McKay from J. Reuben Clark, Jr., May 22, 1951, "Amounts Paid to Earl J. Glade by KSL and Amounts Received and Expenses Incurred by Mr. Glade in the Operation of Radio Broadcasters Inc., January 1, 1929- August 31, 1945 Inclusive," tabulated on September 29, 1945.

CHAPTER 6: TRANSITION AND CHANGE OF FORTUNES

1. D. Michael Quinn (2002), Elder Statesman: A Biography of J. Reuben Clark, Salt Lake City: Signature Books, 384.

2. D. Michael Quinn (2002), Elder Statesman: A Biography of J. Reuben Clark, Salt Lake City: Signature Books, 393.

3. D. Michael Quinn (2002), Elder Statesman: A Biography of J. Reuben Clark, Salt Lake City: Signature Books, 389.

4. D. Michael Quinn (2002), Elder Statesman: A Biography of J. Reuben Clark, Salt Lake City: Signature Books, 394.

5.   D. Michael Quinn (2002), Elder Statesman: A Biography of J. Reuben Clark, Salt Lake City: Signature Books, 400-401

6.   Minutes of the Radio Service Corporation of Utah Board of Directors Meeting, October 12, 1938.

7.   Minutes of the Radio Service Corporation of Utah Board of Directors Meeting, October 1, 1938.

8.   Ibid.

9.   Ivor Sharp, Personal notes written in 1944 concerning the events surrounding his coming to KSL in 1938.

10. Ibid.

11. D. Michael Quinn, *J. Reuben Clark: The Church Years*, (Provo, Utah: Brigham Young University Press 1983), 85.

12. Personal, unpublished notes of Ivor Sharp written in 1944 concerning the events surrounding his coming to KSL in 1938.

13. J. Reuben Clark, letter to LDS President David O'McKay, May 22, 1951.

14. Minutes of the Radio Service Corporation of Utah Board of Directors Meeting, October 12, 1938, and December 31, 1938.

15. *Davis County Clipper*, April 30, 1937.

16. *New York Times*, Oct. 1, 1939.

17. Radio Service Corporation minutes, July 25, 1939.

18. *Deseret News*, November 30, 1943.

19. Minutes of the Radio Service Corporation of Utah Board of Directors Meeting, November 22, 1939.

CHAPTER 7: RISKS, DISAPPOINTMENTS OF ENTREPRENEURIAL INNOVATION IN RADIO

1.   Ivor Sharp, letter to Edmund B. Abbott of KNX Radio and the Columbia Broadcasting System, February 28, 1940.

2.   Edmund B. Abbott, letter to Ivor Sharp, March 1, 1940.

3.   Edmund B. Abbott, report to Ivor Sharp entitled "KSL An Estimate," May 15, 1940.

4.   "KSL Artist Bureau – Glade Artist Bureau and Continental Broadcasting Company," in the personal files of Ivor Sharp, 1943, 10.

5.   Earl J. Glade, letter to J. Reuben Clark Jr., March 21, 1941.

6. Earl J. Glade, letter to J. Reuben Clark Jr., May 4, 1941, personal files of Ivor Sharp.

7. J. Reuben Clark Jr., letter to Earl J. Glade, May 23, 1941, personal files of Ivor Sharp.

8. Radio Service Corporation, "Memorandum for Mr. Vincent," June 5, 1941.

9. Ivor Sharp, "Draft Considerations for Cancellation of Artists' Bureau Agreement," March 6, 1941.

10. Earl J. Glade, letter to J. Reuben Clark Jr., March 21, 1941, personal files of Ivor Sharp.

11. Ivor Sharp, letter to Mr. Ernest L. Wilkinson, September 8, 1941.

12. Federal Communications Commission, Washington, D.C., "In the matter of: Application of the Continental Broadcasting Company, a Corporation of Salt Lake City, Utah, for Construction Permit, requesting facilities 610 kilocycles, one kilowatt, directional antenna unlimited time." File No. B5-P-3276, September 30, 1941.

13. Ibid.

14. Ernest L. Wilkinson, letter to Ivor Sharp, September 3, 1941.

15. Ernest L. Wilkinson, letter to Ivor Sharp, September 8, 1941.

16. Ernest L. Wilkinson, letter to Ivor Sharp, September 3, 1941.

17. Tim Larson, interview with Frank C. Carman, June 27, 1986, Salt Lake City, Utah.

18. Ivor Sharp, "Principal Activities and Accomplishments," report to J. Reuben Clark, August 12, 1943.

19. Ibid.

20. Ibid.

CHAPTER 8: A CHANGE OF CIVIC VENUE AWAY FROM RADIO

1. Memorandum to President J. Reuben Clark, Jr., 47 East South Temple, January 3, 1942, Copy to Mr. Sharp.

2. Tim Larson and Craig Wirth, Interview with John W. Gallivan, Park City, UT, September 6, 2007.

3. D. Michael Quinn (2002), Elder Statesman: A Biography of J. Reuben Clark, Salt Lake City: Signature Books, p. 121-122.

4. *David O. McKay and the Rise of Modern Mormonism,*Gregory A. Prince Wm. Robert Wright, The University of Utah Press, Salt Lake City 2005, p. 124.)

5. *David O. McKay and the Rise of Modern Mormonism*, Gregory A. Prince, Wm. Robert Wright, The University of Utah Press, Salt Lake City 2005, p. 125.)

6. Michael Quinn (2002), Elder Statesman: A Biography of J. Reuben Clark, Salt Lake City: Signature Books, p. 420.

CHAPTER 9: THE CIVIC-MINDED UNIVERSITY REGENT

1. Tim Larson, Interview with Jay W. Wright, February 13, 1992, Seattle, WA 98112.

2. LeRoy E. Cowles, *University of Utah and World War II*, (Salt Lake City: The Deseret News Press, 1949), 27-28.

3. Minutes of the University of Utah Board of Regents, November 14, 1941, 110. Glade evidently was convincing because the Association withdrew its protest of Walker's appointment.

4. A. Ray Olpin, letter to Mrs. Earl J. Glade upon the death of Earl J. Glade, September 1966.

5. Paul Hodson, *Crisis on Campus*, (Salt Lake City: Keban Corp. 1987).

6. Earl J. Glade, notes on President Cowles's Administration, February 1950.

7. Paul Hodson, *Crisis on Campus*, (Salt Lake City: Keeban Corp. 1987), 6-7.

8. Minutes of the Salt Lake City Board of Commission meeting, October 28, 1948.

9. Earl J. Glade, Notes on the Olpin Administration, March 2, 1950.

10. Paul Hodson, *Crisis on Campus*, (Salt Lake City: Keban Corp. 1987), 7.

11. Ibid.

CHAPTER 10: CAMPAIGN FOR MAYOR

1. Ibid.

2. Ivor Sharp, diary excerpts "Concerning Earl J. Glade's Candidacy for Mayor," September 16, 1943, written on the days indicated and later compiled by Sharp as a single document.

3. Earl J. Glade, statement on "Sunday Evening on Temple Square," broadcast, September 19, 1943.

4. Ivor Sharp, Diary excerpts "Concerning Earl J. Glade's Candidacy for Mayor," September 30, 1943, written on the days indicated and later compiled by Sharp as a single document.

5.   Ibid.

6.   *The Salt Lake Tribune*, May 22, 1943.

7.   Ibid.

8.   *The Salt Lake Tribune*, October 20, 1943.

9.   *The Salt Lake Tribune*, November 3, 1943.

10. Dixie S. Huefner, "A Report on Politics in Salt Lake City," reported by Edward C. Banfield, Joint Center for Urban Studies of the Massachusetts Institute of Technology and Harvard University, (Cambridge, MA: 1961), II-1.

11. *The Salt Lake Tribune,* December 30, 1943.

CHAPTER 11: MR. MAYOR

1.   J. Reuben Clark, letter to LDS President David O'McKay, May 22, 1951.

2.   Minutes of the Board of the Commissioners of Salt Lake City, January 3, 1943.

3.   Minutes of the Board of Commissioners of Salt Lake City, December 30, 1943.

4.   Minutes of the Board of the Commissioners of Salt Lake City, January 3, 1944.

5.   Minutes of the Board of the Commissioners of Salt Lake City, January 13, 1944.

6.   *The Salt Lake Tribune*, January 29, 1944.

7.   *The Salt Lake Tribune*, January 18, 1944.

8.   *Piute County News,* October 29, 1943.

9.   *The Salt Lake Tribune*, January 17, 1944.

10. *The Salt Lake Tribune*, March 24, 1944.

11. *Rich County News*, September 22, 1944.

12. *The Salt Lake Tribune*, June 14, 1944.

CHAPTER 12: SALT LAKE CITY'S POSTWAR PERIOD

1.   *The Salt Lake Tribune*, June 14, 1944.

2.   *The Salt Lake Tribune*, January 11, 1953.

3.   *Morgan County News*, March 8, 1946.

4.   *The Salt Lake Tribune*, August 30, 1951.

5.   Cissie Dore Hill, "Voices of Hope: The Story of Radio Free Europe and Radio Liberty," *The Hoover Digest*, (Palo Alto: Standford University, 2001), No. 4.

6.   *The Salt Lake Tribune*, "Ideal Salesmen: Workers in S.L. Prepare '51 Crusade for Freedom" August 21, 1951, 24.

7.   *The Salt Lake Tribune,* "S.L. Launches Crusade For Freedom," September. 3, 1951, 9.

8.   *The Salt Lake Tribune,* "U. Girls to Assist Crusade Drive," September 29, 1951, 17.

9.   *The Salt Lake Tribune,* "Teen-Ager Dance Will Do Bit To Aid Freedom Crusade," September, 29, 1951.

10. *The Salt Lake Tribune,* "Rotary Speakers Acclaim Crusade for Freedom", September 12, 1951, 13.

11. *The Salt Lake Tribune,* Editorial, September 13, 1951, 10.

12. Earl J. Glade, *Deseret News,* July 12, 1941 as reprinted in *Journal of History,* The Church of Jesus Christ of Latter-Day Saints.

13. Ibid.

CHAPTER 13: PAST AND PRESENT: THE UTAH CENTENNIAL AND WATER ISSUES

1.   Ibid.

2.   "Bosone Hits 'McCarthyism' At Liberty Park Outing," *Salt Lake Tribune.*

3.   *The Salt Lake Tribune,* January 7, 1949.
     The Salt Lake Tribune, October 18, 1951.

4.   Minutes of the Board of Commission of Salt Lake City Meeting, December 30, 1946.

5.   *Deseret News,* December 28, 1951.

6.   *The Salt Lake Tribune,* Sept. 23, 1953.

7.   "Little Dam and Reservoir Project," *Bulletin Board,* March 7, 2000, http:// www.ci.slc.ut.us/utilities/NewsEvents/news2000/news03142000.htm

8.   *New York Times,* May 4, 1952.

CHAPTER 14: GLADE'S SECOND TERM: SAFETY, LAW ENFORCEMENT AND YOUTH CRIMES

1.   *The Salt Lake Tribune,* October 3, 1951.

2.   *The Salt Lake Tribune,* March 18, 1947.

3.   Earl J. Glade, "Truly Great Men Recognize Spiritual Power," reprinted in the Church of Jesus Christ of Latter-day Saints, *Journal of History,* from the *Deseret News,* July 26, 1941.

4. *Vernal Express*, June 23, 1948.

5. Earl J. Glade, "Ours is a Practical Faith: How an Inspired Religion Can serve the Community in Meeting the World Crisis," (a series), reprinted in the Church of Jesus Christ of Latter-day Saints, *Journal of History,* from the *Deseret News*, July 12, 1941.

6. Earl J. Glade, "The Youth and the Church," address in the Salt Lake Tabernacle, July 17, 1938.

7. *Murray Eagle*, July 11, 1946.

8. *Salt Lake Tribune*, November. 6, 1948.

9. Ibid. But Utah was not alone in feeling a loss of control. *Time* magazine reported even hardened New Yorkers were also alarmed at what they were seeing. In this case, it was an epidemic, a new youthful curse --- drug use: "During the past year, authorities have become aware of a tremendous and frightening spread of narcotic addiction among teenagers. In one New York court alone, during 1949, there were 41 narcotics arrests of youths between 16 and 18; in 1950 the figure jumped to 161. And there is no telling how many others are using narcotics." *Time*, "High and Light," February 26, 1951.

10. *The Salt Lake Tribune,* January 6, 1951.

11. Ibid.

12. *The Salt lake Tribune,* January 9, 1951.

13. *The Salt Lake Tribune,* January 17, 1951 and January 22, 1951.

14. *The Salt Lake Tribune,* May 24, p. 18; May 11, p. 21; May 28, p. 12; May 30, p. 22, 1951.

15. *The Salt Lake Tribune,* Editorial, July 26, 1951.

16. *The Salt Lake Tribune*, July 22, 1951.

17. *The Salt Lake Tribune*, July 26, 1951.

18. *The Salt Lake Tribune*, August 5, 1951.

19. *The Salt Lake Tribune*, August 4, 1951.

20. *The Salt Lake Tribune,* August 15, 1951.

21. Ibid.

22. *The Salt Lake Tribune*, October 19, 1951.

23. *The Salt Lake Tribune*, August 26, 1951.

24. *Salt Lake Telegram*, August 24, 1951.

25. Ibid.

26. *The Salt Lake Tribune,* October. 6 and October 19, 1951.

27. *The Salt Lake Tribune*, October 20, 1951.

28. *Desert News,* Editorial, October 20, 1951.

29. Ibid.

30. Ibid.

31. *Deseret News,* October 20, 1951.

32. Earl J. Glade, response to the *Deseret News* "Open Letter" of October 20, 1951, published in the *Deseret News,* October 21, 1951.

33. *The Salt Lake Tribune,* October 22, 1951.

34. Ibid.

35. Ibid.

36. *Salt Lake Telegram,* October 24, 1951.

37. *The Salt Lake Tribune,* October 25, 1951.

38. *The Salt Lake Tribune,* October 24, 1951.

39. "Salt Lake City Police records," *Salt Lake Telegram,* Nov. 5, 1951.

CHAPTER 15: GLADE'S STATEWIDE AMBITIONS

1. The Salt Lake Tribune, November 2, 1951.

2. *The Salt Lake Tribune,* February 9, 1952.

3. *Morgan County News,* April 18, 1952.

4. *San Juan Record, April 24, 1952.*

5. *New York Times, September 7, 1952.*

6. *The Salt Lake Tribune, September 3, 1952.*

7. *The Salt Lake Tribune, September 3, 1952.*

8. *The Salt Lake Tribune, August 23, 1952.*

9. *The Salt Lake Tribune, October 1, 1952.*

10. *The Salt Lake Tribune,* September 28, 1952.

11. Ibid.

12. *The Salt Lake Tribune,* September 26, 1952.

13. *The Salt Lake Tribune,* October 9, 1952.

14. *The Salt Lake Tribune,* August 22, 1952.

15. *The Salt Lake Tribune,* October 3, 1952.

16. *The Salt Lake Tribune,* October 19, 1952.

17. *The Salt Lake Tribune,* October 28, 1952.

18. *The Salt Lake Tribune,* November 1, 1952.

19. *The Salt Lake Tribune,* October 26, 1952.

20. *Salt Lake Tribune*, September 23, 1952.Dennis L. Lythgoe, *Let 'em Holler: A Political Biography of J. Bracken Lee* (Salt Lake City: Utah State Historical Society, 1982).

21. *Deseret News,* September 13, 1966.

CHAPTER 16: BACK TO OFFICE AS MAYOR

1. Dixie S. Huefner, "A Report on Politics in Salt Lake City," reported by Edward C. Banfield, Joint Center for Urban Studies of the Massachusetts Institute of Technology and Harvard University, (Cambridge, MA: 1961), II-1.

2. *The Salt Lake Tribune*, June 13, 1954.

3. *The Salt Lake Tribune*, February 23, 1954.

4. *Vernal Express*, August 7, 1952.

5. Dixie S. Huefner, "A Report on Politics in Salt Lake City," reported by Edward C. Banfield, Joint Center for Urban Studies of the Massachusetts Institute of Technology and Harvard University, (Cambridge, MA: 1961), II-1.

6. *The Salt Lake Tribune*, September 25, 1955.

7. 'Hizzoner' is 70, *Deseret News*, December 2, 1955.

8. Earl J. Glade, Salt Lake City Corporation, Department of Parks and Public Property, letter to Ivor Sharp dated January 3, 1955. (It should have been dated January 3, 1956.)

9. *Time*, August 15, 1955.

10. "SLC's Great Goodwill Ambassador, Glade Gives his Mayoralty Valedictory," *Deseret News*, Jan 16, 1956.

CHAPTER 17: GLADE'S FINAL YEARS

1. Earl J. Glade, "Truly Great Men Recognize Spiritual Power," reprinted in the Church of Jesus Christ of Latter-day Saints, Journal of History, from the Deseret News, July 26, 1941. Although difficult to precisely define, Eternal Progression refers to everything that LDS adherers believe and experience by their choices and actions as they progress from pre-existence, to life on Earth, to a resurrected state of growth in the spirit afterlife. The essential middle part of Eternal Progression Glade applied to his earthly life is based on the proposition espoused in the discourse of LDS President Brigham Young that there is no such thing as principle, power, wisdom, knowledge, life, position, or anything that can be imagined that remains stationary --they must increase

or decrease. In countless situations over decades, Glade's communication and activities respected and informed this core LDS principle.

2.   *Deseret News*, May 31, 1951.

3.   Arch L. Madsen with Blaine M. Yorgason and Richard Peterson, "The Infinite Journey: A Brief Overview of the Earthly Life of Arch L Madsen," (1996), 157, 422.

4.   "Howard Pearson's Television Highlights," *Deseret News*, February 9, 1962.

5.   Personal letter to Mr. Earl J. Glade, 2610 Highland Drive, Salt Lake City, Utah, December 31, 1957.

6.   Interview with Marianne Sharp at her Salt Lake City home by Tim Larson, August 7, 1989.

7.   Tim Larson, interview with Blaine Whipple, August 23, 2011, in Bountiful, UT.

8.   Sara R. Glade, Personal Letter to Blaine Whipple, November 7, 1966.

INDEX

www.ingramcontent.com/pod-product-compliance
Lightning Source LLC
Chambersburg PA
CBHW032003050726
47590CB00006B/2025